Get the eBook FREE!

(PDF, ePub, Kindle, and liveBook all included)

We believe that once you buy a book from us, you should be able to read it in any format we have available. To get electronic versions of this book at no additional cost to you, purchase and then register this book at the Manning website.

Go to https://www.manning.com/freebook and follow the instructions to complete your pBook registration.

That's it!
Thanks from Manning!

Graph Algorithms
for Data Science

WITH EXAMPLES IN NEO4J

TOMAŽ BRATANIČ

MANNING

SHELTER ISLAND

For online information and ordering of this and other Manning books, please visit
www.manning.com. The publisher offers discounts on this book when ordered in quantity.
For more information, please contact

Special Sales Department
Manning Publications Co.
20 Baldwin Road
PO Box 761
Shelter Island, NY 11964
Email: orders@manning.com

Manning Publications Co.
20 Baldwin Road
PO Box 761
Shelter Island, NY 11964

Development editor:	Dustin Archibald
Technical Editor:	Arturo Geigel
Technical development editor:	Ninoslav Cerkez
Review editor:	Aleksandar Dragosavljević
Production editor:	Deirdre S. Hiam
Copy editor:	Christian Berk
Proofreader:	Katie Tennant
Technical proofreader:	Jerry Kuch
Typesetter:	Dennis Dalinnik
Cover designer:	Marija Tudor

ISBN: 9781617299469
Printed in the United States of America

brief contents

contents

v

  11.1   Knowledge graph embedding model   279
         Triple   279 ▪ TransE   280 ▪ TransE limitations   281

  11.2   Knowledge graph completion   283
         *Hetionet   284 ▪ Dataset split   287 ▪ Train a PairRE
         model   287 ▪ Drug application predictions   288
         Explaining predictions   289*

  11.3   Solutions to exercises   291

12 **Constructing a graph using natural language
      processing techniques   293**

  12.1   Coreference resolution   297

  12.2   Named entity recognition   297
         Entity linking   298

  12.3   Relation extraction   299

  12.4   Implementation of information extraction pipeline   300
         *SpaCy   301 ▪ Corefence resolution   301 ▪ End-to-end relation
         extraction   303 ▪ Entity linking   305 ▪ External data
         enrichment   308*

  12.5   Solutions to exercises   308

  appendix   *The Neo4j environment   310*

             references   318

             index   323

foreword

When you read this book, I hope you are as astonished by the power of relationships and connected information as I was when I first met Emil Eifrém, one of the founders of Neo4j, 15 years ago on a geek cruise on the Baltic Sea. Ten years later, a similarly inspiring and impactful meeting happened when Tomaž and I met for the first time in person in London. He'd been active in the Neo4j community for a while. After that meeting, his contributions skyrocketed, initially helping test and document the predecessor of the Graph Data Science library and at the same time becoming a prolific author on data science topics related to graphs, NLP, and their practical applications (bratanic-tomaz.medium.com). Tomaž must have published hundreds of articles by the time we were contacted by Manning to discuss creating a book on graph analytics—the one you're holding right now. Tomaž was the obvious choice to become its author, and he did an amazing job, distilling his experience, educational writing style, and real-world examples into an insightful and entertaining book. This book is a journey into the hidden depths of connected data using graph algorithms and new ML techniques—like node embeddings—and graph machine learnings, like link prediction and node classification, many of which now find applications in areas like vector search or large-language models based on transformers like GPT.

I've often said that in the real world, there is no such thing as isolation; everything is connected—people, events, devices, content and products, art, history, politics, markets, biological pathways, and climate tipping points, from the smallest subatomic particles (relational quantum dynamics) to the largest structures in the universe (galactic pathways). Humans have accelerated the volume and density of those connections by adding information technology, the internet, social networks, mobile computing, IoT, and widespread use of ML models. Our lives depend on all those networks working properly, even if we are unaware of most of them. How does one make sense of all these obvious and hidden relationships, which add context and meaning to all individual data points? Sure, you can query for patterns that you already know, but what about the unknown unknowns? This is where graph analytics and graph-based ML techniques shine. They help you find the insights you need. We start with centrality or clustering algorithms, like PageRank or Louvain, which can be used for unsupervised learning about the structure and importance of elements in your data. One of my favorite examples is still *Network of Thrones* by Andrew Beveridge, where he used spatial closeness of characters in the natural-language-processed texts of the *Game of Thrones* books to determine importance, groups, and dependencies. Those algorithms achieved results impressively similar to what you as a human would find if you read the books. Using results from those algorithms as feature vectors in your ML models already improves the accuracy of your predictions, as they capture the context of your entities both structurally and behaviorally. But you can even go a step further and explicitly compute embeddings for nodes based on graph operations. One of the first algorithms in this space was node2vec, which used the word2vec embeddings on paths from random walks out of your starting point (an approach conceptually similar to PageRank). Now, we are much further along, with knowledge graph embeddings using graphs as inputs and outputs that can make real use of the richness of connected data. And in current ML papers and architectures, you will commonly find mentions of graph structures and algorithms, so this is now a kind of foundational technology. Tomaž will take you along the learning journey, starting from data modeling, ingestion, and querying; to the first applications of graph algorithms; all the way to extracting knowledge graphs from text using NLP; and, finally, utilizing embeddings of nodes and graphs in ML training applications. Enjoy the ride to its graph epiphany, and I hope you will come out on the other side a graph addict, as we all turned out to be.

MICHAEL HUNGER, senior director of user innovation, Neo4j

preface

I transitioned to software development in my professional path about seven years ago. As if the universe had a plan for me, I was gently pushed toward graphs in my first developer job. I am probably one of the few people who can claim Cypher query language was the first language they were introduced to and started using, even before SQL or any scripting language, like Python. Kristjan Pećanac, my boss at the time, foresaw that graphs, particularly labeled-property graphs, were the future.

At the time, there weren't many native graph databases out there, so Neo4j felt like a clear-cut choice. The more I learned about graphs and Neo4j, the more I liked them. However, one thing was rather obvious. Even though there were so many awesome things I could do with graphs, the documentation could have been much better. I started writing a blog to showcase all the remarkable things one can do with graphs and to spare people the effort of searching the internet and source code to learn how to implement various features and workflows. Additionally, I treated the blog as a repository of code I could use and copy in my projects.

Fast-forward five years: after more than 70 published blog posts, I authored a post about combining natural language processing and graphs. It was probably my best post to date, and interestingly, I wrote in the summary that if I ever wrote a book, that post would be a chapter in it. Life is a combination of lucky coincidences. Michael Hunger read my NLP post and asked if I was serious about writing a book. I half-jokingly replied that writing a book might be a good idea and would help me advance in my career. Michael took it seriously, and we met with Manning the next month. The rest is history, and the book before you is the result of my journey to make graphs and graph data science easier to learn, understand, and implement in your projects.

acknowledgments

At first, I didn't realize how much work goes into writing a book. After writing this book, I have gained considerable respect for any author who has published a book. Luckily, I had great people around me who helped improve the book with their ideas, reviews, and feedback.

First, I would like to thank my development editor at Manning, Dustin Archibald, for helping me become a better writer and guiding and introducing me to the many concepts that make a great book even better. Thank you as well, Deirdre Hiam, my project editor; Christian Berk, my copyeditor; Katie Tennant, my proofreader; and Aleksandar Dragosavljević, my reviewing editor. I would also like to thank, in no particular order, the many people who contributed their ideas and helped with reviews: Ljubica Lazarevic, Gopi Krishna Phani Dathar, David Allen, Charles Tapley Hoyt, Pere-Lluís Huguet Cabot, Amy Hodler, Vlad Batushkov, Jaglan Gaurav, Megan Tomlin, Al Krinker, Andrea Paciolla, Atilla Ozgur, Avinash Tiwari, Carl Yu, Chris Allan, Clair Sullivan, Daivid Morgan, Dinesh Ghanta, Hakan Lofquist, Ian Long, Ioannis Atsonios, Jan Pieter Herweijer, Karthik Rajan, Katie Roberts, Lokesh Kumar, Marcin Sęk, Mark Needham, Mike Fowler, Ninoslav Cerkez, Pethuru Raj, Philip Patterson, Prasad Seemakurthi, Richard Tobias, Sergio Govoni, Simone Sguazza, Subhash Talluri, Sumit Pal, Syed Nouman Hasany, Thomas Joseph Heiman, Tim Wooldridge, Tom Kelly, Viron Dadala, and Yogesh Kulkarni. I would also like to extend my gratitude to Jerry Kuch and Arturo Geigel for their invaluable technical comments. Arturo is an independent researcher from Puerto Rico. He received his PhD in computer science from Nova Southeastern University, is recognized for being the inventor of Neural Trojans, and currently carries out research machine learning, graph theory, and technological analysis.

about this book

Graph Algorithms for Data Science was written to help you incorporate graph analytic toolkits into your analytics workflows. The idea behind the book is to take a person who has never heard of graphs before and walk them through their first graph model and graph aggregations, eventually arriving at more advanced, graph, machine learning workflows, like node classification and link prediction.

Who should read this book

Graph Algorithms for Data Science is intended for data analysts and developers looking to augment their data analytics toolkit by incorporating graph algorithms to explore relationships between data points. This book is perfect for individuals with a basic understanding of Python and machine learning concepts, like classification models, eager to enhance their data analysis capabilities. With its structured approach, this book caters to a wide range of readers, aiding junior analysts in building a strong foundation in graph algorithms while also providing more experienced analysts with new perspectives and advanced techniques, thereby broadening their data science competencies.

How this book is organized

The book has 3 sections that cover 12 chapters. Part 1 introduces graphs and walks you through a graph modeling task:

- Chapter 1 introduces the concept of graphs and how to spot a graph-shaped problem. It also introduces the types of graph algorithms you will learn about throughout the book.

- Chapter 2 starts by presenting basic graph terminology you can use to describe a graph. It continues by introducing a labeled-property graph model and walking you through a graph modeling task.

Part 2 introduces Cypher query language and frequently used graph algorithms:

- Chapter 3 covers the basic Cypher query language syntax and clauses. It also demonstrates how to import a graph from CSV files.
- Chapter 4 walks you through an exploratory graph analysis. You will learn how to retrieve, filter, and aggregate data using Cypher query language.
- Chapter 5 demonstrates how to use Cypher query language and graph algorithms to characterize a graph. It also shows how to find the most important nodes by using the PageRank algorithm.
- Chapter 6 illustrates how to transform indirect relationships between data points to a direct one, which can be used as input to graph algorithms. Additionally, it introduces the weighted variants of some graph algorithms, like node degree and PageRank.
- Chapter 7 displays how to project a co-occurrence network, where the number of common neighbors between a pair of nodes defines how similar they are.
- Chapter 8 demonstrates how to characterize node roles in the network using various features and metrics. Later in the chapter, you will learn how to construct a k-nearest neighbor graph and find communities of nodes with similar roles.

Part 3 covers more advanced graph machine learning workflows, such as node classification and link prediction:

- Chapter 9 introduces node embedding models and walks you through a node classification task.
- Chapter 10 walks you through link prediction tasks, where you use Cypher query language to extract relevant features and use them to train a link prediction model.
- Chapter 11 covers the difference between link prediction in simple versus complex graphs and introduces knowledge graph embedding models, which can be used to predicts links in complex networks.
- Chapter 12 shows how to construct a graph using natural language processing techniques, like named entity recognition and relationship extraction.

In overview, the first two chapters introduce you to basic graph theory and terminology while also discussing the Twitter graph model that will be used in chapters 3–8. Chapters 3 and 4 are intended to familiarize you with Cypher query language. The following chapters are designed as individual analyst assignments, introducing relevant graph algorithms where needed.

About the code

This book contains many examples of source code both in numbered listings and in line with normal text. In both cases, source code is formatted in a `fixed-width font like this` to separate it from ordinary text. Sometimes code is also **in bold** to highlight code that has changed from previous steps in the chapter, such as when a new feature adds to an existing line of code. In many cases, the original source code has been reformatted; we've added line breaks and reworked indentation to accommodate the available page space in the book. In rare cases, even this was not enough, and listings include line-continuation markers (➥). Additionally, comments in the source code have often been removed from the listings when the code is described in the text. Code annotations accompany many of the listings, highlighting important concepts.

The source code for chapters 3–8 is only available as part of the book, while the source code for chapters 9–12 is provided as Jupyter notebooks on this GitHub repository: https://github.com/tomasonjo/graphs-network-science.

liveBook discussion forum

Purchase of *Graph Algorithms for Data Science* includes free access to liveBook, Manning's online reading platform. Using liveBook's exclusive discussion features, you can attach comments to the book globally or to specific sections or paragraphs. It's a snap to make notes for yourself, ask and answer technical questions, and receive help from the author and other users. To access the forum, go to https://livebook.manning .com/book/graph-algorithms-for-data-science/discussion. You can also learn more about Manning's forums and the rules of conduct at https://livebook.manning.com/ discussion.

Manning's commitment to our readers is to provide a venue where a meaningful dialogue between individual readers and between readers and the author can take place. It is not a commitment to any specific amount of participation on the part of the author, whose contribution to the forum remains voluntary (and unpaid). We suggest you try asking him some challenging questions lest his interest stray! The forum and the archives of previous discussions will be accessible from the publisher's website as long as the book is in print.

about the author

TOMAŽ BRATANIČ is a network scientist at heart, working at the intersection of graphs and machine learning. He has applied these graph techniques to projects in various domains, including fraud detection, biomedicine, business-oriented analytics, and recommendations.

about the cover illustration

The figure on the cover of *Graph Algorithms for Data Science* is "Femme de Lima" or "Woman from Lima," taken from a collection by Jacques Grasset de Saint-Sauveur, published in 1797. Each illustration is finely drawn and colored by hand.

In those days, it was easy to identify where people lived and what their trade or station in life was just by their dress. Manning celebrates the inventiveness and initiative of the computer business with book covers based on the rich diversity of regional culture centuries ago, brought back to life by pictures from collections such as this one.

Part 1

Introduction to graphs

Have you ever marveled at the complex connections between routers that make the internet, navigated through an unfamiliar city using a mapping app, or discovered a hidden gem through a recommendation engine? If so, you've experienced the power of graph algorithms and data science in action. Graphs are everywhere, underlying the complex connections and relationships that shape our world, from social networks and the internet to biological systems and transportation networks. In the last couple of years, the field of graph data science has grown exponentially, driven by the increasing availability of large datasets and rapid advancements in computing power. The heart of these applications lies in the art of modeling, analyzing, and mining data to uncover hidden patterns and gain valuable insights. In essence, graph data science focuses on exploring the relationships and interactions between data points instead of studying them individually, as this approach allows for a deeper understanding of the context and significance of each element within the larger network. The first part of this book will introduce you to the fascinating world of graph algorithms and data science, equipping you with the fundamental knowledge to harness their potential and transform your data-driven projects. Chapter 1 provides an overview of identifying graph-related problems and offers a categorization of graph algorithms that will be used throughout the book. Chapter 2 introduces graph terminology and then dives straight into the action, showing how to approach graph modeling through a practical example.

Graphs and network science: An introduction

This chapter covers

- Introducing graph modeling and visualizations
- Understanding data through relationships
- Spotting graph-shaped problems

If you have ever done any analysis, you have probably used a table representation of data, like an Excel spreadsheet or SQL database. Additionally, if you are dealing with large numbers of documents, you might have used parquet format or JSON-like objects to represent the data.

Figure 1.1 shows table and JSON document representations of orders. For example, the table contains information about four orders of various dates and products. Table representations efficiently perform aggregations, like aggregating the total revenue or counting the number of new customers. Likewise, document structures can be great for storing vast amounts of data. In figure 1.1, a JSON object is used to store information about an online order, such as the order status, shipping address, and more. However, data analytics tools designed for tables or documents frequently overlook the relationships between data points.

Sometimes, the relationships are explicitly specified between data points, like a person and their relationships with friends; and in others, the relationships may be

Table representation

JSON document representation

Order	Date	Product	Qty	Cost
#1	2022-05-07	T-shirt	2	15
#2	2022-08-14	Computer	3	2000
#3	2023-01-05	Table	1	450
#4	2023-02-01	Racket	5	212

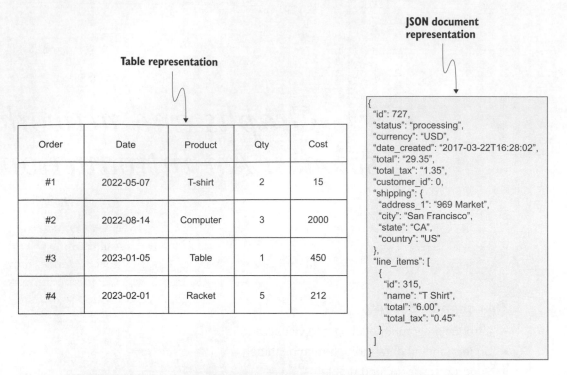

```
{
  "id": 727,
  "status": "processing",
  "currency": "USD",
  "date_created": "2017-03-22T16:28:02",
  "total": "29.35",
  "total_tax": "1.35",
  "customer_id": 0,
  "shipping": {
    "address_1": "969 Market",
    "city": "San Francisco",
    "state": "CA",
    "country": "US"
  },
  "line_items": [
    {
      "id": 315,
      "name": "T Shirt",
      "total": "6.00",
      "total_tax": "0.45"
    }
  ]
}
```

Figure 1.1   Table and document representations of data

indirect or implicit, like when there is a correlation between data points that could be calculated. Whether relationships are explicit or implicit, they contain the additional context of data points that can significantly improve the analysis output.

Figure 1.2 shows a small instance of a *graph*, which consists of five *nodes* connected by five *relationships*. Nodes or vertices can be used to represent various real-world entities, such as persons, companies, or cities; however, you can also use nodes to depict various concepts, ideas, and words.

Graph

Relationships

Nodes

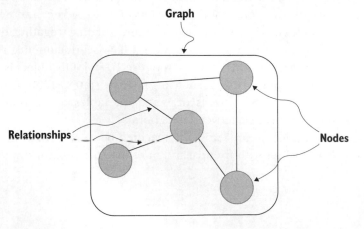

Figure 1.2   Graph representation of data

In most visualizations, nodes are portrayed as circles. Relationships or edges are used to represent various connections between nodes, such as friendships between people or dependencies in software architecture. In this book, we will use the terms *nodes* and *relationships* when discussing the elements of a graph.

Graphs can be used to represent and explore vast amounts of highly connected data. Graph databases, for example, excel in these scenarios, as they are inherently designed to handle complex and variable relationships among entities. In graph theory, nodes and relationships form the core of the model, and the emphasis is on the connections that enable rich, connected queries. Unlike relational databases, graph databases perform these queries without requiring expensive joins or recursive operations. This allows you to efficiently answer questions like, "Who are the friends-of-friends-of-friends?" without suffering from the computational and space complexity typically encountered in the relational model. Additionally, graph databases come with a flexible schema that can accommodate the variations and outliers found in real-world data, providing a more agile solution to evolving business needs. Hence, moving away from the traditional relational paradigm to graph databases can eliminate unnecessary complexity, improve performance, and enable a more intuitive understanding of our data and its relationships.

While the effectiveness of graph databases is apparent in many industries, their application isn't limited to social platforms or e-commerce sectors. They can prove just as instrumental in groundbreaking fields, like space exploration and research. To illustrate, consider one of the world's most renowned space organizations: NASA. NASA's Lessons Learned database (https://llis.nasa.gov/) contains millions of records accumulated over the years, including information about how the organization has responded to difficult projects and their resulting recommendations. The records are invaluable for planning future NASA projects as well as other government and private organizations. Additionally, the database includes metadata about the person who recorded the lesson, the center at which the lesson was submitted, and the topics discussed. One example of such a NASA lesson, shown in figure 1.3, can be accessed via the following NASA web page (https://llis.nasa.gov/lesson/31901).

While the records contain a vast amount of knowledge, the database has grown to a tremendous size, making it increasingly difficult to quickly locate records relevant to a given situation (Marr, 2017; CKO News Staff, 2017). Initially, their search approach used keyword information and access frequency, meaning that records more frequently viewed would be higher in the search results. However, just because a record is frequently viewed doesn't mean it contains relevant information for a specific use case. And while a keyword search would significantly narrow down the results, it could still leave an engineer with up to 1,000 records to inspect for relevant information.

Around 2015, a gentleman named Dr. David Meza embarked on a mission to find and develop a better approach for finding relevant information in the Lessons Learned database. David came across graph-based tools and technologies during his

Subject

For NASA programs using risk-based independent verification and validation (IV&V), detailed NASA-developed/supported simulation of key flight phases provides deeper government insight and certification ability.

Abstract

For NASA programs engaging in risk-based IV&V of contractor-provided flight systems, a detailed, independently developed simulation of deorbit, entry, descent, and landing (DEDL) phases proved invaluable to the Commercial Crew Program (CCP) in providing government insight into and certification of the flight systems. The independent DEDL simulation also informed the CCP by allowing government investigation into areas of concern with the flight system design and/or operation during DEDL. Rapid post-flight support of a CCP spacecraft in-flight anomaly (IFA) was possible with this independent DEDL simulation, demonstrating its potential application for future flights.

Driving Event

Recent application of risk-based IV&V on NASA flight programs (e.g., CCP, Artemis Human Landing System (HLS)) relies heavily on government insight and certification of contractor-developed flight systems. One element to insight involves government review of contractor-provided detailed verification objectives demonstrating flight system acceptability relative to Program-defined constraints. Review of contractor-provided flight system descriptions and results alone provides a limited understanding of key flight system elements and operation.

Lesson(s) Learned

Review of contractor-provided system documentation and detailed verification objective results alone did not provide sufficient insight into the flight system for certification 6 degree-of-freedom DEDL simulation, using contractor-provided detailed descriptions of the flight system and its operation and using the simulation to independently generate critical detailed verification objective results, provided the depth of understanding needed for government insight and vehicle certification. As part of the development process, interaction with contractor personnel to confirm that the government simulation models correctly reflected the flight system and provided results consistent with the contractor simulations led to confidence in both government and contractor simulation-generated results. Another byproduct of this process was the good communication and interactions between NASA and contractor engineering teams (e.g., Guidance, Navigation, and Control (GNC)) that persisted throughout development, certification, and operational flights. Once developed, the independent DEDL simulation allowed NASA to investigate challenging cases in the flight system operational space without distracting the contractor during final flight system development and operations unless an issue was uncovered. A more NESC-focused capability afforded by this independent DEDL simulation was the ability of the team to rapidly participate in an IFA investigation by looking into several possible causes using the previously developed and checked out simulation.

Recommendation(s)

NASA programs using risk-based IV&V to certify a contractor-provided flight system (e.g., CCP and Artemis HLS) should independently develop detailed simulations in key flight phases (e.g., DEDL, ascent, and rendezvous/proximity operations) to model, investigate, and confirm detailed verification objective results to provide the insight necessary to understand the system for certification. Interaction between government and contractor engineers should be encouraged during the development process to confirm that simulation models and results are consistent between the government and contractor simulations. This simulation capability should be maintained after certification (during operational flights) to permit government assistance to contractor flight systems during an IFA or post-flight investigation of an IFA.

Program Relation

Commercial Crew Program

Program/Project Phase

Implementation – Phase D

Mission Directorate(s)

No directorate(s) listed

Topic(s)

- Mission Operations and Ground Support Systems
- Flight Operations
- Independent Verification and Validation
- Safety & Mission Assurance
- Test & Verification
- Orbiting Vehicles
- Spacecraft and Spacecraft Instruments

Figure 1.3   **An example record from NASA's Lessons Learned database**

research. Interestingly, he realized that graph visualizations can make it more intuitive and easier to see patterns and observe how things connect within the Lessons Learned database. First, he had to model the data as a graph. Figure 1.4 shows a graph model that could be used to represent a Lessons Learned record.

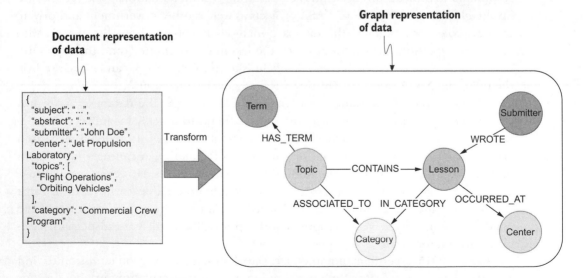

Figure 1.4   **A graph model representing a Lessons Learned record as a graph**

A lesson is described as a node in the graph. Additionally, most of the metadata of the lessons, such as topics, categories, and author, is represented as separate nodes. The nodes are then connected with relationships; for example, the topics are connected to lessons and categories with respective relationships. As you can see, the power of the graph model and visualizations comes from observing how things are connected.

Suppose you are interested in lessons about the valve contamination category, which is represented as a node in the graph shown in figure 1.5. To examine the valve contamination category, you could traverse the relationships from category to lesson nodes to access the lessons in that category.

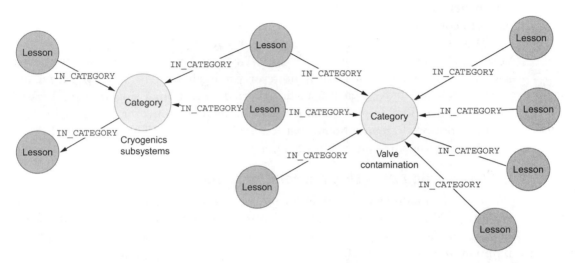

Figure 1.5 The connections between lessons reveal relevant information.

An advantage of graph-based visualizations is that they allow you to look beyond each record individually and, rather, *observe how lessons are connected*. This broader viewpoint often allows you to notice patterns you might not have thought about before. Additionally, it makes searching for relevant information more intuitive, as you can traverse connections between lessons to find the information you are looking for.

An unforeseen consequence of examining the data through its relationships might be that you could see connections you previously didn't think existed. For example, even though there aren't any explicit relationships between categories in the graph, you may see implicit relationships that could be overlooked via traditional analytic approaches. Say you are looking at the graph visualization in figure 1.5 and see that a single lesson can be part of multiple categories, and therefore, categories might overlap. Based on the overlap of categories, you could calculate the correlation between pairs of categories and represent them as relationships, as visualized in figure 1.6.

Interestingly, Dr. David Meza mentions that he couldn't understand how, in this example, valve contamination could end up correlating with a battery fire hazard.

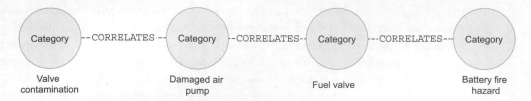

Figure 1.6   Inferring relationships between nodes

After reading through relevant lessons, he learned that there used to be a problem with batteries leaking. Additionally, the batteries were positioned close enough to the valves to contaminate them.

This is just one example of how you might find an unexpected connection between the lessons and dig deeper to learn something new. The knowledge has always been available in the records; however, you might be missing the bigger picture because you are looking at a specific record in isolation. Using the graph-based approach to modeling and visualizations can help you uncover new insights that might be obvious in hindsight but that you might miss if you do not consider the context and patterns surrounding the data points.

1.1   *Understanding data through relationships*

While graph visualizations are great for uncovering new insights, they might lose their value when the number of data points becomes too large to visualize properly. When dealing with large amounts of data, you can use graph algorithms to deliver insights or pinpoint interesting parts of the graph that you can further explore through visualizations. For example, Facebook has more than a billion users on its platform; while you can explore your or other people's surroundings through graph visualizations, it is hard to grasp the overall structure of the graph or find any users who stand out. In these cases, you can use various graph algorithms to inspect the overall structure and find interesting groups of highly connected users, or you can focus on identifying important nodes in the graph that have a significant influence over the information flow.

Finally, you can use the information about node positions or roles to increase the predictive capability of your machine learning models. Consider the context of a social platform like Facebook or Twitter (I use the name *Twitter*, rather than *X*, for the purposes of this text). Examining users through their connections may provide valuable insight; by examining a person's connections, you would likely learn quite a bit about who their friends, family, and role models are. Therefore, the nodes represent users on the platform, and the relationships describe who they follow, like what you would see on Twitter. The graph in figure 1.7 is relatively small so that it fits into a visualization, but you can pretend you are dealing with millions—or even billions—of users. However, even with such a small graph, extracting any meaningful information without properly preparing a graph visualization using graph algorithms is hard. For example, say you want to evaluate the community structure of the graph in figure 1.7.

Figure 1.7 Sample social platform graph

After applying *community detection* (aka *clustering*) algorithms, it is relatively effortless to evaluate the community structure of the graph. For example, you can see in figure 1.8 that two nodes are disconnected and isolated from the main graph.

Additionally, it is easy to observe that nodes in the central graph form multiple communities. A *community* is defined as a densely interconnected group of nodes, similar to how you might imagine a group of friends. The friends form a group that hangs out most of the time; however, some people within the group interact with others only on occasion. For example, say a group member goes boulder climbing once a week. They interact with people at the boulder climbing event, but they don't introduce them to all the other members of the friend group and invite them to their events. The same logic you might apply to a friend group can be applied to communities within a graph. Community detection algorithms are useful to identify groups within the graph that can be used as input to content or friendship recommendations or as a marketing tool to identify and target various segments of users. There may be a case when you want to identify the most important nodes within the graph. A subset of graph algorithms called *centrality algorithms* is designed to identify the most important or central nodes within a graph. There are several different definitions of *node importance*. In the visualization in figure 1.9, the importance is defined as the influence over the information flow in the network. For example, some nodes in the graph provide the only connection between different communities—you likely know them as social media influencers. Since all the information between various communities flows through them, they exert much influence over the flow of information. They can withhold information from reaching others

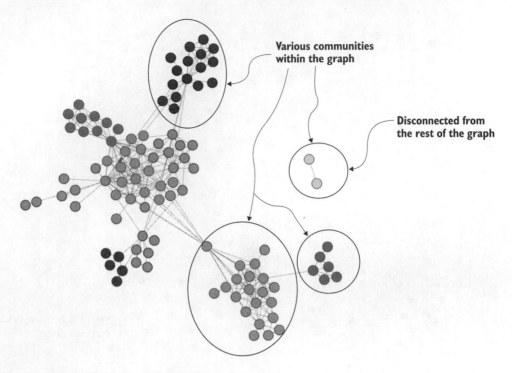

Figure 1.8   Evaluating the community structure of a graph

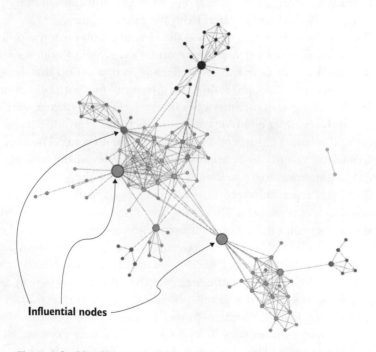

Figure 1.9   Identifying influential nodes

or manipulate one or another community by strategically choosing where to share information or spreading false information.

Identifying important nodes can be used to devise an effective strategy for spreading information through a network for marketing purposes. Another pertinent strategy is to find nodes in a favored position, who have more opportunity to achieve a specific task.

Finally, you could use the information about community structure and influence as a part of your machine learning workflows. Machine learning is becoming a prominent solution for remaining competitive in today's business environment. A compelling motivation for employing machine learning is to accomplish tasks and achieve results that are otherwise unattainable with traditional computational methods. A graph-based approach to machine learning can be used to encode additional context of data points by exploring connections and, consequently, improving the model's accuracy, as shown in figure 1.10.

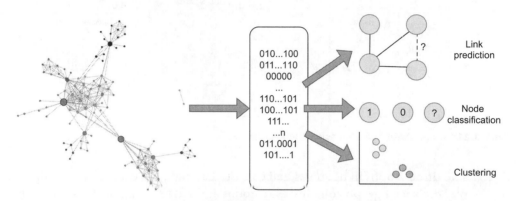

Figure 1.10   Graph-based machine learning

Node classification and regression can be thought of as a traditional classification workflow. The only difference is that you include various features that describe the data point's position or role in the network. Similarly, you could extract different metrics that encode a data point role or position in a network and use it in a clustering workflow. Additionally, there are multiple business scenarios in which you want to predict future links using link prediction workflows.

1.2   *How to spot a graph-shaped problem*

Now, you might be thinking, "I don't run a social network platform! So what do graphs offer me?" While any use case can be modeled as a graph, a specific set of scenarios is uniquely suited for graph-based analysis.

1.2.1   *Self-referencing relationships*

The first scenario deals with self-referencing relationships between entities of the same type. In relational databases, a *self-referencing* relationship occurs between data points within the same table. The self-referencing relationships can be modeled as a single node and relationship type in a graph. Figure 1.11 provides a visualization of three types of graphs.

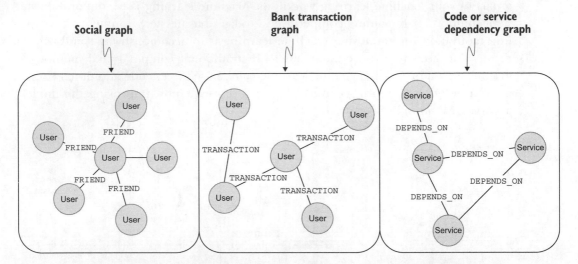

Figure 1.11   Graphs with self-referencing relationships

The three graphs in figure 1.11 all consist of a single node and relationship. For example, the social graph contains `User` nodes and `FRIEND` relationships, while the service dependency graph contains `Service` nodes and `DEPENDS_ON` relationships. The previous section alluded to all the applications of graph algorithms for a social media platform. A great thing about graph algorithms is that they are domain agnostic, meaning it doesn't matter whether the nodes represent people, services, or other entities or concepts. Therefore, you can apply the same graph algorithms in other domains, like bank transaction networks, where fraud detection is a frequent task. Or you can apply the same graph algorithms on a service dependency graph to evaluate how vulnerabilities spread through the graph or how to defend yourself against malicious attacks. There are many scenarios in which a graph with self-referencing relationships would be useful:

- Optimizing supply chains
- Fraud detection
- Social media analysis
- Managing complex telecommunication networks
- Cybersecurity

1.2.2 *Pathfinding networks*

Another fairly common graph scenario is discovering paths or routes between entities or locations. Most of you have probably used navigational systems to find the optimal route for your travels. Figure 1.12 provides a visualization of a transportation network between cities in Belgium and Netherlands.

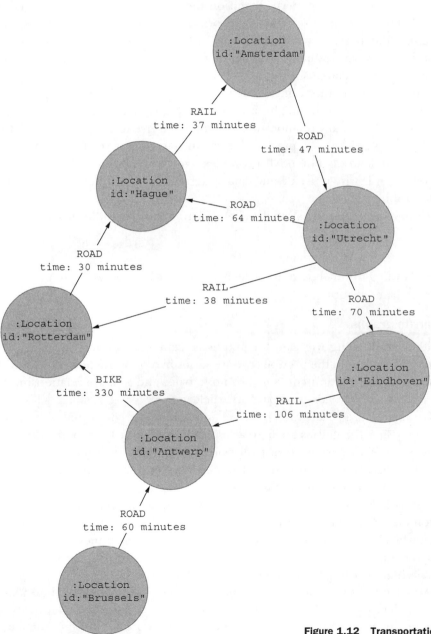

Figure 1.12   Transportation network

The cities are represented as nodes, while the transportation modes are represented as relationships between cities. For example, you could bike from Antwerp to Rotterdam in about 330 minutes or take the train from Hague to Amsterdam for 37 minutes.

As mentioned, you could use a transportation network to calculate the optimal route based on your specifications. The route could be optimized for different factors: time, distance, or cost. You could also analyze the network as a whole and try to predict traffic congestion patterns based on the network structure or find critical locations that would disrupt the whole network if, for example, an accident occurred. In a relational database, you would have to hypothesize the order of relationships you must join to find an available path between two entities. In the example in figure 1.12, there are three relationship options you could choose to traverse: you could travel from one city to another using the road, railroad, or bike network.

Another problem you might face with traditional databases is that you don't know beforehand how many relationships you must traverse to get from node A to node B. Not knowing beforehand precisely which and how many relationships you must traverse could lead to potentially complex and computationally expensive queries. Therefore, it is wise to treat your data as a graph, as it will help you mitigate both of these problems.

Finding optimal routes can be a helpful strategy in the following scenarios:

- Logistics and routing
- Infrastructure management
- Finding optimal paths to make new contacts
- Payment routing

1.2.3   *Bipartite graphs*

Another compelling use case for graphs is examining indirect or hidden relationships. The graphs in the previous two scenarios had only one node type. On the other hand, a bipartite graph contains two node types and a single relationship type. Figure 1.13 depicts a retail graph and an article graph.

For example, a retail graph has `User` and `Item` nodes connected with a `BOUGHT` relationship. Bipartite graphs are a great use case to identify hidden or indirect relationships. While there are no direct relationships between customers, you can compare their purchasing patterns and find similar customers. Essentially, you could define segments of customers using this approach. These types of graphs are also frequently used in collaborative filtering recommender systems, in which you search for similar customers or products commonly purchased together. There are many other scenarios in which retail graphs come in handy, like movie recommendations on Netflix or song recommendations on Spotify. In fact, any scenario that involves a person rating, purchasing, or voting for an item can be modeled as a retail graph.

Article graphs were briefly mentioned in figure 1.5, which covered NASA's Learned Lessons database. Again, there are no direct connections between articles or topics; however, using various data science techniques, you can calculate the similarity of

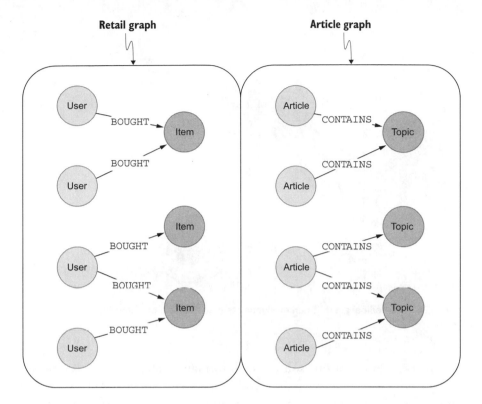

Figure 1.13   Bipartite graphs

articles or correlation of topics, which you can use to improve search or recommenda-tions. As another example, consider app store reviews or parliament members voting on laws and resolutions. You could then, for example, investigate how similarly members of parliament vote and compare their records to their political party associations.

1.2.4   *Complex networks*

The last example is a complex network with many connections between various enti-ties; a biomedical graph is one such scenario. The graph presented in figure 1.14 con-tains various entities, like genes, pathways, compounds, and diseases. Additionally, there are 24 different types of relationships present in the graph.

Explaining all the medical terminology behind medical entities and their relation-ships could be the subject of a whole book. However, you can observe that biomedical concepts are highly interconnected and, therefore, an excellent fit for a graph model. Biomedical graphs are popular for representing existing knowledge and making pre-dictions about new treatments, side effects, and more.

Interestingly, if you work in a product company, you could also construct a highly complex graph representing all the pieces of information about your customers.

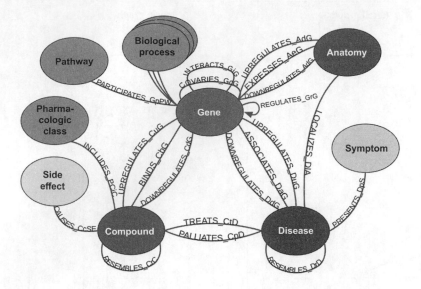

Figure 1.14   Biomedical graph (Source: Himmelstein et al. Licensed under CC BY 4.0)

Typically, you have various sources of information about your customers, like web page analytics, store information, product patterns, and CRM data, that you could combine to create a complete representation of your customers. You could then use this data profile to support analytics or various prediction models in your company.

Summary

- Using relationships in your data model gives your data the context it needs to provide better analytical or prediction results.
- Relationships can be explicitly defined or inferred, like various correlations.
- A graph consists of nodes—which represent entities like people, organizations, locations, or biomedical concepts—and relationships, which describe how things are connected, related, assembled, and more.
- Information in a table or document format can be modeled and transformed into a graph.
- Graph visualizations help you spot patterns you would likely otherwise miss if you looked at data points in isolation.
- Community detection algorithms grant insight regarding the structure of a graph and find disconnected or highly connected groups.
- Centrality algorithms identify the most important, critical, or influential nodes in the graph.
- The output of graph algorithms can be used as input in machine learning workflows in which you predict new links or classify data points.

- Self-referencing graphs, like social graphs containing a single node and relationship type, are excellent fits for graph-based analytics.
- Pathfinding is the core graph problem of identifying optimal paths given particular constraints.
- Frequently, graphs are used to identify hidden, implicit, or indirect relationships between data points that might not be explicitly mentioned or obvious.
- A graph model is an excellent fit for modeling complex, highly connected data, for example, a biomedical graph.

Representing network structure: Designing your first graph model

This chapter covers

- Introducing the learning path to mastering graph algorithms and data science
- Getting familiar with basic graph terminology
- Labeled-property graph model schema design
- Extracting information from tweets

Figure 2.1 illustrates how I envision the learning path to becoming a versatile and experienced graph data practitioner and scientist. This book will take you along this exciting path.

The path illustrated in figure 2.1 takes a bottom-up approach, where you will first learn to describe the data for your domain as a graph, encompassing modeling and constructing a graph. Next, you will learn to identify, retrieve, and aggregate various graph patterns. Once the basics are out of the way, you will dig into descriptive graph analytics, which can help you understand the current state of the graph. In the last couple of chapters, you will learn how to combine all the previous lessons and apply them to predict new patterns in the graph.

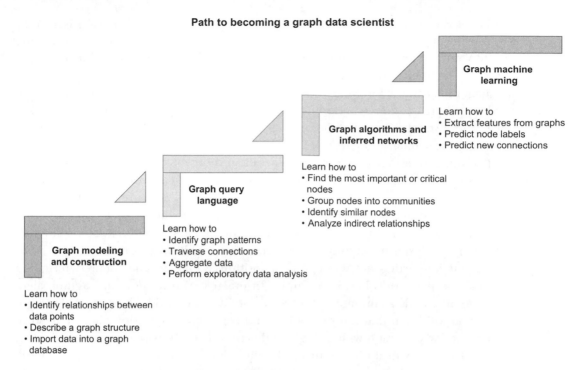

Path to becoming a graph data scientist

Graph machine learning

Learn how to
• Extract features from graphs
• Predict node labels
• Predict new connections

Graph algorithms and inferred networks

Learn how to
• Find the most important or critical nodes
• Group nodes into communities
• Identify similar nodes
• Analyze indirect relationships

Graph query language

Learn how to
• Identify graph patterns
• Traverse connections
• Aggregate data
• Perform exploratory data analysis

Graph modeling and construction

Learn how to
• Identify relationships between data points
• Describe a graph structure
• Import data into a graph database

Figure 2.1   Learning path to mastering graph algorithms and data science

The learning path consists of four major milestones:

- Graph modeling and construction
- Graph query language
- Graph algorithms and inferred networks
- Graph machine learning

The first step is to identify graph-shaped problems and represent your data as a graph. I have already touched on how to spot use cases that fit a graph-based approach in the previous chapter. In this chapter, you will begin by learning how to describe a particular graph structure and how it varies between different datasets.

The first milestone is understanding how to approach graph modeling and importing a dataset into a graph database. While various graph databases use different underlying graph models, I think it is best to focus on one and try to master it; otherwise, I could dedicate a couple of chapters to the differences between graph models. Since I want to get to practical applications and analysis quickly, you will learn how to model and import data only as a *labeled-property graph (LPG) model*.

The most widely adopted graph query language to interact with the LPG model is *Cypher query language*. Cypher query language was developed by Neo4j and has been since adopted by Amazon Neptune, AgensGraph, Katana Graph, Memgraph, Redis-Graph, and SAP HANA (https://opencypher.org/projects/). Cypher query language can be used to read from the LPG database as well as import and transform data. In the third chapter, you will learn Cypher's basics, allowing you to construct your first graph. Your first graph will represent the Twitter social network, which will be used in chapter 4 to teach you how to perform exploratory data analysis with Cypher query language. Learning about and understanding the syntax of Cypher query language will help you reach the second milestone of mastering graph algorithms and data science, where you will be able to identify and retrieve graph patterns, traverse connections, aggregate data, and perform exploratory data analysis.

The third milestone concerns introducing and understanding graph algorithms. In this section of the book, you will learn how to use graph algorithms to describe the current state of the graph and extract valuable insights. There are several categories of graph algorithms. For example, you can use centrality algorithms to identify the most important or influential nodes. On the other hand, you can use community detection or clustering algorithms to recognize highly interconnected groups of nodes. One interesting fact about graph algorithms is that most have a predetermined graph shape that works best as an input. In practice, you do not adjust graph algorithms to fit your data but, rather, transform your data to provide the correct algorithm input. You will learn that most centrality and community detection algorithms were designed to take a graph with a single node and relationship type as input; however, you will frequently deal with graphs with multiple node or relationship types. Therefore, you need to learn techniques that will help you transform various graphs into shapes expected by the graph algorithms.

This idea is not unique to graph algorithms and is also true for most traditional machine learning and data science algorithms. Data science and machine learning practitioners know that feature engineering or data wrangling represents most of the workload in an analytical or machine learning workflow—and dealing with graphs and graph algorithms is no exception. Having to perform data transformations before executing algorithms is also one of the reasons I recommend using a graph database to store your data. Most graph databases have a graph query language or other built-in tools that can help you perform the required data transformations optimally. Chapters 5, 6, and 7 are dedicated to teaching you various techniques on how to transform or *infer* graph structures that best fit the graph algorithms you want to execute.

I have deliberately split graph algorithms and graph machine learning into the third and fourth milestones. In theory, some graph algorithms could also be referred to as *graph machine learning tools*. The term *graph machine learning* is used in this book to refer to workflows in which you predict or classify missing values or future behavior. On the other hand, the term *graph algorithms* is used to refer to descriptive analytics like community detection and centrality algorithms.

The workflow behind graph machine learning is very similar to traditional machine learning workflows, in which you train a model to help you solve the specified task. The major difference between the traditional and graph-based approaches is how to construct the machine learning model features. In general, there are two approaches to extracting machine learning model features from a graph. The first option is to take the manual approach and define the relevant and predictive features. For example, you could use Cypher query language to describe features or use the output of community detection or centrality graph algorithms. The second option is to utilize embedding models that "automagically" encode the network structure as a vector that can be fed into an machine learning model. In chapters 8 through 11, you will learn how to extract and incorporate graph features in a downstream machine learning workflow.

As a bonus, you will learn how to use Natural Language Processing (NLP) techniques to construct a graph in the final chapter. Specifically, you will use named entity recognition (NER) and relation extraction (RE) tools to extract relevant information from a text and store the output as a graph. Let's take the first step on the path to mastering graph algorithms and data science.

2.1   Graph terminology

We'll start our journey by learning some basic graph theory terminology. This section aims to teach you the language required to describe a graph you have at hand.

2.1.1   Directed vs. undirected graph

Figure 2.2(A) is an example of a directed graph, where the direction of the relationship plays an important role. A real-world example of a directed graph is Twitter, on which a user can follow other users that don't necessarily follow them back. In this example, Mark's post will show up on both Jane and Ingrid's feed. On the other hand, Mark will see no posts from either Jane or Ingrid, as he does not follow them. Figure 2.2(B) shows an undirected graph, where the relationship direction is not essential. An *undirected* or a *bidirected relationship* represents a connection between

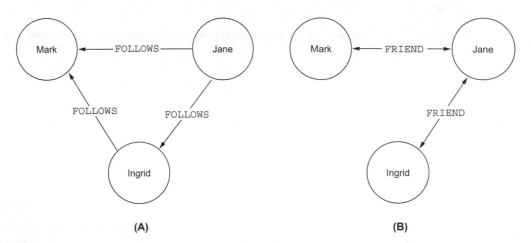

Figure 2.2   **(A) represents a directed graph; (B) represents an undirected graph.**

two entities that can be traversed in both directions. This example could be used to represent Facebook, where a friendship relationship exists only if both parties agree to it.

The notion that every undirected graph can be represented as a directed graph is a crucial concept that will be relevant further down the line. You can simply replace every undirected connection with two directed links in opposite directions.

In the context of graph algorithms, an undirected relationship allows traversal in both directions, while a directed one allows traversal in only a single direction. For example, in figure 2.3(A), you can traverse the undirected connection from Mark to Jane and back. To mimic this functionality in a directed graph, you would create two relationships that point in opposite directions. In figure 2.3(B), having directed relationships in both directions allows you to traverse from Mark to Jane and back. This concept will be essential to understanding graph algorithms' input.

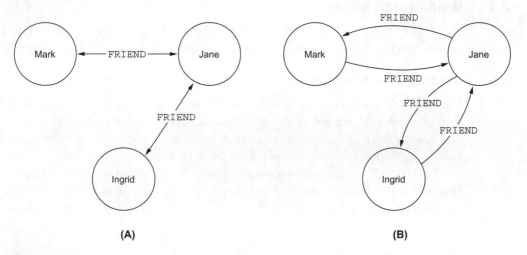

Figure 2.3   **(A) represents an undirected graph; (B) represents a directed graph equivalent of the undirected graph.**

> **NOTE**   In the context of graph algorithms, the traversal of a directed relationship in the opposite direction is typically not permissible. However, in graph databases, the flexibility of Cypher query language allows for the traversal of directed relationships in both directions, making it a versatile tool for navigating complex relational data structures.

2.1.2   *Weighted vs. unweighted graphs*

In an unweighted graph, figure 2.4(A), all relationships have the same strength or associated cost of traversing assigned to them. The notion of stronger or weaker relationships does not exist within an unweighted graph. On the other hand, figure 2.4(B) depicts a weighted graph, where the strength or the cost of traversing the relationships is stored as an attribute (the weight must be a number). In this example, the connection between Jane and Ingrid is stronger than the relationship between Ingrid and Mark. Depending on the domain, sometimes a higher weight value is better, while other times a smaller weight value is preferred. In the example in figure 2.4(B), a higher weight is preferred, as it indicates a stronger friendship relationship. On the other hand, a smaller weight value is preferred in a transportation network, which is a typical application for using a weighted graph, where you are searching for the shortest weighted path between a pair of nodes.

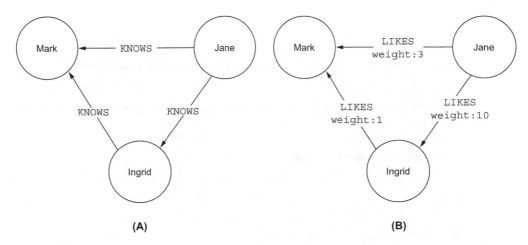

(A) **(B)**

Figure 2.4 **(A) represents an unweighted graph; (B) represents a weighted graph.**

2.1.3 *Bipartite vs. monopartite graphs*

A monopartite graph describes a graph that consists of a single type or class of nodes. In figure 2.5(A), you can observe a monopartite graph containing only a single class of nodes representing persons. As previously mentioned, most graph algorithms are designed to take monopartite graphs as input. The graph in figure 2.5(B) contains two nodes representing persons and a single node representing an organization. As two sets of nodes are present, you can describe this graph as bipartite. Additionally, in a bipartite graph, the relationships always start from one set of nodes and end at the other.

In the example in figure 2.5(B), there are only relationships from persons to organizations—not between persons or between organizations. Bipartite graphs are common in the real world; many user-item interactions can be represented as a graph. For example, on Netflix, a user can rate movies. Both users and movies are represented as nodes, and the rating is described as a relationship. Another example would be the Amazon Marketplace, in which customers can buy various items. Here, customers and

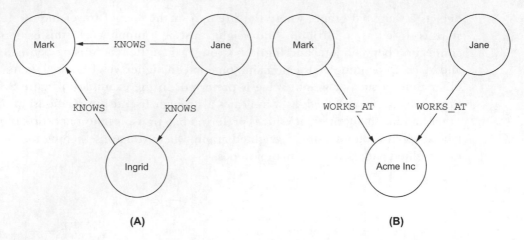

Figure 2.5   (A) represents a monopartite graph; (B) represents a bipartite graph.

products are represented as nodes, and the relationship indicates which items a customer purchased.

2.1.4   *Multigraph vs. simple graph*

A simple graph, as depicted in figure 2.6(A), permits only a single relationship between a pair of nodes in each direction. There are many use cases in which you want to permit multiple relationships between a pair of nodes. In those cases, you would be dealing with a multigraph. An example multigraph is shown in figure 2.6(B).

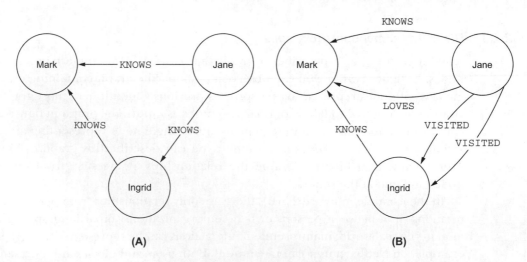

Figure 2.6   (A) represents a simple graph; (B) represents a multigraph.

2.1.5   A complete graph

A complete graph is a graph in which each node is connected to all the other nodes (figure 2.7).

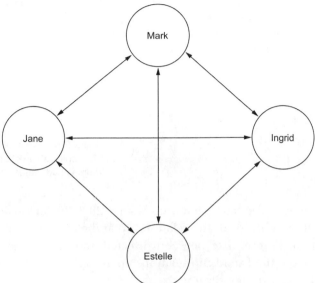

Figure 2.7   A complete graph

2.2   Network representations

Before you learn more about the LPG model, you will also look at the text representation of simple networks. The text representation of networks comes in handy when you want to communicate the network structure via text quickly. We will borrow the syntax from Cypher query language. Cypher's syntax provides a visual way to match patterns of nodes and relationships in the graph using ASCII art syntax. Its syntax describing nodes and relationships is also the basis for the future Graph Query Language (GQL; https://www.gqlstandards.org/home), which aims to unify the graph-pattern query language the same way SQL did for relational databases. An example node representation in Cypher looks like the following:

```
(:Person {name:"Thomas"})
```

To depict nodes in Cypher, surround a node with parentheses—for example, (node). The colon is used to describe the type or a label of a node. In the preceding example, the node label is defined as Person. Nodes can also have properties, which are depicted as key–value pairs inside the brackets of a node. There is a single key–value pair inside the curly brackets, {name:"Thomas"}, that represents the name property of the node.

Relationships in Cypher are surrounded with a square bracket:

```
-[:FRIEND{since:2016}]->
```

Like nodes, you describe the type of the relationship with a colon. Relationships can also have properties defined as key–value pairs inside curly brackets. A relationship can never exist in solitude without existing source and target nodes. For example, you can specify a simple friendship network with the following syntax:

```
(:Person {name:"Thomas"})-[:FRIEND {since:2016}]->(:Person {name:"Elaine"})
```

This Cypher syntax describes a friendship relationship between Thomas and Elaine and can be visualized as the network shown in figure 2.8.

Figure 2.8   Example friendship network between Thomas and Elaine

Thomas and Elaine are people who have been friends since 2016. If you look carefully, you can observe a direction indicator of the relationship at the end of the text representation. With it, you can differentiate between directed and undirected relationships. If you want to describe the friendship relationship as *undirected*, all you have to do is omit the relationship direction indicator:

```
-[:FRIEND{since:"2016"}]-
```

I need to add a small disclaimer here. Many of the graph databases don't directly support storing undirected relationships. However, Cypher query language supports undirected querying, meaning the direction of the relationships is ignored during query runtime. You will learn how to store undirected relationships in the next section.

> **Exercise 2.1**
>
> Try to represent the relation between you and your employer using Cypher syntax. There are two types of nodes present in this graph pattern: a person and an organization or a business. You can also add additional node or relationship properties as you see fit.

I could describe my relationship with Manning Publications using the following Cypher syntax:

```
(:Person {name:"Tomaz"})-[:WRITES_FOR {since:2020}]->(:Organization
    {name:"Manning Publications"})
```

2.2.1   *Labeled-property graph model*

The *labeled-property graph model* (LPG) is one of the graph models used by graph databases. As mentioned, we will use only the LPG model in this book, as the focus is to teach you how to solve and analyze practical problems—not to compare different graph models. I have alluded to the LPG structure a bit in the previous section, where I introduced Cypher text representation.

Nodes have a special type of property called a *label*, which is used to represent node roles in your domain. For example, you could use the label to categorize whether a node represents a person or an organization. Both nodes and relationships can have properties stored as key–value pairs, such as the name of a person as a node property or starting date as relationship property in the previous Cypher text representation.

It is important to note that all relationships in the LPG model are directed and have a single type assigned to them. The type of relationship gives it semantic meaning. So far, the examples used FRIEND and WRITES_FOR as relationship types. Interestingly, with the WRITES_FOR relationship, the direction of the connection is crucial to accurately describe the semantics:

```
(:Person {name:"Tomaz"})<-[:WRITES_FOR {since:2020}]-(:Organization
    {name:"Manning Publications"})
```

If I were to reverse the connection direction, my relationship with Manning Publications would have significantly different semantics. On the other hand, there are some scenarios where the relationship direction is not so important:

```
(:Person {name:"Thomas"})<-[:FRIEND {since:2016}]-(:Person {name:"Elaine"})
```

In this example, where I reversed the relationship direction, the semantics are not as different, as the friendship is usually *bidirectional*. What do I mean by that? When I am friends with someone, that typically implies that they are also friends with me. A bidirectional relationship can also be regarded as *undirected*. I cannot speak for all graph databases but specifically for Neo4j: when storing relationships with bidirectional or undirected semantics, such as friendship, it is enough to create a single directed connection between the two persons, as the relationship also implies the connection in the opposite direction. With Cypher query language, you can ignore the direction of the relationship you want to traverse. You will learn more about this through practical examples.

To demonstrate a simple LPG graph model, let's try to model the following information as a graph:

- Thomas is 40 years old.
- Thomas is friends with Elaine.
- Thomas is a person.
- Elaine is a person.

In the example in figure 2.9, we use the node label to categorize the nodes as persons and store the age information as an internal node property. Since the friendship information indicates a real-world relationship between two persons, we also model it as a relationship in our graph.

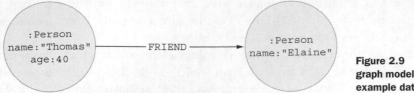

Figure 2.9   Labeled-property graph model representing the example data

Say you wanted to add information about their phone numbers, social security numbers, and addresses to the graph. Usually, you would store literal values like social security number as a node property; however, in some domains, you might want to represent information like social security numbers or phone numbers as separate nodes. A typical example is the fraud detection scenario, where you are interested in examining customers who share the same address, social security number, or phone number (figure 2.10).

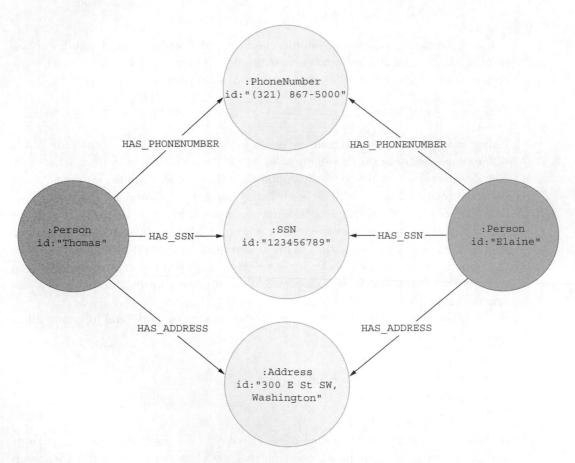

Figure 2.10   Labeled-property graph model representing a fraud investigation domain

The graph model depends on your task, and with the LPG model, you can represent a literal value both as an internal node property (key–value pair) as well as a separate node. Similarly, you have the option to represent the label as a separate node as well. A classic example would be describing class hierarchy with the LPG model. In figure 2.11, the graph schema is modified to support class hierarchy representation that could, for example, be used in biological domains.

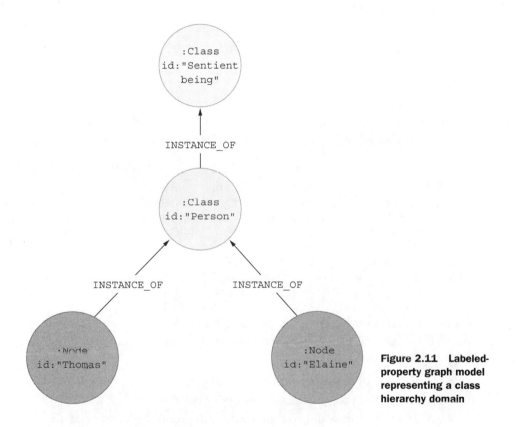

Figure 2.11   Labeled-property graph model representing a class hierarchy domain

As mentioned, the graph model depends on the task you are trying to solve. With labeled-property graphs, the abstraction level is nodes, relationships, labels, and properties.

In this book, you will be using an LPG graph database as a source of truth for graph analysis. It is completely fine if you want to use other graph models as the source of truth in your further graph analysis. However, I won't go through the details of constructing other graph models to best fit your graph analysis task in this book.

2.3   Designing your first labeled-property graph model

Now, imagine a scenario in which a client asks you to perform a network analysis of Twitter. The client will provide all the relevant data; your task is to represent the data as a graph and gain various insights by performing network analysis. You will be using the

LPG model to represent Twitter. A general approach to graph modeling is working backward and starting with the questions you want to answer. Here, unfortunately, no specific questions were posed in the assignment. It is your job as a network scientist to do your best and find as many insights as possible. You can start by trying to describe the domain you have at hand. In the Twitter example, the most basic specifications would be

- A user can follow other users (follower network).
- A user can publish tweets (user–tweet network).
- A user can retweet posts from other users (retweet network).

In this section, you will learn how to develop an LPG graph model.

2.3.1   Follower network

On Twitter, you have the option to follow other users. By following users, you are subscribing to their activity and indicating that you would like to see their tweets on your feed. The follower-network specification is as follows: *A user can follow other users.*

> **Exercise 2.2**
>
> As an exercise, try to design the follower graph model. As a rule of thumb, you would like the entities to be represented as nodes. You can also borrow some logic from English grammar. The subject and object of a sentence are often represented as nodes, and the verb describes the relationship. Adjectives can be translated into properties. When designing a graph model, take into consideration whether the direction of a relationship holds semantic value.

There is no correct or perfect way to design a graph model, but some models can be useful for a specific scenario. When you are designing a graph model, try to answer the following questions:

- How many different types of nodes are present?
- What kind of properties do these nodes have?
- Which property would you use to store the unique identifier of nodes?
- What type of relationships are present?
- Is a single relationship type enough to accurately describe your domain?
- Does the relationship direction hold any semantic value?
- How do properties qualify or quantify relationships?

In the follower-network specification, both the subject and the object of the sentence are users and can be represented as nodes. Relationships can be used to represent the verb of the specification sentence. Here, it makes sense to represent a follow interaction as a relationship between two users. A single relationship pattern from figure 2.12 can be represented with Cypher's pattern syntax as follows:

```
(:User{id:"Vanessa", registeredAt:"2019-03-05"})-[:FOLLOWS{since:"2020-01-
    01"}]->(:User{id:"Thomas", registeredAt:"2011-03-05"})
```

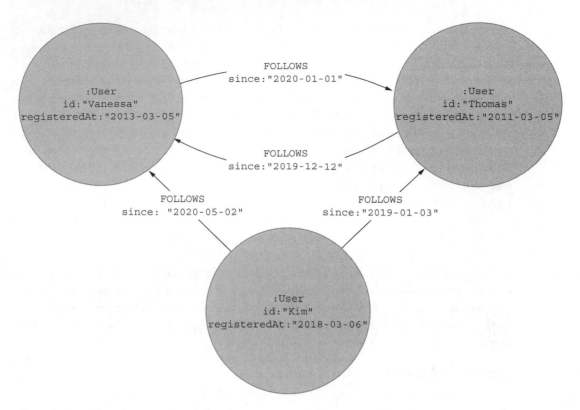

Figure 2.12 **Twitter follower-network model**

Each node in figure 2.12 has the label User attached to it. The node label is used to categorize nodes that represent users. As there is only a single label of nodes present, you are dealing with a monopartite network. A good practice is to have an *unique identifier* for node disambiguation in place for all the nodes of the network. On Twitter, you can use any user's Twitter handle as their unique identifier. The data also contains the sign-up date for users, which you can store as the node's registeredAt property.

In figure 2.12, you can observe that Kim follows Vanessa, but Vanessa does not follow Kim. In other words, Kim will see Vanessa's tweets on her feed, while Vanessa will not see anything from Kim. You can conclude that the direction of the relationships holds semantic value, and as a result, you are dealing with a directed network. The FOLLOWS relationship has no notion of strength assigned to it, which implies the Twitter follower network is unweighted. You do, however, know when the relationship was created. The information about the relationship creation date can be stored as a relationship property.

Before continuing, you can examine the types of questions or insights you could answer using this graph model. When examining a social network, you may want to try to identify influencers. A simple metric to evaluate influencers is a user's direct follower count. The more followers a user has, the more widely their tweets will be distributed; however, whether your followers are also influential makes a difference. For example, a Fortune 500 CEO following you might be more influential than your neighbor.

Likely, the most famous graph algorithm to evaluate the *transitive* influence of a node is PageRank. A transitive relationship is an indirect relationship between two nodes, where, for example, a node A is connected to node B and node B is connected to node C. In this example, node A is not directly related to node C but has an indirect relationship through node B, which implies they are transitively connected. Suppose a Fortune 500 CEO has more connections than your neighbor. In that case, you will gain more transitive relations and, consequently, network influence by having a Fortune 500 CEO follow you than by having your neighbor following you.

Another type of analysis often used for social networks is to deduce community structure. In the last couple of years, it has become increasingly popular to use graphs for predictive analytics. For example, the popular saying is that a person is the average of their five closest friends. You could use this assumption and try to predict a property of a person based on the users they follow. Since the follower's graph contains the time component for both the nodes and relationships, you could also examine how the network evolved over time and use that information to predict how it will grow in the future.

2.3.2 *User–tweet network*

Tweets are the primary way to share content on Twitter. The simplest description of the user–tweet network is as follows: A user can publish a tweet.

> **Exercise 2.3**
> To get into the flow of designing graph models, try to develop a graph model that describes the preceding specification. In the long run, it will be beneficial for you if you take a whiteboard or a sketchbook and draw some basic graph models.

If you again try to develop a graph model from the specification, you might come up with the following graph pattern:

```
(:User)-[:PUBLISH]->(:Tweet)
```

For a more compact text representation of the model, you can usually leave the node and relationship properties out of the Cypher pattern syntax. There are two types of nodes present: users and tweets. All you need to add is a relationship between them to indicate the author of the tweet. A good practice is to describe your graph model as domain specifically as possible. For example, you could have also used a more generic label for tweets such as `Post`. With more generic labels, you might run into issues along the way if you are asked to add additional information about users from Facebook, LinkedIn, or Stack Overflow. Each social media platform is unique and generates distinct data. For instance, a tweet has different attributes than a Facebook post, LinkedIn update, or Stack Overflow question. This means a `Post` node could have numerous optional attributes and relationships, many of which remain unused, depending on the type of the post, leading to potential complications and inefficiencies. Therefore, it's often beneficial to have specific node labels for different types of posts. This way, the graph database is modeled more closely to the domain-specific data it's handling, allowing for more efficient and simpler querying If you follow the guideline to model the graph as close to the domain as possible, you will end up with node types `User` and `Tweet`, as shown in figure 2.13..

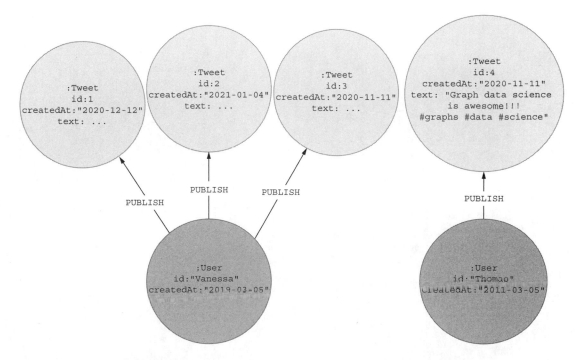

Figure 2.13 User–tweet network

You already established a unique identifier for users in the previous exercise. Now, you can do something similar and assume there is a unique ID created for each tweet when it is created. The tweet's unique identifier, creation time, and text are stored as the properties of a `Tweet` node. As there are two distinct labels of nodes present, you are dealing with a bipartite network. In this example, the direction of the relationship is not very important. You could turn the relationship direction around and change the relationship type to something more appropriate like `PUBLISHED_BY`. Both approaches are correct; you need to pick one and stick to it. My preference is to define relationship types in active voice, which is `PUBLISH` in this example. What you don't want to have is both modeling options present at the same time. You don't have to worry about query performance, as there is no penalty for traversing a relationship in the opposite direction in a native graph database.

The right-side example in figure 2.14 demonstrates what you should avoid when you are developing a graph model. When the relationship in the opposite direction adds no semantic value, it is a good practice to avoid adding it to the model in a labeled-property graph database. You also don't have to worry about getting from a Tweet to a User node. With Cypher query language syntax, you can traverse any relationship in the opposite direction, or you can completely ignore direction.

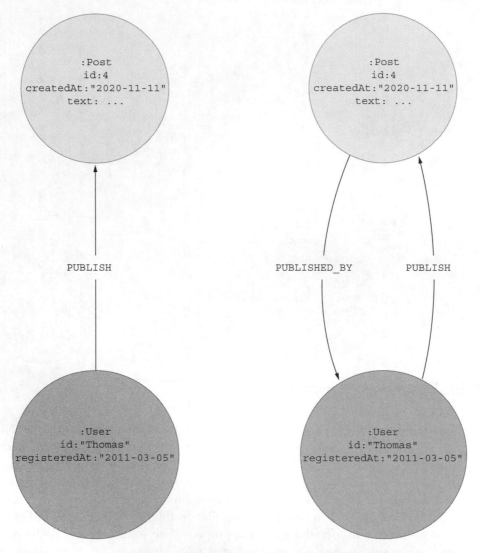

Figure 2.14   A comparison of two graph models, where the left model has a single relationship type to capture all the relevant information, and the right model uses a redundant relationship type in opposite direction

Another question that might come up is why you store the tweet creation date as a property of the node and not the relationship. It is a valid question, and as always, it mostly depends on the domain you are dealing with. In the Twitter universe, a tweet can have only a single author. Having a single author implies that a tweet will have precisely one PUBLISH relationship pointing to it; therefore, a tweet is created only once. When you are making such decisions, you should always include the types of queries you want to execute on this graph model. If you think of the most basic use case, where you want to count the number of tweets per day, it is simpler to have the creation date stored as a property of the tweet node instead of the PUBLISH relationship. You will learn more about how graph-pattern query languages work in chapter 3.

Users liking a tweet would be an example for which adding the creation date on the relationship makes more sense. While there can be only a single tweet author, many users can like a given tweet. To capture the creation time of a like from a particular user, it makes sense to store the creation time information as a relationship property, as shown in figure 2.15. If you wanted to store the time information about the likes on the Tweet node in the form of an array of dates, you would lose the information about which users gave a like at that time.

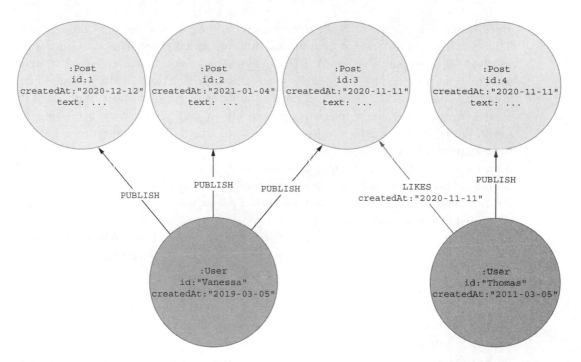

Figure 2.15   An example of a Twitter post LIKE relationship, when it makes sense to store the creation date as a property of the relationship

From the network science perspective, having only PUBLISH relationships between users and tweets is not so interesting. As each tweet has only a single relationship pointing to it, there are no overlaps or similarities between tweets you could try to analyze. However, if you added LIKES relationships to the model, you could analyze which users like the same or similar content and create segments of users based on the content they like.

2.3.3   Retweet network

The only remaining task specification is the definition of a graph model for retweets. When users strongly react to a tweet, they might want to share it with their followers to amplify its reach. In this case, they have the option of retweeting the original tweet. Optionally, users can like the retweet, and those likes do not count toward the original tweet. The task specification is defined as follows: *A user can retweet posts from other users.*

This specification is a bit more complex than the previous two. You can't just extract the subject and the object of the sentence and use that to describe the nodes. The user–tweet network is already defined, so you can expand on that and add the retweets in the graph model. There are several graph model variations you can choose from. A simple option is to add the RETWEET relationship between the user and the original tweet.

Cypher syntax to describe this pattern looks like this:

```
(:User)-[:PUBLISH]->(:Tweet)<-[:RETWEETS]-(:User)
```

Here, you are using the RETWEET relationship between a user and the original tweet. This graph schema does not treat a retweet as an actual tweet. This is neither good nor bad—it all depends on your use case and what you want to achieve with the analysis. There is, however, a slight problem with this approach. On Twitter, a retweet can also have likes that are tied to the retweet and not the original post. With the LPG model, you can't create a relationship pointing to another relationship. Using the graph model in figure 2.16, you lose the ability to attach likes to the retweet. Later in this chapter, you will extract information from retweets text, such as hashtags and mentions. There, you will again face the issue of not having the ability to attach hashtags and mention information to the retweet relationship. If the Twitter domain did not allow separate likes that are not counted separately, then having a retweet as a relationship would make sense. Unfortunately, that is not the case when dealing with the Twitter domain. To solve this issue, you can treat the retweet as a separate tweet that references the original tweet. This way, you keep the graph consistency while still being able to add additional information to retweets later on.

You can still easily differentiate between tweets and retweets. For now, don't worry about the underlying data and how you can retrieve it. You will learn more about the Twitter data source in the next chapter. When retweeting a tweet on Twitter, a user can optionally add their comment to the retweet. In this example, we have skipped this scenario because it was not a part of the specifications; however, we will examine how to model quote tweet interactions in the next chapter. A retweet has an outgoing RETWEETS relationship, and the original tweet can only have an incoming RETWEETS relationship. The graph model where you store the retweet as a separate node (shown in figure 2.17) also allows you to add other relationships to it later in the analysis, if needed. Again, you

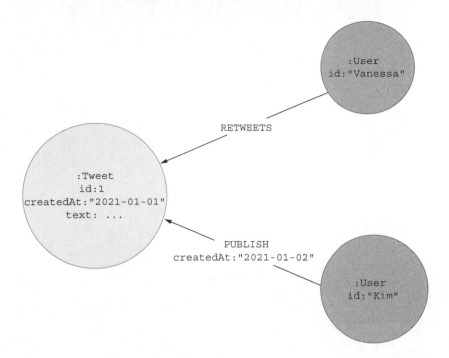

**Figure 2.16   Graph model of the retweet network, where the RETWEET relationship
is defined between the original tweet and the user who retweeted it**

want to evaluate how you can use this graph to extract insights. Remember, most often, users retweet a tweet when they strongly react to its content and want to share it with their followers. You could count the retweets and try to identify the most popular tweet topics or their authors. You could also infer a new direct relationship between users based on the retweet pattern. Translating indirect graph patterns to direct relationships is a frequent intermediate step in the network analysis. In the retweet network case, you could infer a direct relationship between users based on how often they retweet other users.

Figure 2.17 demonstrates a scenario in which Vanessa just retweeted a tweet from Kim. If you assume a retweet is always a positive interaction, you could presume that Vanessa actively promotes Kim's tweet and amplifies its reach. This indirect amplification pattern can be translated to a direct relationship between Kim and Vanessa, as shown in figure 2.18.

You can use the text representation to show that you take the following graph pattern:

```
(:User)-[:PUBLISH]->(:Tweet)<-[:RETWEETS]-(:User)
```

You can then translate this indirect relationship pattern into a direct relationship between users:

```
(:User)-[:AMPLIFY]->(:User)
```

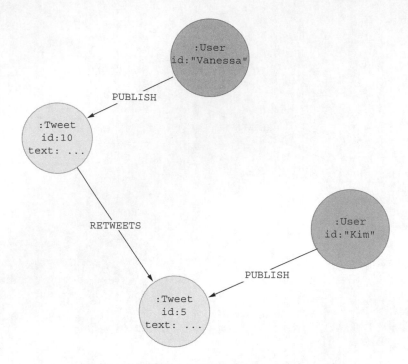

Figure 2.17   Graph model of the retweet network, where the retweet is treated as a tweet that references the original tweet

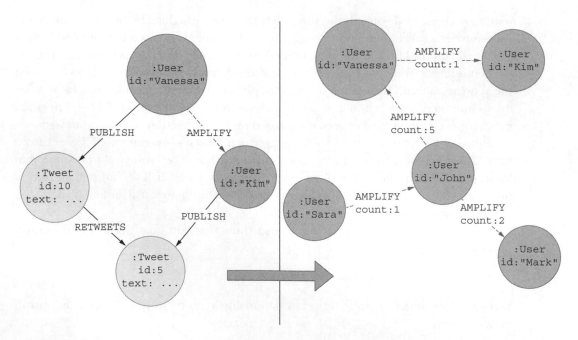

Figure 2.18   Inferring a new network from an indirect pattern of retweet relationships

By translating an indirect pattern to a direct relationship, you are creating a new inferred network. The type of the inferred relationship depends on your domain use case. Here, I have chosen the AMPLIFY type, as the retweet amplifies the reach of the original tweet. The new inferred AMPLIFY relationship is directed, as the direction of the relationship holds semantic value. It is also weighted, as you can quantify the strength of the AMPLIFY relationship by counting the number of retweets. If a user retweets a post from another user a single time, then the weight of the AMPLIFY relationships is 1. However, if a user regularly retweets posts from another user, the weight would be equal to the number of retweets. You could, again, search for influencers within this inferred network or try to find communities of users who actively support each other by promoting their content.

2.3.4 Representing graph schema

The beauty of the graph approach to data modeling is that you can always connect new information to an existing graph. You can now combine all the graph model decisions so far into a single graph model. Figure 2.19 visualizes the graph with

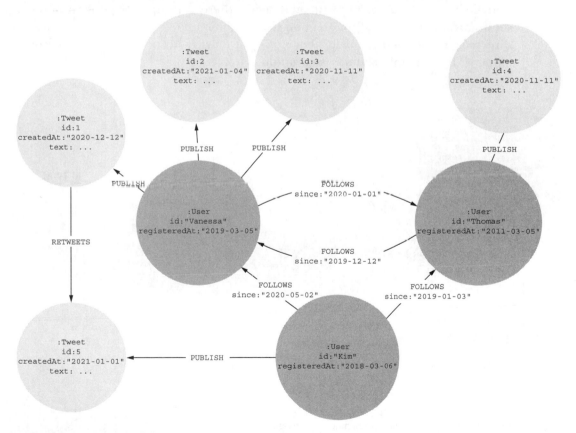

Figure 2.19 Labeled-property graph representing a Twitter network, where users can follow one another as well as publish and retweet posts

combined data that follows your decision on how to model users, their followers, tweets, and retweets.

Over the years, people have come up with ways to represent an LPG graph schema. There is no official standard to present an LPG graph schema, but we will now discuss perhaps the most common approach.

Each node type or label is represented as a single node. There are two different labels of nodes present in the current Twitter network representation. You can describe them as two nodes in the graph schema representation as shown in figure 2.20. The node properties are then added to the node representing each label. Optionally, you can add example values to the node properties, but I prefer to add their data type as the value. For now, there is no agreed-upon way to visualize whether a node property is optional or whether it is used as a unique identifier. Relationships between the same label of nodes are represented as a self-loop. A self-loop is a relationship that has the same start and end node. On the right side of figure 2.20, there are two self-loops present. The FOLLOWS relationship starts and points to nodes with the User type. Additionally, the RETWEETS relationships starts and points to nodes with a type Tweet. Unfortunately, again, there is no agreed-upon way of representing when a relationship direction has semantic value (i.e., should be treated as directed or undirected) or not. For now, you must read the fine print that comes along with the graph schema visualization.

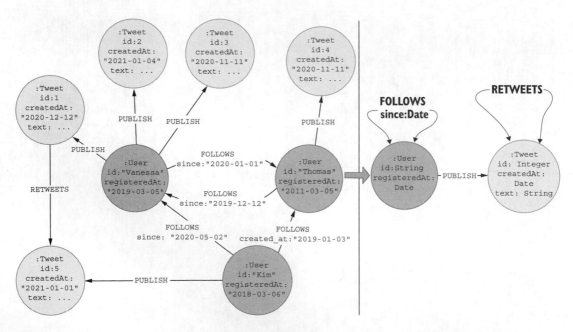

Figure 2.20   Twitter social network graph model representation

2.4   *Extracting knowledge from text*

You have learned how to construct a graph model based on the graph-based features of the data. Next, you will learn how you can extract relevant information from the text and incorporate them into your knowledge graph model. To get a sense of what information you can extract from the tweet content, let's look at an example tweet.

The tweet in figure 2.21 incorporates several elements to maximize its reach and interactivity. The hashtags, such as #KnowledgeGraph, #NamedEntityLinking, #Wikipedia, #NLP, #DataScience, and #Graphs are tools for categorizing the content and making it discoverable to users interested in these specific topics, thereby increasing its visibility on Twitter's platform. Links, like the Medium article URL, provide direct access to additional relevant content, allowing followers to explore the topic in depth. Mentions, represented by the @ symbol followed by a Twitter username (e.g., @tb_tomaz and @CatedraBOB), are used to directly address or reference specific

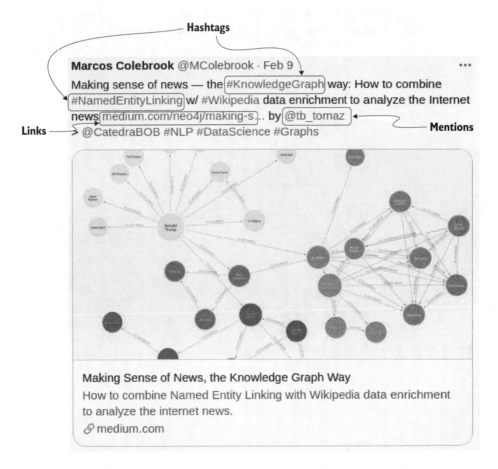

Figure 2.21   An example tweet, where mentions, links, and hashtags are present

individuals or organizations, creating a conversation and fostering engagement within the Twitter community.

2.4.1 Links

The first information you could extract from tweet content is any links included in the tweet. It should be pretty straightforward to process any links from the text.

> **Exercise 2.4**
>
> Now that you have some experience developing a labeled-property graph (LPG) model, what do you think is the best approach to add the link information in the Twitter graph model? You have already defined the tweet in the model; now you only need to add the extracted links information to them.

I can think of two options. You could either store the URL as a tweet node property or store it as a separate node and add a relationship between the link and the tweet (figure 2.22).

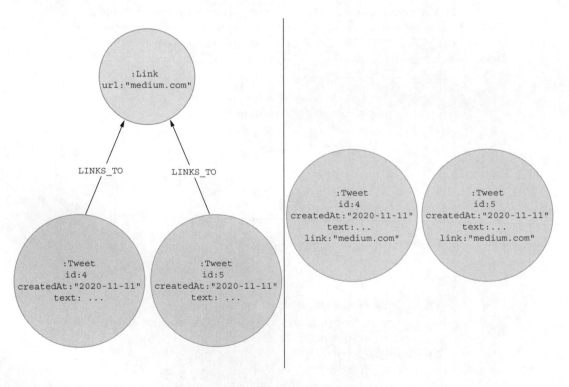

Figure 2.22   Two options for storing the extracted link from the tweet

Which approach do you think is better? With both approaches, you have the option to store one or many links, as you can use a list of strings as a node property. The real answer depends on your queries. Do you want to group tweets with the same links in your analysis or not? If you store links as node properties, it will be computationally more expensive to find tweets with the same link, as you need to compare all elements in a list between all pairs of tweets. You can avoid that by storing links as separate nodes. By using separate nodes to represent links, you only need to traverse two relationships to get from one tweet to another or even all tweets with the same links. This approach will scale much better if you are interested in grouping nodes with the same links.

Graph modeling considerations

When considering whether you want to store information as separate nodes or node properties, it is important to examine whether the values are standardized. Take a look at the example of links in a tweet. When discrete values are not standardized, storing that information as separate nodes doesn't make sense. The whole point of using separate nodes to store information is to allow faster traversals at query runtime. When values are not standardized, you lose the ability to traverse fast between persons that live in the same city. A rule of thumb is that a single real-world entity or concept should be represented as a single node in the graph. In the following figure, the Medium website is represented as three different nodes, which would return invalid information if you were trying to find tweets with the same links. While storing the link information as a node property does not solve the issue of finding tweets with the same links, at least you don't represent a single real-world entity as multiple nodes in your graph. The solution is to either clean and standardize the link information so that you can model links as separate nodes or store the link information as a node property to avoid having a single entity represented as multiple nodes in the graph.

Another topic to consider is how specific that information is. For example, suppose the information is very unspecific and doesn't add much value from the information point of view, like the gender of a user. In that case, it is better to store that information as a node property. One reason for this is that you avoid having nodes that can be connected to large parts of the graph. With the gender example, you could have nodes connected to almost half of the users in the graph. Nodes connected to large parts of the graph are called *super nodes*, and you generally want to avoid them in your graph, as they can hinder query performance, due to the sheer number of relationships attached to them.

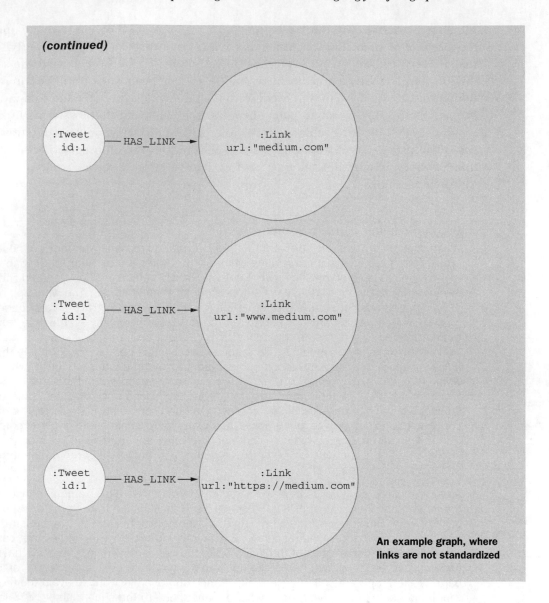

(continued)

An example graph, where links are not standardized

2.4.2   Hashtags

The other information you can extract from tweet content is the hashtags. People use the hashtag symbol (#) before a relevant keyword or phrase in their tweet to categorize them. A tweet can contain many hashtags; it makes sense to store them as separate nodes and connect tweets to them, as shown in figure 2.23.

An important consideration is that you want to avoid generic relationship types like HAS, where you could use it in many scenarios. You want your relationship types to have meaning (e.g., if you traverse a LINKS_TO relationship from a tweet, you will

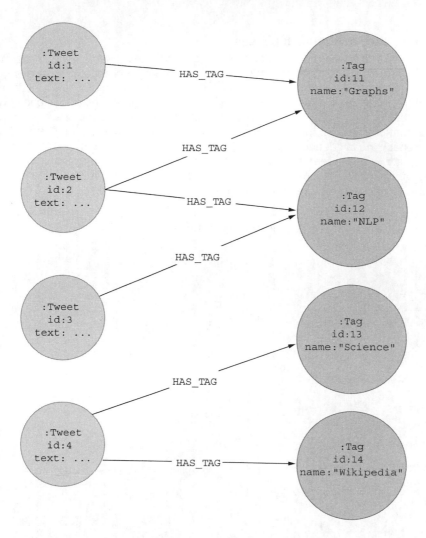

Figure 2.23 Graph model of tweet's hashtags

always land at a Link node). Similarly, if you traverse a HAS_TAG relationship from a tweet, you will always arrive at a Tag node. It's important to keep in mind that you don't want to end up with a single relationship type that can lead to many different node types. Using a generic relationship type can hinder the expressiveness of a graph model and negatively affect query processing times.

Avoiding generic relationship types

Suppose you were dealing with a graph model of Twitter that used a generic HAS relationship between various types of nodes. For example, say you want to retrieve all tweet hashtags. The engine must expand all outgoing HAS relationships of a Tweet node and check if the node at the end of the relationship is a Tag node. On the other hand, if you used a specific HAS_TAG relationship to connect tags to tweets, you would avoid traversing relationships that do not point to a Tag node. Additionally, the engine does not need to check the target node type, since it is guaranteed that the HAS_TAG relationship points to a Tag node. Therefore, using generic relationship types may result in slower query performance, as the database needs to search through a greater number of relationships to find the graph patterns that match the query.

Using a generic relationship type can also hinder the clarity and maintainability of a graph. In the example in the following figure, the HAS relationship is used to indicate

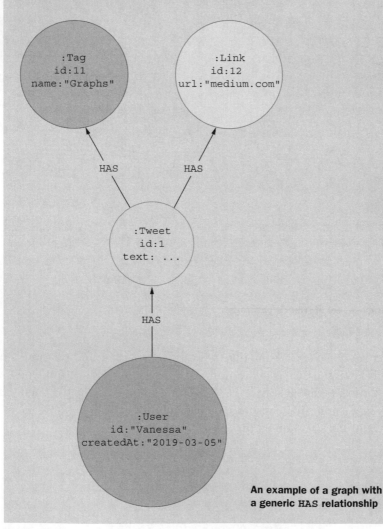

**An example of a graph with
a generic HAS relationship**

the author of a tweet as well as its hashtags and links. Using a generic relationship type can lead to confusion or errors when querying or modifying the graph. Instead, defining specific relationship types that describe the nature of the relationship can make the graph easier to understand and work with and, consequently, help ensure the graph remains consistent and correct over time, due to a less error-prone schema.

The graph in figure 2.24 is a bipartite network consisting of tweet and hashtag nodes. When dealing with a bipartite network, it is a common analysis workflow step to project it to a monopartite network. For example, if a pair of tweets share the same hashtag, you could assume they are somehow connected. This is a process similar to the one you saw in the retweet network, where you translated indirect graph patterns to direct relationships. The transformation of a bipartite network of hashtags and tweets to a monopartite network is visualized in figure 2.24.

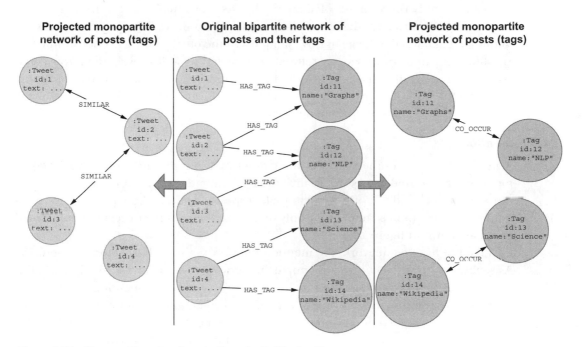

Figure 2.24   Monopartite network projection of a Twitter hashtag

You can observe that you always have the option to project a bipartite network to both types of nodes. In a bipartite network of tweets and their hashtags, you can project it to a monopartite network of tweets or hashtags. How you name the new inferred relationship depends on the domain. I have added a SIMILAR relationship between tweets, as I assume that tweets with more overlapping hashtags can be deemed more similar. On the other hand, hashtags can also be similar if they frequently co-occur. To put it in text representation of networks, you can transform the following indirect graph pattern:

```
(:Tweet)-[:HAS_TAG]->(:Tag)<-[:HAS_TAG]-(:Tweet)
```

You can transform it to a more direct graph pattern:

```
(:Tweet)-[:SIMILAR]-(:Tweet)
```

You might have noticed that a common approach to network analysis is to reduce a complex graph pattern to a network with a single type of nodes and relationships. This is because most classical graph algorithms, like centrality or community detection algorithms, are designed to have a monopartite network as an input. With monopartite projections, the direction of the relationship often does not hold any semantic value. If tweet A is similar to tweet B, then tweet B is also similar to tweet A. You can quantify the strength of similarity between two tweets by counting the number of common hashtags they have. As a result, most inferred similarity networks are undirected and weighted, like in this example. On the other hand, a previously inferred amplification network based on retweets is directed as well as weighted. You could analyze the inferred similarity network of tweets and try to find users who publish similar content. Note that you could also combine information from other parts of the graph to infer a new monopartite network.

2.4.3   Mentions

A user can mention other users in their tweet by using the mention symbol (@). A mention can be understood as an invitation to comment or a callout, while at other times, it can be used to notify users to look at specific content. You already have users defined in the graph schema, so it only makes sense to connect tweets to mentioned users, as shown in figure 2.25.

Like the hashtag network, the mention network is also a classic bipartite network. As such, you can project it to a monopartite network of users or tweets (figure 2.26). For example, you could analyze which users are frequently co-mentioned and try to examine the community structure of the inferred co-mention network between users. Something else you could examine is whether the mentioned person interacted with the tweet. You could also combine mention information with other information in the graph and inspect the most common hashtags of tweets in which a user is mentioned. One strategy you could use is to take the mention information and integrate it into follower recommendations.

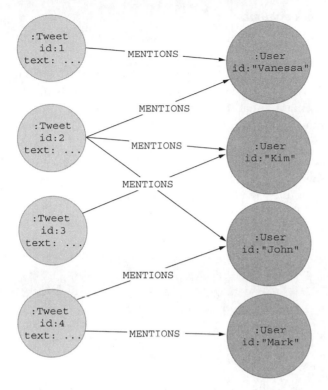

Figure 2.25 Graph model of tweet's mentions

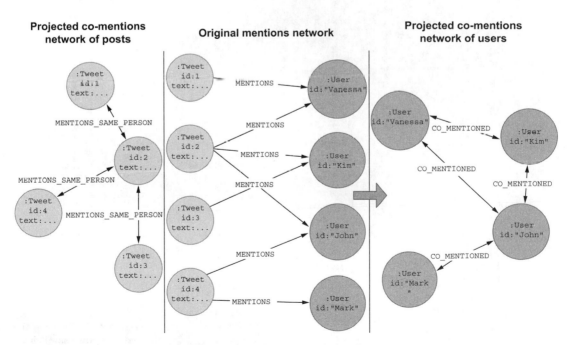

Figure 2.26 Twitter mention network folding or monopartite projection

2.4.4   *Final Twitter social network schema*

Designing a graph model schema is an iterative process. You have slowly added additional information to the graph model, and it has gradually become richer in knowledge. When adding new data to the graph model, designing a self-describing graph schema is recommended. With a self-describing graph model, you can avoid additional work to create a schema manual for others to learn about the information the graph stores and how to query it. Finally, the graph schema might change, depending on the queries you will be executing, as you might want to optimize the performance of specific queries. You can observe the following graph structure if you put all the graph model design considerations you have made so far into a single visualization.

Figure 2.27 shows an example Twitter network, where there are four distinct types or labels of nodes present. There are users, tweets, hashtags, and link nodes in the

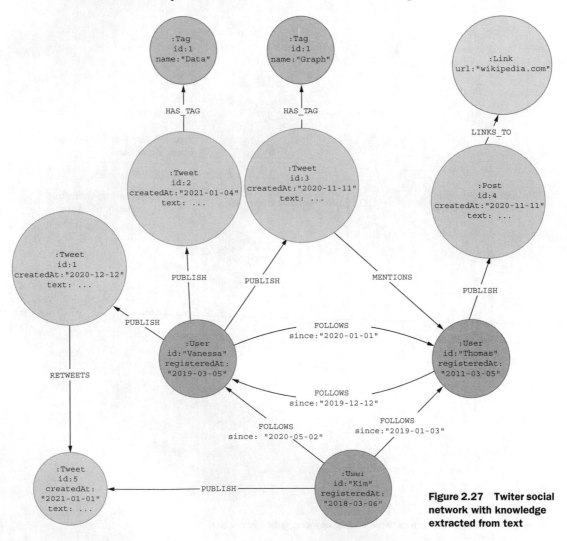

Figure 2.27   Twiter social network with knowledge extracted from text

final Twitter graph model. Along the way, you have also introduced six different types of relationships. If you sum it up, you can represent this example network with the graph schema shown in figure 2.28.

You only want to add the inferred relationships that will be instantiated to the graph schema. Inferred relationships and similarity networks are created based on assumptions you might make during the network analysis. You don't know which inferred relationships will be instantiated yet, so it makes sense to leave them out of the graph schema for now. The final graph schema representation can be viewed in figure 2.28.

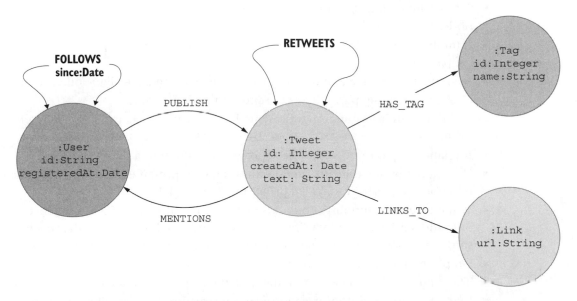

Figure 2.28 Final Twitter social network graph schema representation

You might have noticed that a common theme in network analysis is to translate indirect graph patterns and relationships to direct ones. Using a graph database with a dedicated graph-pattern query language makes it easier for you to instantiate those network transformations. For example, you can translate the retweet links between tweets to direct amplification relationships between users. Another frequent scenario is translating a bipartite network to a monopartite network. Monopartite projections are used because most graph algorithms are designed to work on networks with a single type of nodes and relationships. In the next chapter, you will learn the basics of Cypher and how to import a network based on the graph model you derived in this chapter.

Summary

- The labeled-property graph model is represented by a set of nodes, relationships, node labels, and properties.
- An undirected relationship can be traversed in both directions.
- An undirected graph can be represented as a directed graph, where each relationship is replaced by two that point in the opposite direction.
- A relationship can be weighted, where the weight represents the strength or cost of traversing the relationship.
- A monopartite graph contains only a single node and relationship type.
- A bipartite graph contains two sets of nodes, and no relationship exist between nodes in the same sets.
- A multigraph is a type of graph that allows multiple relationships between a single pair of nodes.
- A complete graph is a graph in which nodes are connected to all the other nodes.
- Cypher syntax uses parentheses to represent nodes: `(:Node)`.
- Relationships in Cypher are represented with square brackets: `()-[:RELATION-SHIP]-()`.
- A relationship cannot exist or be represented without its adjacent nodes.
- Depending on the domain, literal values can be represented as a separate node or a node property in a labeled-property graph model.
- When a relationship direction adds no semantic value, it is a good practice to only add a relationship in a single direction and avoid duplicating the relationship in the opposite direction when using a labeled-property graph database.
- Graph modeling is an iterative process.
- The graph model can be represented with the graph model schema visualization.
- Extracting structured information from unstructured text is valuable for most data analysis.
- Reducing indirect graph patterns to direct relationships (monopartite projection) is a frequent step in network analysis.

Part 2

Network analysis

Now that you are equipped with the fundamental knowledge of graph terminology and modeling, you are ready to learn how to use a graph query language and graph algorithms to perform a social network analysis and uncover hidden or indirect patterns that might be missed with traditional analytical approaches. Chapters 3 and 4 are designed to introduce you to Cypher query language and show you how to use it in exploratory graph analysis. In chapter 5, you will learn how to characterize a network by examining a social graph of Twitter followers. You'll look at the node degree distribution and use graph algorithms, like weakly connected components and local clustering coefficient algorithms, followed by identifying the most important nodes in the graph with the Page-Rank algorithm. A significant part of graph analysis involves the transformation of a graph to align with the structure the graph algorithms expect. Therefore, you will learn how to transform an indirect relationship to a direct one in chapter 6, construct and analyze a co-occurrence network in chapter 7, and manually define and extract node role features and use them to produce a nearest neighbor graph in chapter 8.

3

Your first steps with Cypher query language

This chapter covers

- Introducing the Cypher query language syntax
- Creating nodes and relationships with Cypher
- Matching and retrieving data from the database
- Removing properties and deleting nodes and relationships
- Best practices for importing a CSV into a graph database

So far, you have learned a bit of graph theory and how to approach the labeled-property graph modeling process. Now, you will begin to learn how to perform network analysis through practical use cases. To follow the examples in this book, you need to set up a Neo4j development environment. If you need some help getting started with the setup, see the appendix.

This chapter will introduce Cypher query language clauses and best practices for importing data into a graph database. First, I will do a quick recap of using Cypher query language syntax to represent networks in a textual format. If you are already familiar with the Cypher query syntax, you can skip most of the chapter and just import the data as shown in the last section. Remember from the previous chapter that the Cypher syntax uses parentheses to encapsulate a representation of a node. A quick reminder how to describe a node with Cypher syntax is shown in figure 3.1.

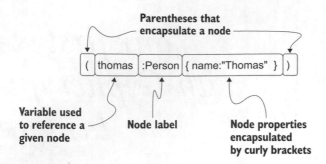

Figure 3.1   Cypher query language syntax to represent a node with its label and properties

In this example, I have described a node with a label `Person`. The label of the node is always preceded by a colon. Node properties are key–value pairs wrapped inside the curly brackets. The example node has only a single property with a key, `name`, and its value, `Thomas`. In Cypher, you can also add a variable, which is used as a reference to the specific node, at the start of the node. You can choose any name for the reference variable; in this example, I have chosen the reference variable `thomas`. The node variable allows you to refer to this particular node later in the Cypher statement, and it is only valid within the context of a single Cypher statement. You can use the node variable to access its properties and labels; use it in expressions; or create new patterns related to a given node. In Cypher, the relationships are represented with square brackets.

A relationship can only exist when it is adjacent to both a source node and a target node. When you are describing a relationship with Cypher, you always need to include the adjacent nodes. Each relationship has a single type; like node labels, the relationship type is also preceded by a colon. The example in figure 3.2 describes a relationship with a `FRIEND` type. Relationship properties are described like node properties, and each relationship can be assigned a variable (in this example, `f`) that can be used later in the Cypher statement to refer to the given connection.

NOTE   In Neo4j, each relationship is stored as directed. You can, however, ignore the relationship direction when executing a Cypher query or a graph algorithm on top of the stored graph. A common practice in Neo4j is to store an undirected relationship as a single directed relationship. When executing Cypher queries, you can then ignore the direction of the relationship and treat it as undirected. While this is a relevant aspect in Neo4j, it can be difficult to understand at first, so throughout the book, I will show you practical examples of how to differentiate between storing the graph and how to query it.

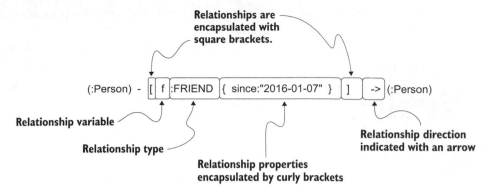

Figure 3.2 Cypher query language syntax to represent a relationship with its type and properties

3.1 *Cypher query language clauses*

Armed with the knowledge of how to describe a node and a relationship in Cypher, we will now begin our discussion of Cypher clauses. To follow along with the examples, you need to have a working Neo4j environment ready. I recommend you use the Neo4j Browser to execute Cypher queries. Again, if you need some help with setting up a Neo4j environment and accessing the Neo4j Browser, I suggest reviewing the appendix.

3.1.1 *CREATE clause*

You will begin by learning how to create data with Cypher. The CREATE clause is used to store nodes and relationships in the graph database. While Cypher query language clauses are not case sensitive, it is a best practice to write Cypher clauses in uppercase for easier readability. For more information on the Cypher style guide, see this Neo4j web page: https://neo4j.com/developer/cypher/style-guide/. You can store any graph pattern by using Cypher syntax to describe node and relationship patterns.

You will begin by creating a single node in the graph. The statement in the following listing creates a new node with a label Person and a single node property.

> **Listing 3.1 Cypher query that stores a node with a label Person and a property name with the value Satish**

```
CREATE (p:Person{name:'Satish'})
```

With every execution of the query in listing 3.1, a new node will be created in the database. The CREATE clause does not check for existing data in the graph database; it blindly follows the command to create a new pattern in the database.

If you want to retrieve the created graph elements and visualize them in Neo4j Browser, you can use the RETURN clause. There can be only a single RETURN clause in a Cypher query and only as the last clause of a query. As always, there are some exceptions where you can have multiple RETURN clauses in a query. Those exceptions are unions and subqueries, which you will learn about later.

The Cypher statement in the following listing starts by creating a node with the Person label and the name property.

> **Listing 3.2   Cypher query that creates a node and fetches its information with the RETURN clause**

```
CREATE (p:Person{name:'Frodo'})
RETURN p
```

The created node is referenced with the p variable. To fetch the information about the created node from the database, you can use the RETURN clause and define which variables you want to retrieve. In this example, you want to retrieve the p variable.

The Cypher statement in listing 3.2 produces the output shown in figure 3.3 in the Neo4j Browser. This visualization depicts a single node that is returned by the Cypher statement in listing 3.2. Additionally, Neo4j Browser has a few visualization options, like node color and size options, along with the caption definition. Learn more about Neo4j Browser styling in the browser manual (http://mng.bz/j1ge).

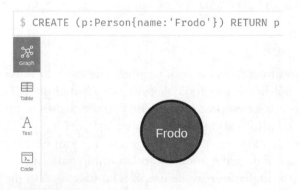

Figure 3.3   The output of the Cypher statement in listing 3.2

> **Exercise 3.1**
>
> To get practice creating graphs, create a new node in the graph with a label Person and two node properties. The first node property holds the information about your name, and the second node property holds the information about your age.

You can use multiple CREATE clauses in a single Cypher statement. By using the variable of nodes and relationships, you can modify and connect them in the subsequent CREATE queries.

The Cypher statement in the following listing demonstrates how to create two nodes and a relationship between them.

> **Listing 3.3 Cypher query that stores two nodes and a relationship between them in the database**

```
CREATE (elaine:Person{name:'Elaine'}), (michael:Person {name: 'Michael'})
CREATE (elaine)-[f:FRIEND]->(michael)
RETURN *
```

In the first CREATE clause, two nodes are created, and in the second CREATE clause, a relationship between them is added. While you could combine these two CREATE clauses into a single clause, it is recommended as a best practice to create nodes and relationships separately.

You might have noticed that the Cypher statement in listing 3.3 uses a * wildcard operator in the RETURN clause. The wildcard operator * will return all variables in scope.

Exercise 3.2

Try to create two nodes, one that represents you and one that represents the organization you work at. You will likely want to use different node labels to describe a person and an organization. Then, in the same Cypher statement, create a relationship between yourself and your employer. You can try to add a relationship property indicating when you started to work in your current role.

Remember, you can only store directed relationships in the Neo4j graph database. Let's see what happens when you try to create an undirected relationship in the following listing.

> **Listing 3.4 Cypher query that tries to stores an undirected relationship in the database and fails**

```
CREATE (elaine:Person{name:'Elaine'}), (michael:Person {name: 'Michael'})
CREATE (elaine)-[:FRIEND]-(michael)
RETURN *
```

The Cypher statement in listing 3.4 fails due to only being able to store directed relationships in the database. While the relationship direction arrow seems to be such a small part of the query, it is very influential to how the query will behave.

Another common misconception among beginners is that they forget that reference variables are only visible within the same Cypher statement. As stated previously, the CREATE statement performs no database lookup before inserting new data in the graph. The following Cypher statement looks OK at first glance, but it is actually quite awful.

> **Listing 3.5 Cypher query that stores two empty nodes with no labels and a relationship between them in the database**

```
CREATE (ankit)-[f:FRIEND]->(elaine)
RETURN *
```

Can you deduce why? As the CREATE statement performs no database lookups and does not have variable reference visibility between Cypher queries, it will just create a new pattern we have described. Therefore, the Cypher statement in listing 3.5 creates a FRIEND relationship between two nodes with no labels and no properties. You must be very careful to avoid these types of situations. There are no situations in the labeled property graph model in which you would want to have nodes without any labels stored in the database. At a minimum, you can add a generic Node label to each node.

> **NOTE**   The labeled-property graph model is so flexible that it allows you to create nodes without labels or properties. However, you should always strive to, at the very least, add a label to every node you store in the database. Having labeled nodes will help with model readability as well as query execution performances. I can safely say that if you have nodes without a label in your graph, something is wrong with either your model or your import process.

Exercise 3.3

The goal of this exercise is to create three nodes and two relationships between them. The nodes should represent the city, country, and continent you currently live in. Add one relationship between the city and the country and the second relationship between the country and the continent. Take a couple of minutes to decide what relationship types you want to use and the direction of relationships.

3.1.2   *MATCH clause*

You can search for existing graph patterns stored in the database using the MATCH clause. Cypher is a declarative query language, which means you only need to specify the pattern you are interested in and let the query engine take care of how to retrieve those patterns from the database. In the previous section, you created at least three nodes with the label Person and different name property values. If you want to find a Person node with a specific name property value, you can use the following query.

> **Listing 3.6   Cypher statement that searches and retrieves any nodes with a label Person and a name property with a value of Satish**

```
MATCH (p:Person {name:'Satish'})
RETURN p
```

You can observe why it was critical first to learn how to describe node and relationship patterns with Cypher before you wrote your first Cypher clause. When you know how to describe a graph pattern, you can use the MATCH clause to retrieve it from the database. The query in listing 3.6 uses *inline* graph pattern matching. Inline pattern matching uses Cypher pattern syntax to describe a node or relationship pattern with its labels and properties. The opposite of inline pattern matching is using a WHERE clause to describe a graph pattern.

> **Listing 3.7 Cypher statement that searches and retrieves any nodes with a label `Person` and a `name` property with a value of `Satish` using a `WHERE` clause**

```
MATCH (p)
WHERE p:Person AND p.name = 'Satish'
RETURN p
```

The query in listing 3.7 will produce the exact same query plan and results as the query in listing 3.6. The inline syntax is just syntactic sugar that improves readability. Using the WHERE clause, you have described you want to retrieve a node with the label Person and the name property with a value of Satish. My personal preference is to describe the node label with inline graph pattern and provide additional matching filters in the WHERE clause.

> **Listing 3.8 Cypher statement that combines inline graph pattern matching with a `WHERE` clause to describe a graph pattern**

```
MATCH (p:Person)
WHERE p.name = 'Satish' OR p.name = 'Elaine'
RETURN p.name AS person
```

The Cypher statement in listing 3.8 introduces the AS operator. With the AS operator, you can name or alias a variable reference, which allows you to produce more readable query outputs.

Exercise 3.4

As an exercise, try to retrieve all the nodes with a label Person from the database. You can use the inline graph pattern description, or you can use a WHERE clause. In the RETURN statement, only return the name properties of the nodes. Use the AS operator to alias the name property to produce a more readable column name.

You can always have multiple MATCH clauses in a sequence; however, the WHERE clause only applies to the previous MATCH clause. If you use many MATCH clauses in a sequence, make sure to append a WHERE clause to each MATCH clause, where needed.

> **Listing 3.9 Cypher statement that combines inline graph pattern matching with a `WHERE` clause to describe a graph pattern**

```
MATCH (satish:Person)
WHERE satish.name = 'Satish'
MATCH (elaine:Person)
WHERE elaine.name = 'Elaine'
RETURN *
```

NOTE A WHERE clause can only exist when it follows a WITH, a MATCH, or an OPTIONAL MATCH clause. When you have many MATCH or WITH clauses in sequence, make sure to append the WHERE clause after each of them, where needed. You might sometimes get the same results even if you only use a single WHERE clause after multiple MATCH statements, but the query performance will most likely be worse.

The MATCH clause is often used to find existing nodes or relationships in the database and then insert additional data with a CREATE or MERGE clause. For example, you could use the MATCH clause to find nodes labeled Person with names Elaine and Satish and create a new relationship between them.

> **Listing 3.10   Cypher query that find two nodes in the database and creates a new FRIEND relationship between them**

```
MATCH (from:Person), (to:Person)
WHERE from.name = 'Satish' AND to.name = 'Elaine'
CREATE (from)-[f:FRIEND]->(to)
RETURN *
```

The statement in listing 3.10 combines the MATCH and CREATE clauses to create a new relationship between existing nodes in the database.

> **Exercise 3.5**
>
> If you haven't yet created a Person node with your name as the value of the name node property, please do that first. Next, in a separate query, use the MATCH clause to find the Person nodes with your name and Elaine, which also needs to exist in your database, and create a new FRIENDS relationship between them. You can add any additional relationship properties you think are appropriate.

A crucial concept when using the MATCH clause is to recognize that if a single MATCH clause within the query does not find any data matching the provided pattern in the database, the query will return no results. If you use a single MATCH clause to retrieve a nonexisting graph pattern from the database, you will get no results.

> **Listing 3.11   Cypher query that matches a nonexistent graph pattern in the database**

```
MATCH (org:Organization)
WHERE org.name = 'Acme Inc'
RETURN *
```

It is intuitive that when you try to retrieve a nonexistent graph pattern from the database, you will get no results. What is not so intuitive is that when you have multiple MATCH clauses in sequence, if only a single MATCH clause tries to retrieve a nonexistent pattern from the database, the whole query will return no results.

Listing 3.12 Cypher query that matches both an existing and a nonexisting graph pattern in the database

```
MATCH (p:Person)
WHERE p.name = 'Satish'
MATCH (b:Book)
WHERE org.title = 'Catcher in the rye'
RETURN *
```

The query in listing 3.12 first tries to find a `Person` node with a `name` property `Satish`. You have already executed this part of the query before, so you know this pattern exists in the database. The second `MATCH` clause tries to retrieve a nonexistent pattern from the database. If even a single `MATCH` clause in the query retrieves no pattern from the database, the result of the query will be empty.

OPTIONAL MATCH CLAUSE

If you do not want your query to stop when a single `MATCH` clause finds no existing graph patterns in the database, you can use the `OPTIONAL MATCH` clause. The `OPTIONAL MATCH` clause would return a `null` value if no matching patterns were found in the database instead of returning no results, behaving similarly to an `OUTER JOIN` in SQL. You can rewrite the query in listing 3.12 to expect and handle a nonexisting `Organization` pattern by using the `OPTIONAL MATCH` clause.

Listing 3.13 Cypher statement that matches both an existing and a nonexisting graph pattern in the database

```
MATCH (p:Person)
WHERE p.name = 'Satish'
OPTIONAL MATCH (b:Book)
WHERE b.title = 'Catcher in the rye'
RETURN *
```

By using the `OPTIONAL MATCH` clause as shown in listing 3.13, the statement does not return empty results when no graph patterns are found. Instead, the `null` value is returned for nonexisting graph patterns while the matched patterns are still retrieved.

The `OPTIONAL MATCH` can also be used to retrieve node relationships if they exist.

Listing 3.14 Cypher statement that matches both an existing and a nonexisting graph pattern in the database

```
MATCH (p:Person)
WHERE p.name = 'Satish'
OPTIONAL MATCH (p)-[f:FRIEND]->(f1)
RETURN *
```

The Cypher statement in listing 3.14 first matches on a `Person` node that has the `name` property value of `Satish`. Next, it uses the `OPTIONAL MATCH` to match any outgoing

FRIENDS relationships. If the FRIENDS relationships are found, it returns the relationships and the original node. However, if no FRIENDS relationships are found, the Cypher statement in listing 3.14 still returns the Person node with the name property value Satish.

> ### Exercise 3.6
> Determine whether the node representing yourself has any FRIENDS relationships in the database. Start by using the MATCH clause to match the Person node with your name. Next, use the OPTIONAL MATCH to evaluate whether there are any FRIENDS relationships attached to the node. Finally, return the specified graph patterns with the RETURN clause.

3.1.3 WITH clause

Using the WITH clause, you can manipulate the data as an intermediate step before passing the results to the next part of the Cypher query. The intermediate data manipulations within a Cypher statement before passing them on to the next part can be one or more of the following:

- Filter results
- Select results
- Aggregate results
- Paginate results
- Limit results

For example, you can use the WITH clause in combination with LIMIT to limit the number of rows.

Listing 3.15 Cypher statement that uses the WITH clause to limit the number of rows

```
MATCH (p:Person)
WITH p LIMIT 1
RETURN *
```

You can also use the WITH clause to define and calculate intermediate variables.

Listing 3.16 Cypher statement that uses the WITH clause to calculate new variables

```
CREATE (p:Person {name: "Johann", born: 1988})
WITH p.name AS name, 2023 - p.born AS age
RETURN name, age
```

The Cypher statement in listing 3.16 starts by creating a Person node with name and born properties. You can use the intermediate WITH clause to calculate the age based on the year Johann was born. Additionally, you can select any variables and alias them, like the example with the `name` property in listing 3.16.

If you wanted to, you could also use the `WITH` clause in combination with the `WHERE` clause to filter intermediate results based on existing or newly defined variables.

Listing 3.17 Cypher statement that uses the `WITH` clause in combination with `WHERE` to filter results

```
MATCH (p:Person)
WITH p.name AS name, 2023 - p.born AS age
WHERE age > 12
RETURN name, age
```

The Cypher statement in listing 3.17 introduces the calculated `age` variable in the `WITH` clause. You can use the `WHERE` clause that immediately follows the `WITH` clause to filter results based on existing or newly defined variables.

The `WITH` clause is also useful when aggregating data. In chapter 4, we will discuss data aggregation in greater depth.

3.1.4 SET clause

A `SET` clause is used to update labels of nodes and properties of both nodes and relationships. The `SET` clause is very often used in combination with the `MATCH` clause to update existing node or relationship properties.

Listing 3.18 Cypher statement that uses a `SET` clause to update existing node properties

```
MATCH (t:Person)
WHERE t.name = 'Satish'
SET t.interest = 'Gardening',
    t.hungry = True
```

There is also a special syntax for a `SET` clause to change or mutate many properties using a map data structure. The *map* data structure originated from Java and is identical to a dictionary in Python or a JSON object in JavaScript.

Listing 3.19 Cypher statement that uses a map data structure in combination with the `SET` clause to update several node properties

```
MATCH (e:Person)
WHERE e.name = 'Elaine'
SET e += {hungry: false, pet: 'dog'}
```

Note that if the `+=` operator of the `SET` clause is replaced with only `=`, it overrides all existing properties with only those provided in the map.

With the `SET` clause, you can also add additional labels to nodes.

Listing 3.20   Cypher statement that adds a secondary label to an existing node

```
MATCH (p:Person)
WHERE p.name = 'Satish'
SET p:Student
```

Multiple node labels are helpful when you want to tag your nodes for faster and easier retrieval. In the example in listing 3.20, you have added the `Student` label to the `Satish` node, and in the following exercise, you will add an appropriate label to the node representing you, such as `Student`, `Employee`, or other. A good guideline to follow when using multiple node labels is that node labels should be semantically orthogonal. *Semantically orthogonal* refers to node labels not holding the same or similar meaning and having nothing to do with one another. Secondary node labels are used to group nodes into different buckets to make each subset easily accessible. Note that a single node can have multiple secondary labels; for instance, a person could be both employed and attending college simultaneously. In that case, you could assign both `Student` and `Employee` labels to it. However, you should avoid adding more than a couple of node labels to a single node for modeling and performance reasons.

In my work, I have also noticed that using multiple labels is helpful in scenarios in which you precalculate some values and assign additional node labels based on those values. For example, if you work with a customer in a marketing funnel, you can add the secondary label to a node according to its funnel stage. Figure 3.4 shows three `Person` nodes; however, all the nodes have a secondary node label. If you had a graph of people on your website, you could use the secondary node label to tag their position in the marketing funnel. For example, people who have already made the purchase could be tagged with a secondary `Customer` label.

Figure 3.4   Using multiple node labels to assign customer funnel stage

> ### Exercise 3.8
> Match the `Person` node representing you (i.e., it has your name as the `name` property value). Then, add a secondary `Reader` label to it.

3.1.5 REMOVE clause

The `REMOVE` clause is the opposite of the `SET` clause. It is used to remove node labels and node and relationship properties. Removing a node property can also be understood as setting its value to `null`. If you want to remove the `hungry` property from the `Person` node with the name `Satish`, you can execute the following Cypher query.

> **Listing 3.21 Cypher statement that removes a node property from an existing node in the database**

```
MATCH (t:Person)
WHERE t.name = 'Satish'
REMOVE t.hungry
```

With the `REMOVE` clause, you can also remove labels from existing nodes.

> **Listing 3.22 Cypher statement that removes a node label from an existing node in the database**

```
MATCH (t:Person)
WHERE t.name = 'Satish'
REMOVE t:Author
```

3.1.6 DELETE clause

The `DELETE` clause is used to delete nodes and relationships in the database. You can first inspect the content of your graph database (if the graph is very tiny) with the following Cypher query.

> **Listing 3.23 Cypher statement that retrieves all nodes and relationships in the database**

```
MATCH (n)
OPTIONAL MATCH (n)-[r]->(m)
RETURN n, r, m
```

If you run the query in the listing 3.23 in Neo4j Browser, you should get a graph visualization similar to the one in figure 3.5.

There are currently only a few nodes and relationships in the database, with the exact number depending on how many exercises you completed. It is OK if you haven't completed any exercises; however, you need to at least execute the Cypher statements in listings 3.3, 3.6, and 3.10 to populate the database with relevant data. First, you will delete the relationship between `Person` nodes with the `name` properties

```
MATCH (n) OPTIONAL MATCH (n)-[r]→(m) RETURN n, r, m
```

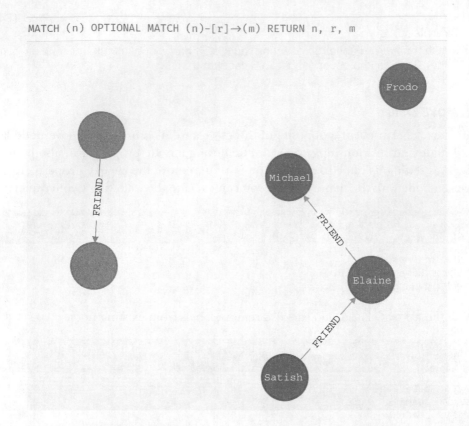

Figure 3.5   Visual representation of the current stored graph in the database

`Satish` and `Elaine`. To perform a graph pattern deletion, you must first use the MATCH clause to find the graph pattern and then use the DELETE clause to delete it from the database.

Listing 3.24   Cypher statement that deletes a relationship between `Person` nodes with the `name` properties `Satish` and `Elaine`

```
MATCH (n:Person)-[r]->(m:Person)
WHERE n.name = 'Satish' AND m.name = 'Elaine'
DELETE r
```

In listing 3.24, the MATCH clause first matches any relationships directed from the `Person` node representing Satish to the node representing Elaine. Notice that you didn't define any relationship type in the MATCH clause. When you omit the relationship type in the graph pattern description, the MATCH clause will search for relationships of any type between described nodes. Similarly, you can also delete a node from a database, as shown in the following listing.

Listing 3.25   Cypher query that deletes a single node from the database

```
MATCH (n:Person)
WHERE n.name = 'Satish'
DELETE n
```

Now, what would happen if you tried to delete the Elaine node from the database?

Listing 3.26   Cypher query that deletes a single node from the database

```
MATCH (n:Person)
WHERE n.name = 'Elaine'
DELETE n
```

You might wonder why you could delete the node representing Satish but cannot delete the node representing Elaine. Luckily, the error, shown in figure 3.6, is very descriptive: you cannot delete a node that still has relationships attached to it.

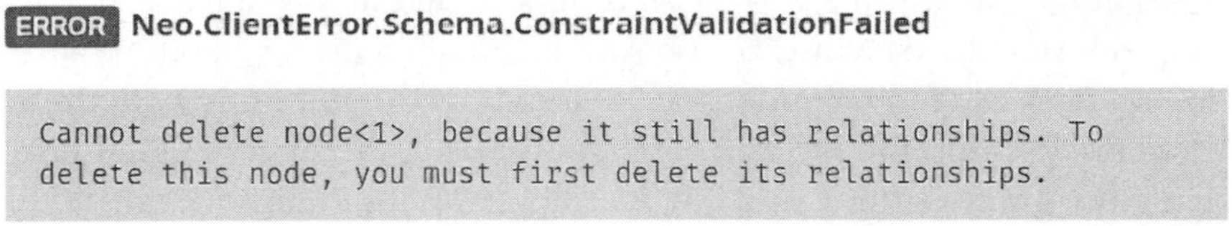

ERROR   **Neo.ClientError.Schema.ConstraintValidationFailed**

```
Cannot delete node<1>, because it still has relationships. To
delete this node, you must first delete its relationships.
```

Figure 3.6   An error that occurs when you want to delete a node that has existing relationships to other nodes

DETACH DELETE CLAUSE

As deleting nodes with existing relationships is a frequent procedure, Cypher query language provides a DETACH DELETE clause that first deletes all the relationships attached to a node and then deletes the node itself. You can try to delete the node representing Elaine with the DETACH DELETE clause.

Listing 3.27   Cypher statement that deletes a single node and all its relationships from the database by using the DETACH DELETE clause

```
MATCH (n:Person)
WHERE n.name = 'Elaine'
DETACH DELETE n
```

The Cypher statement in listing 3.27 deleted both the relationships attached to the node as well as the node itself.

Exercise 3.9

Try to delete the node representing yourself or the node representing a `Person` with the name `Michael`. If the given node still has existing relationships, you must use the DETACH DELETE clause to first delete the relationships and then delete the node.

A Cypher statement that might come in handy when you are toying around with a graph database, hopefully not in production, is to delete all the nodes and relationships in the database.

> **Listing 3.28   Cypher statement that deletes all the nodes and relationships in the database**

```
MATCH (n)
DETACH DELETE n
```

The query in listing 3.28 will first use the MATCH clause to find all the nodes in the database. As you don't include any node label in the node description, the query engine will return all nodes in the database. With the DETACH DELETE clause, you instruct the query engine first to delete all attached relationships to a node and then the node itself. Once the statement is finished, you should be left with an empty database.

3.1.7   *MERGE clause*

In this section, I will assume you are starting with an empty database. If you still have data stored inside the database, please run the query in listing 3.28.

The MERGE clause can be understood as a combination of using both the MATCH and CREATE clauses. Using the MERGE clause, you instruct the query engine first to try to match a given graph pattern, and if it does not exist, it should then create the pattern shown in the following listing.

> **Listing 3.29   Cypher query that uses the MERGE clause to ensure a Person node with a name Alicia exists in the database**

```
MERGE (a:Person {name:'Alicia'})
```

The MERGE clause only supports inline graph pattern description and cannot be used in combination with a WHERE clause. The statement in listing 3.29 ensures a Person node with the name property Alicia exists in the database. You can rerun this query multiple times, and there will always be precisely one Person node with the name Alicia in the database. A statement that can be rerun multiple times and always output the same results is also known as an *idempotent* statement. When you import data into the graph database, it is advisable to use the MERGE instead of the CREATE clause. Using the MERGE clause, you don't have to worry about later deduplication of nodes and can rerun a query several times without corrupting your database structure. What do you think will happen if we try to use the MERGE clause to describe a Person node with the name Alicia and an additional node property location? Let's examine this in the following listing.

> **Listing 3.30   Cypher query merges a single node with two node properties**

```
MERGE (t:Person {name:'Alicia', location:'Chicago'})
```

> **Exercise 3.10**
> Try to match and retrieve all nodes in the database that have a `Person` label and a `name` property with value `Alicia`.

By completing exercise 3.10, you can quickly observe that there exist two nodes, with the label `Person` and `name` property `Alicia`, in the graph visualization shown in figure 3.7.

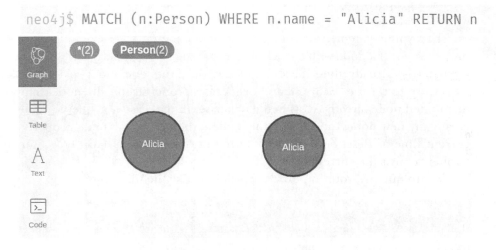

Figure 3.7   Visualization of all the Alicia nodes in the database

There are two `Person` nodes with the same `name` property in the database. Didn't we just discuss that the `MERGE` clause is idempotent? Remember, the `MERGE` clause first tries to match an existing graph pattern, and it only creates the full given graph pattern if it does not exist. When you executed the query in listing 3.30 to merge a `Person` node with two node properties, the query engine first searched for the given pattern. A `Person` node with the `name` property `Alicia` and `location` property `Chicago` did not exist in the database at that moment. Following the `MERGE` logic, it then created a new `Person` node with those two properties.

When designing a graph model, the best practice is to define a unique identifier for each node label. A unique identifier consists of defining a unique property value for each node in the graph. For example, if you assumed that the `name` property of the `Person` nodes is unique, you could use the following `MERGE` clause to import `Person` nodes.

Listing 3.31   Cypher query that merges a node on its unique identifier property and then adds additional properties to the node

```
MERGE (t:Person{name:"Amy"})
ON CREATE SET t.location = "Taj Mahal", t.createdAt = datetime()
ON MATCH SET t.updatedAt = datetime()
```

A MERGE clause can be followed by an optional ON CREATE SET and ON MATCH SET. In the MERGE clause, you used the unique identifier of nodes to merge the nodes. If the node is created during this query, you can define additional node properties that should be set with the ON CREATE SET clause. Conversely, if the node with the label Person and the name property Amy already existed in the database, then the ON MATCH SET clause will be invoked.

The Cypher statement in listing 3.31 will first merge a Person node with the name property Amy. If a node with a label Person and the name property Amy does not exist in the database already, then the MERGE clause will create one and invoke the ON CREATE SET clause to set the location and createdAt properties on the node. Suppose the mentioned node already exists in the database. In that case, the query engine will not create any new nodes, and it will only update the updatedAt node property with the current time as described in the ON MATCH SET clause. The datetime() function in Cypher returns the current time.

Very frequently, your import query will look like the following listing.

Listing 3.32   Cypher query that merges two nodes and then merges a relationship between them

```
MERGE (j:Person{name:"Jane"})
MERGE (s:Person{name:"Samay"})
MERGE (j)-[:FRIEND]->(s)
```

The most frequent Cypher structure when importing data into Neo4j is first to merge the nodes separately and then merge any relationships between them. Using the MERGE clause, you don't have to worry about data duplication or multiple query executions. The statement in listing 3.32 ensures there are three graph patterns in the database: two nodes describing Jane and Samay and a FRIEND relationship existing between them. You can rerun this query multiple times, and the output will always be the same.

The MERGE clause also supports merging an undirected relationship. The fact that you can omit the relation direction in the MERGE clause might be a bit confusing. At the beginning of the chapter, I mentioned you can only store a directed relationship in the Neo4j database. Let's see what happens if you run the following query.

Listing 3.33   Cypher query that merges two nodes and then merges an undirected relationship between them

```
MERGE (j:Person{name:"Alex"})
MERGE (s:Person{name:"Andrea"})
MERGE (j)-[f:FRIEND]-(s)
RETURN *
```

You can observe that two new `Person` nodes were created. When you describe an undirected relationship in the `MERGE` clause, the query engine first tries to match the relationship while ignoring the direction. Practically, it searches for a relationship in both directions. If there are no relationships between the nodes in any direction, it then creates a new relationship with an arbitrary direction. Having the ability to describe an undirected relationship in the `MERGE` clause allows us to import undirected networks more conveniently. If you assume the `FRIEND` relationship is undirected—meaning that if Alex is friends with Andrea, then Andrea is also friends with Alex—then you should store only a single directed relationship between them and treat it as undirected when you are executing graph algorithms or queries. You will learn more about this approach in the following chapters. For now, it is enough that you are aware that it is possible to describe an undirected relationship in the `MERGE` clause.

> **NOTE** When creating or importing data to Neo4j, you typically want to split a Cypher statement into multiple `MERGE` clauses and merge nodes and relationships separately to enhance performance. When merging nodes, the best approach is to include only the node's unique identifier property in the `MERGE` clause and add additional node properties with the `ON MATCH SET` or `ON CREATE SET` clauses.
>
> Handling relationships is a bit different. If there can be at most a single relationship of one type between two nodes, like in the `FRIEND` example, then do not include any relationship properties in the `MERGE` clause. Instead, use the `ON CREATE SET` or `ON MATCH SET` clauses to set any relationship properties. However, if your graph model contains multiple relationships of the same type between a pair of nodes, then use only the unique identifier property of the relationship in the `MERGE` statement and set any additional properties the same as previously discussed.

3.2 Importing CSV files with Cypher

You have learned the basic Cypher clauses that will help you get started. Now, you will learn how to import data from external sources. Two frequent input data structures for a graph database are the CSV and JSON formats. In this chapter, you will learn how to import the CSV-like data structure. Interestingly, dealing with CSV files and importing data from a relational database is almost identical. In both scenarios, you are dealing with a table that has, hopefully, named columns. In this section, you will define unique constraints and import a Twitter dataset into a Neo4j graph database.

3.2.1 Clean up the database

You need to empty the database before continuing, as you don't want random nodes from the previous examples to persist.

> **Listing 3.34 Cypher query that deletes all the nodes and relationships in the database**

```
MATCH (n)
DETACH DELETE n
```

3.2.2   *Twitter graph model*

In the previous chapter, you went through a graph model design process and developed the graph model shown in figure 3.8. There were no data limitations; you just assumed you could get any relevant data. Like anything in life, you can't always get exactly what you asked for, but there might be some additional data that wasn't previously considered.

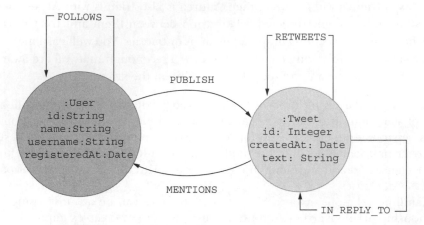

Figure 3.8   Initial Twitter graph model you will import

You will start by importing the follower network between users. There was a `since` property of the `FOLLOWS` relationship in the initial graph model. Unfortunately, the Twitter API doesn't provide the date of creating the `FOLLOWS` relationship, so you will have to remove it from the model. See the reference for the Twitter API `FOLLOWS` endpoint (http://mng.bz/W1PW) for more information.

There may be a discrepancy between the initial graph modeling design and the provided data if you made some assumptions that later didn't hold up. That is why the graph modeling process is iterative. You start with some assumptions and change the graph model accordingly as you learn more. On the other hand, the assumption that there can only be a single author of a given tweet turns out to be valid. And you did not consider that a user can also reply to a given tweet and not just retweet it. The graph model has been

Figure 3.9   Add a comment to the retweet via a quote tweet.

updated to support storing the information when a tweet was made in response to another tweet by adding an `IN_REPLY_TO` relationship. It is also important to note the difference between just retweeting a post and adding a comment to the retweet. The Twitter interface allows you to add a comment to the retweet via a quote tweet (figure 3.9).

Because adding a comment has different semantics than just retweeting a post, it is important to differentiate between the two scenarios by using different relationship types, as shown in figure 3.10.

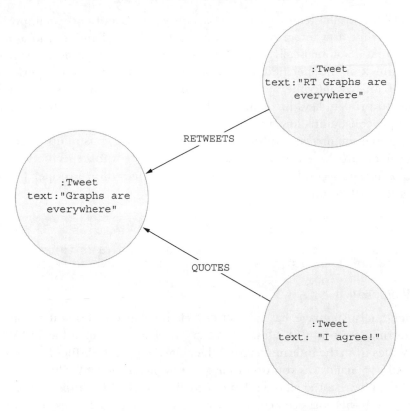

Figure 3.10 Differentiating between retweets and quotes by using different relationship types

By clearly differentiating between retweets and quotes, it will be easier for you to find quotes in the graph and analyze their responses. For example, you could use NLP techniques to detect the sentiment of the comments and examine which tweets or users are most likely to receive comments with positive or negative sentiment. Unfortunately, while I was thinking of including them in our graph import, I did not fetch any quote tweets during my scraping process, so we will skip importing and analyzing them. In the initial import, you will also ignore the hashtags, mentions, and links of a tweet.

3.2.3 *Unique constraints*

The Neo4j graph database model is considered *schemaless*, meaning you can add any type of nodes and relationships without defining the graph schema model. There are, however, some constraints you can add to your graph model to ensure data integrity. In my graph journey, I have only used the *unique node property constraint* so far. There are two benefits of using the unique node property constraint. The first is that it ensures the value of a given node property is unique for all the nodes with a specific label. For a beginner, this feature is handy, as it informs you and stops an import query that would corrupt data integrity. An additional benefit of defining a unique node constraint is that it automatically creates an index on the specified node property. By creating an index on the specified node property, you will optimize the performance of import and analytical Cypher queries. You can think of unique constraints as a concept similar to primary keys in relational databases, although the difference is that Neo4j's unique constraint allows null values.

For the initial import, you will define two unique node constraints. One unique constraint will ensure there can only be a single User node with a specific id property in the database. The second unique constraint guarantees the id property of nodes with label Tweet will be unique for each node.

> **Listing 3.35   Cypher query that defines two unique node constraints**

```
CREATE CONSTRAINT IF NOT EXISTS FOR (u:User) REQUIRE u.id IS UNIQUE;
CREATE CONSTRAINT IF NOT EXISTS FOR (p:Tweet) REQUIRE p.id IS UNIQUE;
```

3.2.4   *LOAD CSV clause*

The Cypher query language has a LOAD CSV clause that enables you to open and retrieve information from CSV files. The LOAD CSV clause can fetch local CSV files as well as CSV files from the internet. Having the ability to fetch CSV files from the internet comes in very handy, as you don't have to download the CSV files to your local computer first. I have stored all the relevant CSV files on GitHub (https://github.com/ tomasonjo/graphs-network-science) for easier access. The LOAD CSV clause can load CSV files whether or not they contain a header. If the header is present, each row of the CSV file will be available as a map data structure that can be used later in the query. Conversely, when there is no header present, the rows will be available as lists. The LOAD CSV clause can also be used in combination with a FIELDTERMINATOR clause to set a custom delimiter, where you are, for example, dealing with a tab-separated value format.

To retrieve information from a specific CSV file, you can use the following query.

> **Listing 3.36   Cypher query that fetches and displays information from a CSV file**

```
LOAD CSV WITH HEADERS FROM "https://bit.ly/39JYakC" AS row
WITH row
LIMIT 5
RETURN row
```

The CSV file must be publicly accessible, as the LOAD CSV clause does not feature any authorization support. The statement in listing 3.36 also uses the LIMIT clause. As mentioned, the LIMIT clause is used to limit the number of results you want to retrieve.

It is important to note that the LOAD CSV clause returns all values as strings and makes no attempt to identify data types. You must convert the values to the correct data type in your Cypher import statements.

3.2.5 Importing the Twitter social network

I have prepared five CSV files that contain the following information:

- User information
- Follower network
- Information about tweets and their authors
- Information about the MENTIONS relationships between posts and users
- Information about the RETWEETS relationships between posts
- Information about the IN_REPLY_TO relationships between posts

It is a good practice to split the graph import into multiple statements; I could have probably prepared a single CSV file with all the relevant information. Still, it makes more sense to split the import into multiple statements for better readability and faster import performance. If you are dealing with graphs with millions of nodes, then it is advisable to split the import of nodes and relationships. In this case, you are dealing with only thousands of nodes, so you don't have to worry about query optimization that much. My general rule of thumb is to split the import queries by node labels and relationship types as much as possible.

To begin with, you will import user information into Neo4j. As mentioned, all the data is publicly available on GitHub, so there is no need to download any files. The CSV structure for user information has the structure shown in table 3.1.

Table 3.1 User CSV structure

id	name	username	createdAt
333011425	ADEYEMO ADEKUNLE King	ADEYEMOADEKUNL2	2011-07-10T20:36:58
1355257214529892352	Wajdi Alkayal	wajdiAlkayal	2021-01-29T20:51:28
171172327	NLP Excellence	excellenceNLP	2010-07-26T18:48:47

You can use the following Cypher statement to import user information into the Neo4j database.

Listing 3.37 Cypher query that imports user information from a CSV file

```
LOAD CSV WITH HEADERS FROM "https://bit.ly/39JYakC" AS row
MERGE (u:User {id:row.id})
ON CREATE SET u.name = row.name,
              u.username = row.username,
              u.registeredAt = datetime(row.createdAt)
```

You could have used the CREATE clause to import user information. If you started with an empty database and trust that I have prepared a CSV file without duplicates, the result would be identical.

Dealing with real-world datasets, you often can't afford the luxury of assuming you have clean data present. Hence, it makes sense to write Cypher statements that can handle duplicates or other anomalies and are also idempotent. In the Cypher statement in listing 3.37, the LOAD CSV clause first fetches the CSV information from the GitHub repository. LOAD CSV then iterates over every row in the file and executes the Cypher statement that follows. In this example, it executes the MERGE clause in combination with ON CREATE SET for every row in the CSV file.

Exercise 3.11

Retrieve five random users from the database to inspect the results and validate that the import process of users worked correctly.

Currently, you only have nodes without any relationships in the database; you will continue by importing FOLLOWS relationships between users. The CSV file that contains the information about the followers has the structure shown in table 3.2.

Table 3.2   Follower's CSV structure

source	target
14847675	1355257214529892352
1342812984234680320	1355257214529892352
1398820162732793859	1355257214529892352

The followers' CSV file has only two columns. The source column describes the start node ID, and the target column describes the end node ID of the follower relationships. When dealing with larger CSV files, you can use the IN TRANSACTIONS clause in combination with a Cypher subquery to split the import into several transactions, where x represents the batch size. Splitting the import into several transactions can spare you the headache of running out of memory when doing large imports. The follower's CSV has almost 25,000 rows. By default, the IN TRANSACTIONS clause will split the transaction for every 1,000 rows. Instead of importing the whole CSV file in a single transaction, you should use the transaction batching clause in combination with a Cypher subquery to, effectively, split it into 25 transactions. For some reason, you need to prepend :auto when using transaction batching in Neo4j Browser. In other cases (e.g., when using a Neo4j Python driver to import the data), you don't need to prepend the :auto operator, as shown in the following listing.

Listing 3.38 Cypher query that imports the follower network from a CSV file

Starts a Cypher subquery using the CALL clause

Prepends the :auto operator and uses the LOAD CSV clause, as usual

```
:auto LOAD CSV WITH HEADERS FROM "https://bit.ly/3n08lEL" AS row
CALL {
    WITH row
    MATCH (s:User {id:row.source})
      MATCH (t:User {id:row.target})
    MERGE (s)-[:FOLLOWS]->(t)
} IN TRANSACTIONS
```

To use any variables from the enclosing query, you need to explicitly import them using a WITH clause.

Matches start and source users

The IN TRANSACTIONS clause indicates the subquery should be batched into single transactions for every 1,000 rows.

Merges a relationship between source and target users

The statement in listing 3.38 first retrieves the information from a CSV file located on GitHub. To define that the import should be split into multiple transactions, use the CALL {} clause to define a Cypher subquery that has the IN TRANSACTIONS clause appended. Any variables used in a Cypher subquery from the enclosing query must be explicitly defined and imported using the WITH clause. The query steps in the Cypher subquery will be executed for every row in the CSV file. For each row, it matches the source and the target User node. Here, you assume all the User nodes are already present in the database. Remember, if the MATCH clause does not find a pattern, it skips the execution of the rest of the query for a specific row.

In the statement in listing 3.38, if, for example, a source node was not found by the MATCH clause, the Cypher query would skip the creation of the FOLLOWS relationship. You could avoid this limitation by using the MERGE clause instead of the MATCH clause to identify the source and target User nodes. There is, however, a drawback: any node created by the MERGE clause in listing 3.38 would have only the id property and no other information, as they were missing from the CSV file containing user information.

Once both the source and the target nodes are identified, the query merges a FOLLOWS relationship between them. Using the MERGE clause, you ensure there will be exactly one FOLLOWS relationship from the source to the target User node in the database. This way, you don't have to worry about having duplicates in the input CSV file or rerunning the query multiple times. Another critical consideration is that the direction of the FOLLOWS relationship in the Twitter domain has a semantic value. For example, if user A follows user B, that does not imply that user B follows user A. For this reason, you need to add the relationship direction indicator in the MERGE clause to ensure the relationship is imported correctly.

> **NOTE** When you are using the MATCH clause to identify nodes in Cypher import queries, be aware that no additional nodes will be created during the import. Therefore, all the relationships between nodes that do not exist in the database will also be skipped during the import process.

Exercise 3.12
Retrieve five FOLLOWS relationships from the database to validate the import process.

Next, you will import the tweets and their authors. The CSV structure of the tweets is as shown in table 3.3.

Table 3.3   Twitter posts CSV structure

id	text	createdAt	author
12345	Example text	2021-06-01T08:53:22	134281298
1399649667567	Graph data science is cool!	2021-06-01T08:53:18	54353345
13996423457567	Exploring social networks	2021-06-01T08:45:23	4324323

The id column of the Tweets CSV file describes the Twitter post ID that will be used as the unique identifier. The file also includes the text and the date of creation as well as the ID of the author. There are 12,000 rows in the CSV file, so you will again use the CALL {} clause in combination with the IN TRANSACTIONS clause for batching purposes.

Listing 3.39   Cypher query that imports tweets from a CSV file

Starts a Cypher subquery
with a CALL clause

```
:auto LOAD CSV WITH HEADERS FROM "https://bit.ly/3y3ODyc" AS row
CALL {
    WITH row                          ← Imports the row variable
    MATCH (a:User{id:row.author})       explicitly in the WITH clause
    MERGE (p:Tweet{id:row.id})        ←
    ON CREATE SET p.text = row.text,       Merges Tweet
                p.createdAt = datetime(row.createdAt)   node and sets
    MERGE (a)-[:PUBLISH]->(p)         ←    additional
} IN TRANSACTIONS                          properties
```

Matches
author
User node

Uses the IN TRANSACTIONS clause
to indicate transaction batching

Merges a
relationship
between a user
and a tweet

If you look closely, you can observe that the query structure in listing 3.39 is similar to the query in listing 3.38. When you are importing any relationship into the database, you will most likely match or merge both source and target nodes and then connect them. In the first step, the query matches on the User node. Next, you use the MERGE clause to create the Tweet nodes. Although all the Tweet nodes need to be created, as there are none in the database beforehand, I still like to use the MERGE clause to have idempotent queries. It is the best experience for you as a user, and it is an excellent practice to follow. Finally, a relationship between the user and the tweet is created.

Exercise 3.13

To validate the import process, retrieve the `text` property of three random `Tweet` nodes.

Now that you have both tweets and users in the database, you can import `MENTIONS` relationships between a tweet and user. The `MENTIONS` relationship indicates a user has tagged another user in their post. The CSV containing this information has the structure shown in table 3.4.

Table 3.4 Mentions CSV structure

post	user
333011425	134281298
1355257214529892352	54353345
171172327	4324323

The import query is relatively simple. First, use the `MATCH` clause to identify the tweet and the mentioned user, and then `MERGE` a relationship between them.

Listing 3.40 Cypher query that imports `MENTIONS` relationships from a CSV file

```
LOAD CSV WITH HEADERS FROM "https://bit.ly/3tINZ6D" AS row
MATCH (t:Tweet {id:row.post})          ◄          Matches the
MATCH (u:User {id:row.user})           ◄          Tweet node
MERGE (t)-[:MENTIONS]->(u);            ◄

        Merges a relationship                Matches the mentioned
        between a tweet and a user           User node
```

In the last two import queries, you will import additional `RETWEETS` and `IN_REPLY_OF` relationships. Both the Retweets and In Reply To CSV files have the same structure, as shown in table 3.5

Table 3.5 Retweets and In Reply To CSV file structure

source	target
14847675	1355257214529892352
1342812984234680320	1355257214529892352
1398820162732793859	1355257214529892352

Begin by importing the `RETWEETS` relationship, as in listing 3.41.

Listing 3.41   Cypher query that imports retweets relationships from a CSV file

```
LOAD CSV WITH HEADERS FROM "https://bit.ly/3QyDrRl" AS row
MATCH (source:Tweet {id:row.source})       ◁────────    Matches the
MATCH (target:Tweet {id:row.target})       ◁────────    source tweet
MERGE (source)-[:RETWEETS]->(target);      ◁────────
```

Merges a retweet relationship   **Matches the**
between source and target tweets   **target tweet**

The query structure to add relationships to a database mostly identifies the source and target nodes and then adds a connection between the two. You must take special care in determining whether to use MATCH or MERGE to identify nodes. If you use the MATCH clause, then no new nodes will be created, so any relationships that don't have both the source and target nodes already in the database will be ignored during the import. On the other hand, if you use the MERGE clause, you might end up with new Tweet nodes with only the id but no text property or even the author connected to it. Using the MERGE clause to add relationships, you ensure there will be precisely one relationship of that type between source and target nodes, no matter how many times the connection occurs in the underlying data or how often you run the import query. There are options to change the query to import more than a single relationship type between a pair of nodes and still use the MERGE clause.

Exercise 3.14
Match five RETWEETS relationships between a pair of tweets from the database. Then, inspect the text of the original and the retweeted post.

The final import statement imports the IN_REPLY_TO relationships, as shown in the following listing. It has a structure almost identical to importing the RETWEETS relationship: only the type of relationship is changed.

Listing 3.42   Cypher query that imports IN_REPLY_TO relationships from a CSV file

```
LOAD CSV WITH HEADERS FROM "https://bit.ly/3b9Wgdx" AS row
MATCH (source:Tweet {id:row.source})       ◁────────    Matches the
MATCH (target:Tweet {id:row.target})       ◁────────    source tweet
MERGE (source)-[:IN_REPLY_TO]->(target);   ◁────────
```

Merges a reply-to relationship   **Matches the**
between the source and target tweets   **target tweet**

Congratulations, you have imported the initial Twitter graph into Neo4j! Neo4j has a special procedure that enables you to inspect and visualize the graph schema of the stored graph in the database.

Listing 3.43   Schema introspection procedure

```
CALL db.schema.visualization()
```

If you run the schema introspection procedure specified in listing 3.43 in Neo4j Browser, you should get the schema visualization shown in figure 3.11.

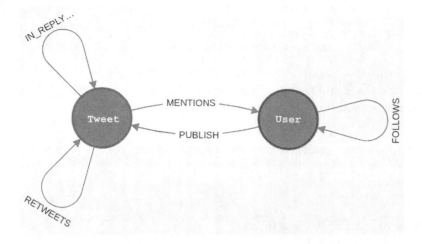

Figure 3.11 Visualization of generated graph schema based on the stored graph

If you get the exact same graph schema visualization, you are ready to learn more about the analytical Cypher queries and graph algorithms, which we cover in the next chapter. If the generated schema is not identical, rerun all the import queries.

3.3 Solutions to exercises

The solution to exercise 3.1 is as follows.

> **Listing 3.44 Cypher statement that creates a node with a label `Person` and properties `name` and `age`**

```
CREATE (p:Person{name:'Tomaz', age: 34})
```

The solution to exercise 3.2 is as follows.

> **Listing 3.45 Cypher statement that creates two nodes representing an employee and their employer and then creates an `EMPLOYED_BY` relationship between the two**

```
CREATE (p:Person{name:'Tomaz'}), (o:Organization {name: "Acme Inc"})
CREATE (p)-[e:EMPLOYED_BY]->(o)
RETURN *
```

The solution to exercise 3.3 is as follows.

Listing 3.46   Creating three nodes representing the city, country, and the continent you reside in and then connecting them with the IS_IN relationship

```
CREATE (city:City {name: "Grosuplje"}),
       (country: Country {name: "Slovenia"}),
       (continent: Continent {name: "Europe"})
CREATE (city)-[i1:IS_IN]->(country)
CREATE (country)-[u2:IS_IN]->(continent)
RETURN *
```

Using different node and relationship types is OK, since the exercise did not specify any labels or types you should use.

The solution to exercise 3.4 is as follows.

Listing 3.47   Retrieving the name property of all Person nodes

```
MATCH (p:Person)
RETURN p.name AS name
```

The solution to exercise 3.5 is as follows.

Listing 3.48   Creating a FRIENDS relationship between node representing yourself and Elaine

```
MATCH (t:Person {name:'Tomaz'}), (e:Person {name:'Elaine'})
CREATE (t)-[f:FRIENDS]->(e)
RETURN *
```

The solution to exercise 3.6 is as follows.

Listing 3.49   Using OPTIONAL MATCH to identify whether there are any FRIENDS relationships attached to the node representing you

```
MATCH (t:Person {name:'Tomaz'})
OPTIONAL MATCH (t)-[f:FRIENDS]->(e)
RETURN *
```

The solution to exercise 3.7 is as follows.

Listing 3.50   Using the SET clause to add a node property

```
MATCH (t:Person{name:'Tomaz'})
SET t.favouriteFood = 'Steak'
RETURN t
```

The solution to exercise 3.8 is as follows.

Listing 3.51   Using the SET clause to add a secondary Reader label

```
MATCH (t:Person{name:'Tomaz'})
SET t:Reader
RETURN t
```

The solution to exercise 3.9 is as follows.

Listing 3.52 Deleting the node representing yourself

```
MATCH (t:Person{name:'Tomaz'})
DETACH DELETE t
```

The solution to exercise 3.10 is as follows.

Listing 3.53 Retrieving all nodes with a label `Person` and name property `Alicia`

```
MATCH (n:Person)
WHERE n.name = 'Alicia'
RETURN n
```

The solution to exercise 3.11 is as follows.

Listing 3.54 Retrieving five `User` nodes

```
MATCH (u:User)
WITH u
LIMIT 5
RETURN u
```

The solution to exercise 3.12 is as follows.

Listing 3.55 Retrieving five `FOLLOWS` relationships

```
MATCH (u:User)-[f:FOLLOWS]->(u2:User)
WITH u, f, u2
LIMIT 5
RETURN *
```

The solution to exercise 3.13 is as follows.

Listing 3.56 Retrieving the `text` property of three random `Tweet` nodes

```
MATCH (t:Tweet)
WITH t.text AS text
LIMIT 3
RETURN text
```

The solution to exercise 3.14 is as follows.

Listing 3.57 Comparing the text of an original tweet and its retweet

```
MATCH (retweet:Tweet)-[:RETWEETS]->(original:Tweet)
WITH original.text AS originalText, retweet.text AS retweetText
LIMIT 3
RETURN text
```

Summary

- Cypher syntax uses parentheses, (), to encapsulate a node.
- Cypher syntax uses square brackets, [], to encapsulate a relationship.
- A relationship cannot exist on its own but needs to be described with adjacent nodes.
- In Neo4j, all relationships are stored as directed, although you can ignore the direction at query time.
- It is not advisable to ever create any nodes without node labels.
- The CREATE clause is used to create data.
- The MATCH clause is used to identify existing patterns in the database.
- The WHERE clause can be used in combination with MATCH or WITH clauses to specify various filters.
- If a MATCH clause doesn't find the specified graph pattern, the whole Cypher statement returns no results.
- You can use OPTIONAL MATCH when you are not certain whether a graph pattern exists in the database, but you still want to return other variables in the query output.
- The WITH clause can be used to filter, aggregate, select, paginate, or limit intermediate rows in the Cypher statement.
- The SET clause is used to add node properties and labels.
- The REMOVE clause is used to remove node properties and labels.
- The DELETE clause is used to delete nodes and relationships.
- If you want to delete a node with existing relationship patterns, you need to use the DETACH DELETE clause.
- The MERGE clause is a combination of MATCH and CREATE clauses that ensures the specified graph pattern exists in the database.
- The MERGE clause is frequently used for data import, as it allows for idempotent queries and automatic deduplication.
- In Neo4j, you can define unique constraints that ensure unique values for the specified node property of a particular node label.
- It is recommended to import nodes and relationships separately into the database to improve performance and data quality.
- You can easily evaluate the graph schema of existing data with the db.schema .visualization() procedure.

Exploratory
graph analysis

This chapter covers

- Exploring a graph with Cypher query language
- Aggregating data with Cypher query language
- Using existential subqueries to filter by graph patterns
- Using counting subqueries to count graph patterns
- Handling query cardinality when using multiple clauses in a single Cypher statement

This chapter will teach you how to perform an exploratory data analysis of the imported Twitter social network using Cypher query language. Imagine you are working as a social media consultant and want to find as many insights as possible. As is typical with any analysis, you begin with an exploratory data analysis to get an overview of the data you are working with.

I will present how I collected the data to give you a sense of the data you will be working on in this chapter. The imported Twitter social network was retrieved using the official Twitter API. I have fetched tweets that are part of the NLP or Knowledge graph topics. At this time, I had information about tweets and users who either were mentioned or published tweets. Next, I fetched additional metadata about users in the graph, such as their registration date and follower relationships. All the users in the imported Twitter subgraph have either published a tweet or have been mentioned by one. I did not include all the followers because that would explode the graph and the network would end up consisting of a couple of million users.

One part of the exploratory graph analysis consists of counting the number of nodes and relationships in the network. With the Twitter network, it is also essential to know the timeline of the created tweets. In this chapter, you will learn how to aggregate time-based information with Cypher query language. As the last part of the exploratory analysis, you will examine some interesting nodes in the dataset, like users who posted the most tweets or were mentioned the most.

Now that we've covered an overview of what you will be learning in this chapter, let's start with some practical examples. To follow along with the examples in this chapter, you must have a Neo4j database instance with Twitter network data imported as described in chapter 3.

4.1 Exploring the Twitter network

The goal of the exploratory analysis is to get to know the dataset and teach you Cypher query syntax that will allow you to aggregate and filter data. I recommend you use the Neo4j Browser environment, which can be used to develop Cypher queries and return the query results in the form of a table as well as a graph visualization.

If you open Neo4j Browser and select the database tab in the top-right corner, it will show a simple report indicating the number and the type of nodes and relationships in the database, as shown in figure 4.1.

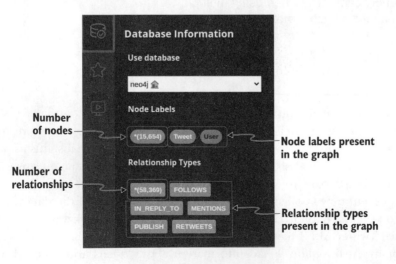

Figure 4.1   Neo4j Browser database report

After the upload of Twitter data, as shown in chapter 3, there should be a total of 15,654 nodes in the database. As you already know, nodes are labeled either `Tweet` or

User. In addition, there are also 58,369 connections across four relationship types. Both the node labels and the relationship types in the left-side toolbar are clickable. For example, if you click the FOLLOWS relationship type, the tool will generate a Cypher statement that returns a sample of 25 FOLLOWS relationships.

> **Listing 4.1   Generated Cypher query that visualizes a sample of 25 FOLLOWS relationships**

```
MATCH p=()-[r :FOLLOWS]->()
RETURN p LIMIT 25;
```

The generated statement in listing 4.1 returns the results as the *path* data object. A sequence of connected nodes and relationships can be represented as a path data type. Cypher query syntax allows paths to be referenced by a variable name in a manner similar to node and relationship variables.

You should get a visualization similar to that shown in figure 4.2 by executing the generated Cypher statement.

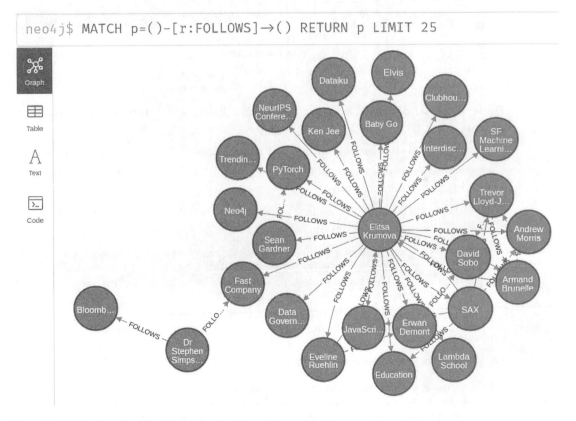

Figure 4.2   A subgraph of the followers network

> ### Exercise 4.1
>
> As an exercise, generate a Cypher statement to visualize sample RETWEETS relationships. You can click on the relationship types in the left-side toolbar, or you can use the statement in listing 4.1 as the template and change the relationship type accordingly.

4.2   Aggregating data with Cypher query language

Aggregating and counting data points is the basis of all data analysis. In the context of graph analysis, you will first learn how to count various graph patterns like the number of nodes and relationships. If you already have some experience with relational databases and SQL query language, you will see that Cypher follows a similar syntax for aggregating data. The first aggregation function you will learn is the count() function, which is used to count the number of rows or values produced by the MATCH clause.

To count the number of the nodes in the database, you can execute the following Cypher statement.

Listing 4.2   Counting the number of nodes

```
MATCH (n)                                    Matches all the nodes
RETURN count(n) AS numberOfNodes;            in the database

                                             Returns the total
                                             count of nodes
```

There is a total of 15,654 nodes in the graph. The count() function appears in two variants:

- count(*)—Returns the number of rows produced by the Cypher statement
- count(variable or expression)—Returns the number of non-null values produced by an expression

To test both variants of the count() function, you will count the number of User nodes and the non-null values of their registeredAt properties.

Listing 4.3   Counting the number of User nodes and their non-null values of registeredAt properties

```
MATCH (u:User)
RETURN count(*) AS numberOfRows,
       count(u.registeredAt) AS numberOfUsersWithRegisteredAtDate
```

Table 4.1 shows the results of listing 4.3.

Table 4.1   Results of the Cypher statement in listing 4.3

numberOfRows	numberOfUsersWithRegisteredAtDate
3,594	3,518

There are 3,594 `User` nodes in the graph, but only 3,518 of them have the non-null `registeredAt` property. The graph is missing the registration date information for 76 users. When preparing a dataset summary, you usually present the number of missing values as a ratio rather than an absolute number. In Neo4j, you must be careful because when you divide an integer by an integer, the result will also be an integer. To avoid this issue, you can cast either of the variables to the float data type.

Execute the following Cypher statement to evaluate the ratio of non-null values for the `registeredAt` node property of `User` nodes.

Listing 4.4 Calculating the ratio of non-null values of `registeredAt` node property

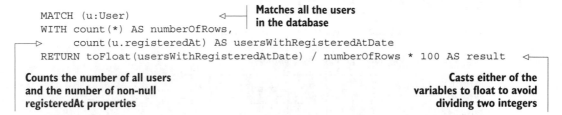

```
MATCH (u:User)                    ◄──┐  Matches all the users
WITH count(*) AS numberOfRows,        │  in the database
     count(u.registeredAt) AS usersWithRegisteredAtDate
RETURN toFloat(usersWithRegisteredAtDate) / numberOfRows * 100 AS result   ◄──┐
```

Counts the number of all users and the number of non-null registeredAt properties

Casts either of the variables to float to avoid dividing two integers

You'll see that 97.88% of users have a non-null value of the `registeredAt` property. If you forgot to cast either the `usersWithRegisteredAtDate` or `numberOfRows` in listing 4.4 to float, the result would be 0.

> **NOTE** In Neo4j, when you divide an integer value by another integer value, the result will also be the integer data type. If you want the result to be of the float type, such as with the ratio example in listing 4.4, you need to cast either of the variables to float using the `toFloat()` function.

Exercise 4.2

Calculate the ratio of missing values for the `createdAt` node property of the `Tweet` nodes. The result of the statement should be a percentage of non-null values divided by the count of tweets.

The correct answer to exercise 4.2 is that there are no missing values for the `createdAt` property of `Tweet` nodes.

As you might be used to from your other data projects, you want to aggregate or count values grouped by specific values more often than not. For those familiar with SQL aggregations, you can define the grouping keys in the GROUP BY statement. *Grouping keys* are non-aggregate expressions used to group the values going into aggregate functions. Aggregation in Cypher is different from aggregation in SQL. In Cypher, you don't need to specify a grouping key explicitly. As soon as any aggregation function is used in the Cypher statement, all non-aggregated columns in the WITH or RETURN clause become grouping keys. With Cypher query language, the grouping keys are implicitly defined, as you don't need to explicitly add a GROUP BY statement after the aggregation functions.

Suppose you want to count the number of nodes grouped by their node label. The function to extract the node labels is labels(). You only need to provide the labels() function as the grouping key alongside an aggregation function that will count the number of nodes.

Listing 4.5   Counting the number of nodes by labels

```
MATCH (n)
RETURN labels(n) AS labels,
       count(n) AS count;
```

Table 4.2 shows the number of nodes for each label.

Table 4.2   Counting nodes grouped by their label

labels	count
["User"]	3594
["Tweet"]	12060

At the moment, there are only two types of nodes in the graph. You can observe that the Cypher statement in listing 4.5 returns the node labels as a list. The list data type indicates that you can have multiple labels on a single node. Assigning a secondary node label is helpful in a network analysis when you want to speed up subsequent queries by tagging relevant subsections of nodes. As previously mentioned, you might notice the lack of a GROUP BY statement. In Cypher, you don't need to explicitly specify a grouping key. As soon as an aggregation function is used, all non-aggregated result columns become grouping keys.

NOTE   With Cypher query language, the grouping keys are defined implicitly, meaning all non-aggregated columns in a WITH or RETURN clause automatically become grouping keys.

Exercise 4.3

Count the number of relationships by their type. To count the number of relationships grouped by their type, you start by describing a relationship pattern with Cypher syntax. Note that you cannot describe a relationship without its adjacent nodes. Because you are interested in counting all the relationship types, you must not specify any node labels or relationship types in the Cypher pattern. In the last part of the statement, you use the type() function to extract the relationship type and use it as a grouping key in combination with the count() aggregation function.

The solution to exercise 4.3 produces the output shown in table 4.3.

Table 4.3 Count of relationships grouped by their type

relationshipType	count
PUBLISH	12,060
FOLLOWS	24,888
RETWEETS	8,619
MENTIONS	12,379
IN_REPLY_TO	423

The number of PUBLISH relationships is identical to the number of Tweet nodes. With the Twitter social network, a single TWEET has precisely one author, indicated by the PUBLISH relationship.

Interestingly, 8,619 out of 12,060 tweets are retweets, and 423 tweets are replies. Only around 30% of the tweets are original content. This is not so unusual; for example, the research by Joshua Hawthorne et al. (2013) shows that while normal users don't have a high count of retweets per tweet, more prominent accounts rake in vast numbers of retweets. Additionally, when researchers examined the tweets by former US presidents (Minot et al., 2021), the number of retweets was at least an order of magnitude higher than usual. Consequently, there is a larger number of retweets than original tweets on the platform due to the significant amount of retweets of tweets by prominent accounts.

What's a bit surprising is that there are more mentions than tweets. I did not manually parse the mentioned information, as that was automatically provided by the official Twitter API. I've also noticed that when a user retweets another user, they are automatically mentioned in the retweet.

> **Exercise 4.4**
> Inspect the text of a retweet and compare it to the original tweet's text. Use the LIMIT clause to limit the number of results to 1.

The solution to exercise 4.4 produces the output shown in table 4.4.

Table 4.4 A single comparison of tweet and retweet's text

retweetText	originalText
RT @Eli_Krumova: 5 Best Practices: Writing Clean & Professional #SQL #Code https://t.co/Y4DepLfOOn v/ @SourabhSKatoch #DataScience #AI #ML...	5 Best Practices: Writing Clean & Professional #SQL #Code https://t.co/Y4DepLfOOn v/ @SourabhSKatoch #DataScience #AI #ML #MachineLearning #IoT #IIoT #IoTPL #Python #RStats #Cloud #CyberSecurity #Serverless #RPA #NLP #programming #coding #100DaysOfCode #DEVCommunity #CodeNewbie https://t.co/ma03V8btZBhttps://t.co/TOnwwHgaHQ

One immediately obvious thing is that the retweet's text is trimmed to a fixed length and does not always contain the original tweet's complete text. Another more subtle difference is that the retweet's text is prepended with RT followed by the original author's handle. It seems that Twitter automatically prepends the original user's handle in the retweet and treats it as a mention—I had no idea this was the case. It is a good practice to always begin with exploratory graph analysis before diving into graph algorithms to spot such abnormalities.

Exercise 4.5

For those of you who are more visually oriented, try to visualize a single graph pattern in which a user retweeted a post from another user. Include the MENTION relationships of both the original and the retweeted post. Follow these hints to help you construct the desired Cypher statement:

- Match a graph pattern that describes a retweet, an original tweet, and their authors.
- Use the WITH clause in combination with the LIMIT clause to limit results to a single described pattern.
- Separately match the MENTION relationships of the original and retweeted post.
- Visualizing networks in Neo4j Browser is easiest by returning one or multiple path objects.

This exercise is a bit more advanced, so take it step by step to construct the final Cypher statement. You can examine the results after each step to make sure you have correctly described the desired graph pattern. The solution to exercise 4.5 produces the network visualization in Neo4j Browser shown in figure 4.3.

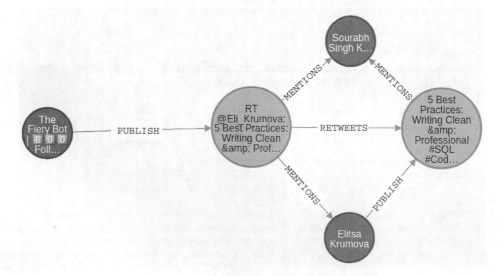

Figure 4.3 By default, a retweet also mentions the original tweet author.

4.2.1   Time aggregations

As with any dataset, it is essential to learn the timeline of the data points. Both the
`User` and the `Tweet` nodes contain the datetime property. First, you will evaluate the
time windows of the tweets. You can use the `min()` and `max()` functions on the datetime property to get the earliest and the last date values.

Listing 4.6   Retrieving the earliest and last created date values of tweets

```
MATCH (n:Tweet)
RETURN min(n.createdAt) AS earliestDate, max(n.createdAt) as lastDate
```

The first tweet in the dataset was on August 12, 2016, and the last was on June 1, 2021.
There is a five-year span between the first and the last tweet. While this information is
nice, it is not very descriptive. To get a better feeling for the time window, you will calculate the distribution of tweets by year.

In Cypher, a datetime property behaves like an object. You can access datetime
attributes, such as the year and the month, by using the following Cypher syntax.

Listing 4.7   Extracting datetime attributes

```
MATCH (t:Tweet)
WITH t LIMIT 1
RETURN t.createdAt.year AS year,
       t.createdAt.month AS month,
       t.createdAt.day AS day,
       t.createdAt.epochSeconds AS epochSeconds;
```

Table 4.5 shows the datetime attributes of this sample tweet.

Table 4.5   Datetime attributes of a sample tweet

year	month	day	epochSeconds
2021	6	1	1622537602

You can then use the datetime attributes in combination with aggregation functions.

> ### Exercise 4.6
> Calculate the distribution of tweets grouped by year created. Remember, Cypher uses
> implicit grouping key aggregations, so all you need to add to the RETURN statement
> is the `year` column and the `count` operator.

The solution to exercise 4.6 produces the output in table 4.6.

Table 4.6   Distribution of tweets by their creation date

year	count
2021	12029
2020	19
2019	6
2018	3
2016	3

Even though the time window between the first and the last tweet is five years, almost all the tweets were created in 2021. Let's drill it down even more.

> **Exercise 4.7**
>
> Use the MATCH clause in combination with the WHERE clause to select all the tweets that were created in 2021. You can filter datetime attributes like you would other node properties. In the next step, calculate the distribution of tweets by their creation month. Use both the creation year and month as grouping keys.

By now, you are probably already in the habit of adding grouping keys as non-aggregate values in the RETURN or WITH clause. Additionally, you just need to be careful to use the WHERE clause to match only tweets that were created in 2021.

The solution to exercise 4.7 produces the output in table 4.7.

Table 4.7   Distribution of tweets by their creation date

year	month	count
2021	6	2695
2021	5	8507
2021	4	376
2021	3	432
2021	2	8
2021	1	11

Around 93% (11,202 of 12,060) of the tweets were created in May and June of 2021.

Exercise 4.8 is designed to test you on the implicit grouping aggregations in Cypher and use some of the previously discussed clauses together. Please take a couple of minutes to try to solve it on your own. I would recommend you return the results after each step of the query to determine whether you are on the right track.

> **Exercise 4.8**
>
> Before you move on to the rest of the chapter, I want to present you with a challenge. Can you prepare a Cypher statement that will return the top four days with the highest count of created tweets? Although you haven't seen this exact example, you already have some experience with all the clauses required to construct this Cypher statement. Here are some hints that should help you:
>
> - Start by matching all tweets.
> - Use the creation year, month, and day as the grouping keys along with the `count()` aggregation.
> - Use the `ORDER BY` clause to order the results based on the count descending.
> - Use the `LIMIT` clause to return only the top four days.

The solution to exercise 4.8 produces the output in table 4.8.

Table 4.8   Distribution of tweets by their creation date

year	month	day	count
2021	5	31	6185
2021	6	1	2695
2021	5	30	1847
2021	5	28	62

Interestingly, you started with a five-year time window and were able to narrow it down to only four days by gradually digging deeper. Most of the tweets in the dataset were created between May 30 and June 1. This information will help you evaluate the number of tweets and mentions given this timeframe.

4.3   Filtering graph patterns

Now, you will investigate the network of mentions more thoroughly. You already know there are 12,379 MENTIONS relationships, but now, you want to determine how many distinct users have been mentioned. How would you construct the Cypher statement to retrieve the number of distinct users that have been mentioned? As a beginner, my first thought would be to use the following statement.

Listing 4.8   Counting the number of occurrences of a user being mentioned

```
MATCH (u:User)<-[:MENTIONS]-(:Tweet)
RETURN count(u) AS countOfMentionedUsers;
```

At first glance, the statement in listing 4.8 appears valid. You matched the users who were mentioned and then returned the count of users. But the `count()` function doesn't count the number of distinct users; it counts the number of occurrences where the user variable is not null. You have actually counted the number of graph patterns where a `User` node has an incoming `MENTIONS` relationship originating from a `Tweet` node, which is 12,379. One way to count the number of distinct users who were mentioned is by using the `distinct` prefix. The `distinct` prefix, shown in the following listing, is used to count the number of unique values of a reference variable or expression.

Listing 4.9   Counting the number of distinct users who were mentioned

```
MATCH (u:User)<-[:MENTIONS]-(:Tweet)
RETURN count(u) AS numberOfOccurences,
       count(distinct u) AS numberOfDistinctUsers;
```

Table 4.9 shows the results of listing 4.9.

Table 4.9   The number of occurrences and count of distinct users mentioned in a tweet

numberOfOccurences	numberOfDistinctUsers
12,379	1,632

There is a total of 1,632 distinct users who were mentioned at least once. When doing any query aggregations, you must also keep in mind the query cardinality and what you are actually counting. *Cardinality* is the number of rows or records of the input stream to the operation. Cypher performs a specific operation for each incoming row. In listing 4.9, the `MATCH` clause produces 12,379 rows. These rows are then used as an input to the `count` operator. Using the `count(u)` operator, you count the number of non-null values the u reference variable. Since the `MATCH` clause will produce no null values for the u variable, the result of the `count(u)` operation is 12,379.

> **NOTE**   The cardinality of the query will also affect its performance. You want to keep the cardinality as low as possible to achieve the best execution speed. In Neo4j, you can prefix your Cypher statement with the `PROFILE` clause to compare the performance of queries. To learn more about the `PROFILE` clause, see the documentation: http://mng.bz/84pD.

You don't have to expand all the `MENTIONS` relationships to get a list of users who were mentioned in at least a single tweet. Using the *existential subqueries* in the `WHERE` clause, you can filter on graph patterns. An existential subquery can be used to determine whether a specified pattern exists at least once in the graph. You can think of it as an expansion or upgrade of the `WHERE` clause in combination with the graph patterns, where you can introduce new reference variables or even use other clauses, like `MATCH`, in the subquery. The subquery begins and ends with curly brackets {}. You can use any of the variables from the outer query to describe a graph pattern; however, any new variables you introduce in the subquery are not carried over to the main query.

Listing 4.10 Counting the number of distinct users who were mentioned in tweets

```
MATCH (n:User)
WHERE EXISTS { (n)<-[:MENTIONS]-() }
RETURN count(n) AS numberOfDistinctUsers;
```

The Cypher statement in listing 4.10 produces the identical count of distinct users to the query result in listing 4.9 and is also more performant. The syntax used in listing 4.10 is useful for finding nodes in the network that are part of at least a single described graph pattern. In this example, you don't care if a user was mentioned once or hundreds of times—you just want to match the distinct users who were mentioned at least once.

> **NOTE** Existential subqueries are usually more performant, since they don't have to expand all relationships. For example, the Cypher statement in listing 4.9 has to expand 12,379 MENTIONS relationships and then use the distinct operator to retrieve the count of distinct User nodes. On the other hand, the existential subquery specified in listing 4.10 does not expand all MENTIONS relationships, as the expression is true if a single MENTIONS relationship is present. If a User node has 100 MENTIONS relationships, the Cypher statement in listing 4.9 will expand all 100 relationships, while the existential subquery specified in listing 4.10 will be satisfied by finding the first MENTIONS relationship and will, therefore, ignore the other 99.

Exercise 4.9
Count the number of distinct users who have published at least one tweet.

Using the existential subqueries in combination with graph patterns is also very helpful when negating a graph pattern. You could match the whole pattern in the previous example and use distinct to get the correct count. However, when you want to negate a graph pattern, you cannot use it in the MATCH clause. Hence, negating graph patterns is a prime example of using the existential subqueries in the WHERE clause to negate a graph pattern.

In this example, shown in the following listing, you will count the number of distinct users who were mentioned but haven't, themselves, published a single tweet. You must negate the outgoing PUBLISH relationships to filter out users without any tweets.

Listing 4.11 Counting the number of users who were mentioned but haven't published a single tweet

```
MATCH (u:User)
WHERE EXISTS { (u)<-[:MENTIONS]-() } AND
  NOT EXISTS { (u)-[:PUBLISH]->() }
RETURN count(*) AS countOfDistinctUsers
```

Around half of the distinct users (809 of 1,632) mentioned in a tweet in our dataset haven't published any tweets themselves. As shown in listing 4.11, you can easily combine multiple graph pattern predicates to filter out nodes that fit the described graph patterns.

As previously mentioned, you can also introduce new reference variables in the existential subquery. For example, if you wanted to count the number of users mentioned in a tweet and discount the mentions that are part of the retweet pattern, you would need to introduce a new reference variable. In the following listing, you will use the existential subquery to count the number of users mentioned in a tweet and ignore the retweet mention pattern.

> **Listing 4.12   Counting the number of users who were mentioned in a tweet and discounting the retweet mention pattern with an existential subquery**

Uses the MATCH clause to identify the pattern in which a User has been mentioned by a Tweet

```
MATCH (u:User)<-[:MENTIONS]-(tweet:Tweet)
WHERE NOT EXISTS {
    (original)<-[:PUBLISH]-(u)<-[:MENTIONS]-(tweet)-[:RETWEETS]->(original)
}
RETURN count(distinct u) AS countOfUsers
```

Uses the existential query to negate graph patterns where the MENTION relationship exists because of a retweet pattern

Uses the distinct operator to return the distinct number of users part of the described graph pattern

You needed to use the existential subquery in listing 4.12 to be able to introduce the reference variable original. The reference to the original is needed, as you only want to discount the specific MENTION relationships that are part of the retweet pattern.

The result of the statement in listing 4.12 is 1,206. Therefore, around 26% (426 of 1,632) of the users who were mentioned have an incoming MENTION relationship only because their posts were retweeted. Interestingly enough, around 33% (1,206 of 3,594) of all users were mentioned in a tweet if you discard retweets. And if you completed exercise 4.9, you know that around 75% (2,764 of 3,594) of all users have published at least one tweet.

> ### Exercise 4.10
> Find the top five users with the most distinct tweets retweeted. To make it easier for you, I have prepared a template Cypher statement you need to fill in, shown in table 4.10.

> **Listing 4.13   Template query for exercise 4.10**

Uses a combination of the WHERE clause with a graph pattern to filter tweets that were retweeted. A tweet that was retweeted has an incoming RETWEETS relationship.

```
MATCH (n:User)-[:PUBLISH]->(t:Tweet)
_Fill in the WHERE_
```

```
WITH n, count(*) AS numberOfRetweets          ◄──────────
_Fill in the ORDER BY_
RETURN n.username AS user, numberOfRetweets    ◄───┐
_Fill in the LIMIT_
```

Uses the ORDER BY clause to order by numberOfRetweets, descending

Uses the LIMIT to return only the top five users

By solving exercise 4.10, you should get the results shown in table 4.10.

Table 4.10 Users with the top five highest counts of retweeted tweets

user	numberOfRetweets
"IainLJBrown"	754
"SuzanneC0leman"	314
"Eli_Krumova"	31
"Paula_Piccard"	31
"Analytics_699"	26

It seems that IainLJBrown has, by far, the most retweeted tweets. In second place, with 354 tweets that were retweeted, is SuzanneC0leman. You could probably think of these users as influencers because they publish a lot but their followers also retweet their posts in high volumes. After that, there is an order of magnitude drop to only 31 retweeted posts from Eli_Krumova and Paula_Piccard.

4.4 Counting subqueries

Next, I will show you how to conveniently count graph patterns with Cypher. Although you already know how to count and filter graph patterns, there is a simple yet performant syntax to remember when counting various graph patterns. For example, you could use the following Cypher statement if you wanted to get the top five most mentioned users.

Listing 4.14 Retrieving the top five most mentioned users

```
MATCH (u:User)<-[:MENTIONS]-(:Tweet)
WITH u, count(*) AS mentions
ORDER BY mentions DESC LIMIT 5
RETURN u.username AS user, mentions
```

There is nothing wrong with the statement in listing 4.14; however, you will frequently be performing multiple aggregations in a single query. When performing multiple aggregations in a query, you must be very mindful of the query cardinality (number of intermediate rows in the query). A simple yet very effective syntax to not increase the cardinality when counting the number of relationships a node has is to use the count {} operator and describe the desired graph pattern you want to count, as shown in the following listing.

> **Listing 4.15 Convenient way of retrieving the top five most mentioned users by not increasing main query cardinality**

```
MATCH (u:User)
WITH u, count { (u)<-[:MENTIONS]-() } AS mentions
ORDER BY mentions DESC LIMIT 5
RETURN u.username AS user, mentions
```

You might have noticed that a common theme in Cypher syntax is to wrap a graph pattern in curly brackets and prepend a desired Cypher clause like count, EXISTS, or CALL, depending on your use case. The results of the Cypher statement in listing 4.15 are shown in table 4.11.

Table 4.11 Top five most mentioned users

user	mentions
"IainLJBrown"	3646
"SuzanneC0leman"	673
"Analytics_699"	476
"Paula_Piccard"	460
"Eli_Krumova"	283

By far, the most mentioned user is IainLJBrown. If you are like me, you are probably wondering what the distribution of those mentioned is. Is this user frequently retweeted, are posts mentioning him frequently retweeted, or do people just like to mention him? From the results of exercise 4.10, you already know he has 754 posts that were retweeted.

4.5   *Multiple aggregations in sequence*

As mentioned, when performing multiple aggregation in sequence, you must be mindful of the intermediate cardinality. For example, say that you have two MATCH clauses in a row.

> **Listing 4.16 How multiple MATCH clauses affect the query cardinality**

```
MATCH (u:User)
MATCH (t:Tweet)
RETURN count(*) AS numberOfRows,
       count(u) AS countOfUsers,
       count(t) AS countOfTweets
```

Table 4.12 shows how the cardinality of a query can explode when performing multiple MATCH statements in sequence if you don't perform any intermediate steps.

Table 4.12   Multiple aggregation in sequence without reducing cardinality

numberOfRows	countOfUsers	countOfTweets
43,343,640	43,343,640	43,343,640

You already know that this result doesn't make sense at all. First, the number of users and tweets is identical, and you definitely don't have 43 million nodes in the graph. So why do you get these results? Each MATCH or OPTIONAL MATCH produces a certain number of rows. Any subsequent MATCH or OPTIONAL MATCH clauses will be executed as many times as the rows produced by the previous MATCH clause. The first MATCH in listing 4.16 produces 3,594 rows. The second MATCH is then executed for each produced row separately. Effectively, the second MATCH will be executed 3,594 times. There are 12,060 tweets in our graph, so if you find the product of 12,060 and 3,594, you will get the 43 million rows.

How do you avoid this problem? In this example, you can reduce the cardinality before the second MATCH clause to 1 so that the second MATCH clause will be executed only once. You can use any of the aggregating functions to reduce the cardinality. Let's say you want to count the number of users and tweets in the graph. In this case, you can use the count() function after the first MATCH clause to reduce the cardinality.

Listing 4.17   Reducing cardinality between multiple MATCH clauses in a sequence

```
MATCH (u:User)                                  Reduces the cardinality to 1 before
WITH count(u) AS countOfUsers                   executing the subsequent MATCH clause
MATCH (t:Tweet)
RETURN count(*) AS numberOfRows, countOfUsers, count(t) AS countOfTweets   ⬅
```

Table 4.13 shows how performing aggregations to reduce the intermediate cardinality of a query can produce valid results.

Table 4.13   Multiple aggregation in sequence with reducing intermediate cardinality

numberOfRows	countOfUsers	countOfUsers
12,060	3,594	12,060

By reducing the intermediate cardinality after the first MATCH to 1, you are making sure any subsequent MATCH clauses will be executed only once. This will help you with query performance as well as getting accurate results. Another trick that will help you keep the cardinality in check is to use the count {} operator, as described in listing 4.15.

Exercise 4.11

Calculate the mention distribution for the user IainLJBrown. Mentions can come in three forms:

- Someone retweeting a post from IainLJBrown
- Someone posting an original tweet that mentions IainLJBrown
- Someone retweeting a post that mentions IainLJBrown

Make sure to reduce the cardinality after each MATCH or OPTIONAL MATCH clause. Because you don't know beforehand if mentions of IainLJBrown fall into all three categories, I advise you to use OPTIONAL MATCH when counting the mentions distribution.

The solution to exercise 4.11 is shown in the following listing.

Listing 4.18   Calculating the distribution of mentions for user IainLJBrown

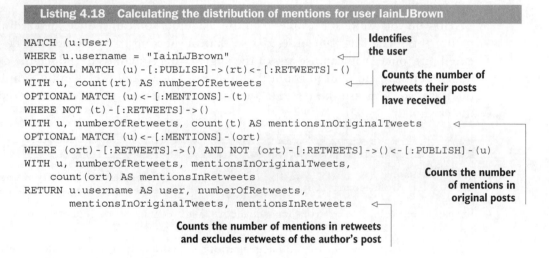

```
MATCH (u:User)                                           Identifies
WHERE u.username = "IainLJBrown"                          the user
OPTIONAL MATCH (u)-[:PUBLISH]->(rt)<-[:RETWEETS]-()
WITH u, count(rt) AS numberOfRetweets                    Counts the number of
OPTIONAL MATCH (u)<-[:MENTIONS]-(t)                      retweets their posts
WHERE NOT (t)-[:RETWEETS]->()                            have received
WITH u, numberOfRetweets, count(t) AS mentionsInOriginalTweets
OPTIONAL MATCH (u)<-[:MENTIONS]-(ort)
WHERE (ort)-[:RETWEETS]->() AND NOT (ort)-[:RETWEETS]->()<-[:PUBLISH]-(u)
WITH u, numberOfRetweets, mentionsInOriginalTweets,
    count(ort) AS mentionsInRetweets                     Counts the number
RETURN u.username AS user, numberOfRetweets,             of mentions in
      mentionsInOriginalTweets, mentionsInRetweets       original posts
```

Counts the number of mentions in retweets
and excludes retweets of the author's post

Table 4.14 shows the resulting distribution of mentions for IainLJBrown.

Table 4.14   Distribution of mentions for IainLJBrown

user	numberOfRetweets	mentionsInOriginalTweets	mentionsInRetweets
"IainLJBrown"	3643	2	1

The fact that you must use the count() operator directly after each OPTIONAL MATCH clause, and not only at the end, is a very important detail. This way, you reduce the in-between cardinality to 1 after each OPTIONAL MATCH clause and your count won't explode. There are a couple of other ways you could get this result, so if your query is a little different but produces the same results, then it's all OK. Almost all of the mentions for the user IainLJBrown come from their posts being retweeted. They were only mentioned in two original tweets, and one of them was likely retweeted once. If you consider the information from exercise 4.10, you know that 754 of his posts were retweeted 3,643 times. In this Twitter subgraph, he can definitely be regarded as an influencer.

Exercise 4.12

Fetch the top five users who have published the most tweets or retweets. Use the `count {}` operator.

Congratulations! By completing all of the exercises, you have learned a considerable amount about Cypher aggregations and filtering.

4.6 Solutions to exercises

The solution to exercise 4.1 is as follows.

Listing 4.19 Generated Cypher query that visualizes a sample of 25 RETWEETS relationships

```
MATCH p=()-[r:RETWEETS]->()
RETURN p LIMIT 25;
```

The solution to exercise 4.2 is as follows.

Listing 4.20 Calculating the ratio of non-null values of the `createdAt` node property of tweets

```
MATCH (u:Tweet)
WITH count(*) AS numberOfRows,
count(u.createdAt) AS tweetsWithCreatedAtDate
RETURN toFloat(tweetsWithCreatedAtDate) / numberOfRows * 100 AS result
```

The solution to exercise 4.3 is as follows.

Listing 4.21 Counting the number of relationships grouped by their type

```
MATCH ()-[r]->()
RETURN type(r) AS relationshipType, count(r) AS countOfRels
```

The solution to exercise 4.4 is as follows.

Listing 4.22 Cypher statement to compare the retweet and original tweet's text property

```
MATCH (rt:Tweet)-[:RETWEETS]->(t:Tweet)
RETURN rt.text AS retweetText, t.text AS originalText
LIMIT 1
```

The solution to exercise 4.5 is as follows.

Listing 4.23   Visualizing a single graph pattern in which a user retweeted a post from another user

```
MATCH p=(:User)-[:PUBLISH]->(rt:Tweet)-[:RETWEETS]->
➥   (t:Tweet)<-[:PUBLISH]-(:User)
WITH p, rt, t LIMIT 1
MATCH prt=(rt)-[:MENTIONS]->()
MATCH pt=(t)-[:MENTIONS]->()
RETURN p,pt,prt
```

The solution to exercise 4.6 is as follows.

Listing 4.24   Calculating the distribution of tweets by year

```
MATCH (t:Tweet)
RETURN t.createdAt.year AS year, count(*) AS count
ORDER BY year DESC
```

The solution to exercise 4.7 is as follows.

Listing 4.25   Calculating the distribution of tweets created in 2021 by month

```
MATCH (t:Tweet)
WHERE t.createdAt.year = 2021
RETURN t.createdAt.year AS year,
       t.createdAt.month AS month,
       count(*) as count
ORDER BY year DESC, month DESC
```

The solution to exercise 4.8 is as follows.

Listing 4.26   Determining the top four days by the number of tweets created

```
MATCH (t:Tweet)
WITH t.createdAt.year AS year,
     t.createdAt.month AS month,
     t.createdAt.day AS day,
     count(*) AS count
ORDER BY count DESC
RETURN year, month, day, count LIMIT 4
```

The solution to exercise 4.9 is as follows.

Listing 4.27   Counting the number of distinct users who have published at least one tweet

```
MATCH (u:User)
WHERE EXISTS { (u)-[:PUBLISH]->() }
RETURN count(*) AS countOfUsers
```

The solution to exercise 4.10 is as follows.

> **Listing 4.28 Finding the top five users who had the most distinct tweets retweeted**

```
MATCH (n:User)-[:PUBLISH]->(t:Tweet)
WHERE EXISTS { (t)<-[:RETWEETS]-() }
WITH n, count(*) AS numberOfRetweets
ORDER BY numberOfRetweets DESC
RETURN n.username AS user, numberOfRetweets
LIMIT 5
```

The solution to exercise 4.11 is as follows.

> **Listing 4.29 Calculating the distribution of mentions for user IainLJBrown**

```
MATCH (u:User)
WHERE u.username = "IainLJBrown"                      ⟵  Identifies the user
OPTIONAL MATCH (u)-[:PUBLISH]->(rt)<-[:RETWEETS]-()   ⟵  Counts the number of
WITH u, count(rt) AS numberOfRetweets                     retweets their posts
OPTIONAL MATCH (u)<-[:MENTIONS]-(t)                       have received
WHERE NOT (t)-[:RETWEETS]->()
WITH u, numberOfRetweets, count(t) AS mentionsInOriginalTweets   ⟵
OPTIONAL MATCH (u)<-[:MENTIONS]-(ort)
WHERE (ort)-[:RETWEETS]->() AND NOT (ort)-[:RETWEETS]->()<-[:PUBLISH]-(u)
WITH u, numberOfRetweets, mentionsInOriginalTweets,
➡  count(ort) AS mentionsInRetweets                      Counts the number
RETURN u.username AS user, numberOfRetweets,             of mentions in
       mentionsInOriginalTweets, mentionsInRetweets  ⟵  original posts
```

Counts the number of mentions in retweets
and excludes retweets of author's post

The solution to exercise 4.12 is as follows.

> **Listing 4.30 Fetching the top five users who have published the most tweets or retweets**

```
MATCH (u:User)
RETURN u.username AS username,
       count{ (u)-[:PUBLISH]->() } AS countOfTweets
ORDER BY countOfTweets DESC
LIMIT 5
```

Summary

- A path data object contains a sequence of connected nodes and relationships.
- Cypher aggregations use implicit grouping keys.
- As soon as an aggregation function is used, all non-aggregated columns become grouping keys.
- Existential subqueries can help you efficiently filter using graph patterns.
- Existential subqueries are especially useful when you want to negate a graph pattern.
- Cardinality is the number of rows or records of the input stream to the operation.

- A datetime object has multiple attributes that you can use to retrieve the year, month, day, or epoch information.
- A `distinct` operator can be used to count the number of distinct patterns, nodes, relationships, or properties.
- Dividing an integer by an integer will return an integer. Therefore you need to cast one of the values to float using the `toFloat` function to avoid returning an integer.
- The `count` operator can be used to count the number of non-null properties or expressions.
- When executing multiple clauses or aggregation functions in sequence, you have to be mindful of the intermediate query cardinality.
- Counting subqueries are useful when you want to count graph patterns without affecting the cardinality of the main query.
- You can prefix any Cypher statement with the `PROFILE` clause to evaluate its performance by examining total database hits.

Introduction to
social network analysis

5

Social network analysis is a process of investigating network structures and node roles using graph theory and algorithms. One of the earliest network science writers was Hungarian author Frigyes Karinthy. One of his most important works is a short story, "Láncszemek," in which he describes that even though we think the world is vast, it is, in fact, very tiny. The story was originally written in Hungarian, but Adam Makkai prepared an English translation (http://mng.bz/E9ER). The short story describes an idea known today as the *small-world concept*. To demonstrate his claim, he presented how he could connect himself to someone far from his perspective in 1929. In Karinthy's example, he showed how he, being in Budapest, could connect to a worker in an American Ford factory. The worker in the Ford factory knows his manager, and that manager probably knows Henry Ford. Henry Ford probably knows an industrialist in Hungary, and that industrialist is, perhaps, a friend of a friend of Karinthy. This way, he demonstrated that a Ford company worker is probably four or five handshakes away from an author in Budapest. Over the years, the small-world concept has been rebranded and popularized as the *six degrees of separation*, from John Guare's play *Six Degrees of Separation*.

In the 1950s and '60s, Paul Erdös and Alfréd Rényi started to work on language for describing a network. In their 1959 paper, they started to examine how large networks behave. Large networks look so complicated that one might assume they are random. Even in a social network, it is hard to predict who is connected to whom. They assumed those networks must be random, as people might randomly meet other people or molecules randomly interact with each other.

An essential aspect of characterizing any network is to look at the node degree distribution. In simple terms, the node degree is the number of links each node has. In a random network, the degree distribution will follow the Gaussian distribution, as shown in figure 5.1.

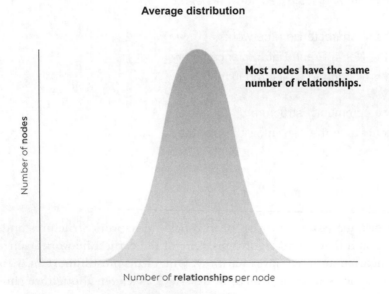

Figure 5.1   **Random network degree distribution**

The vast majority of nodes have roughly the same number of links. There won't be many hugely popular nodes, but there won't be many isolated nodes either. However, the Gaussian distribution is most often used for independent observations. On the other hand, a graph consists of highly interconnected observations that are not independent. It turns out that almost no real-world network follows the random network degree distribution. The idea behind this claim is that networks have profound organizing principles. At about the same time, Google developed its famous graph algorithm PageRank (Brin & Page, 1998) and Albert Barabási and his colleagues examined the structure of the web (Albert et al. 1999). The web consists of web pages and URL links pointing to other sites. This is essentially a network, where nodes represent web pages and relationships represent their URL links. The assumption was that the web would turn out to be a random network as anyone can publish a web page and choose which sites they want to link to. They discovered that the web degree distribution follows a different pattern, as shown in figure 5.2.

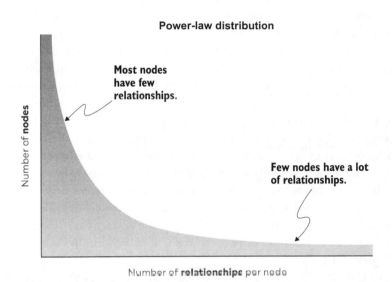

Figure 5.2 Scale-free network degree distribution

This is a very different degree distribution than expected. On the web, the vast majority of pages are very rarely, if ever, visited; they may have one or two links pointing to them. Then, there are some pages, such as Google, Amazon, Yahoo, and others, that have hundreds of millions of links pointing to them. Such a network is incredibly uneven and is, today, known as a *scale-free network*. It was later shown that most real-world networks are scale-free networks, where a few big hubs hold together many tiny nodes. Why is that so? The truth is that networks have profound organizing principles. For example, think of a group of people. Who is more likely to form new connections: a person with only a few friends or a person who already has many friends? It turns out that a person who already has many friends is more likely to form new relationships. A simple explanation is that they are likely to be invited to more events, at which they can mingle with new folks, due to their greater number of existing connections. Also, they are more likely to be introduced to new people by their existing contacts. This network organizing principle is known as the *preferential attachment model*, a term coined by Barabási and Albert (1999).

Traditional analytical tools are frequently designed to work with independent observations that adhere to the Gaussian distribution. However, these tools might be troublesome for analyzing densely and unevenly connected data. Therefore, a set of graph analysis tools was designed to handle highly connected data that adheres to a power-law distribution.

5.1 *Follower network*

Most graph algorithms were designed to be used on monopartite networks. If you recall, a monopartite network contains a single type of nodes and relationships. A typical example is a friendship network, where you only have people and their friendship relationships. Another frequently mentioned example is the web network, where you deal with web pages and hyperlinks connecting them. Even when dealing with a multipartite network, it is common to infer or project a monopartite network using various techniques. The next chapter will focus more on inferring monopartite networks.

Here, you will execute your first graph algorithms on the Twitter followers network. Even though the Twitter social graph contains multiple node types and relationships, you can focus your graph analysis on a specific subgraph. The followers network is monopartite, as it contains only User nodes and FOLLOWS relationships. I've chosen it so you don't have to deal with monopartite projections just yet.

A user can follow another user, but they don't necessarily follow them back. This means you are dealing with a directed network. Also, the relationships don't have any attribute or property that would quantify their strength, which implies you are dealing with an unweighted network.

First, you will learn how to characterize the followers network in terms of connectedness and the density of links. For example, the Stanford Network Analysis Platform (SNAP) repository (http://snap.stanford.edu/index.html) contains a variety of graph datasets. If you open the Pokec social network (http://snap.stanford.edu/data/soc-Pokec.html) dataset web page, you can observe that the following characteristics of a network are given along with the data itself:

- Number of nodes
- Number of relationships
- Number of nodes in the largest weakly connected component
- Number of nodes in the largest strongly connected component
- Average local clustering coefficient

To characterize a network, you will be using Cypher query language and graph algorithms from the Neo4j Graph Data Science library. Specifically, in this chapter, you will learn to use some *community detection* and *centrality* graph algorithms. The community detection algorithms will be used to characterize the network and also find tightly connected groups of users. In the context of networks, a community refers to a densely connected group of nodes, whose members have comparatively fewer connections to other communities in the network. For example, think of a friendship network (figure 5.3).

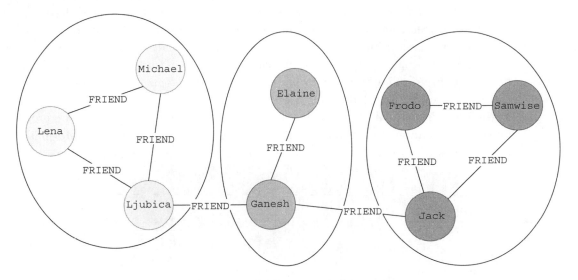

Figure 5.3 Friendship network with nodes with outlined communities

Figure 5.3 visualizes a network of eight people and their friendship connections. The communities are outlined with circles. You can observe that communities form between nodes that are densely interconnected. For example, there are three communities in figure 5.3; on the right side, Frodo, Samwise, and Jack form a community. They all have connections with each other, similar to what you would expect of a group of friends. Although Jack has a connection with Ganesh, they don't belong to the same community, as Ganesh doesn't share any ties to the other friends in Jack's group.

This makes sense if you think about it in terms of real-life friend groups. Imagine you have a group of friends with whom you like to go hiking or play board games. Let's call them your community of friends. Now, even though you might make a friend at your workplace, that doesn't automatically make the work friend part of your community. And likely, the work friend also has a separate group of friends they engage in hobbies with. You could only consider the two communities to be merged and to form a single community with densely connected ties if your community and your work friend's community joined to, for example, play board games or go hiking together. In that case, you would belong to the same community as your work friend, with whom you now also hang out in your free time.

Community detection techniques can be used to detect various segments of users, discover people with common interests, or recommend new connections within a community. Suppose you take a step away from social networks. In that case, you could use community detection algorithms to group proteins with similar roles (Pinkert et al., 2010) or identify physicians' specialties based on prescription data (Shirazi et al., 2020). Another application for community detection algorithms is to examine the network structure of scientific collaboration networks (Newman, 2001; Piedra et al., 2017).

Now, think about what makes a node have influence over the network. There are a couple of procedures to determine whether a node is influential. The metrics used to identify important or influential nodes in the graph are called *centrality measures*, and the algorithms that calculate them are called *centrality algorithms*. For example, the most basic metric to determine a node's importance is *degree centrality*, which simply counts the number of relationships a node has. The higher the count of relationships is, the more influential the node is in the network. Another example of node importance is to examine the amount of influence a node has over the flow of information in a network (figure 5.4).

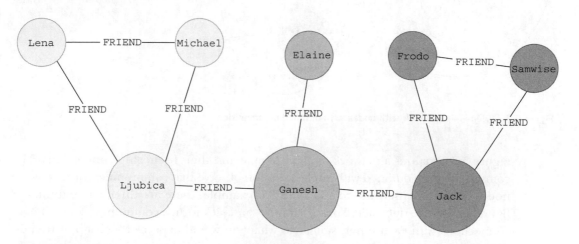

Figure 5.4   Friendship network with node size corresponding to their influence over the information flow

Figure 5.4 shows the same network as figure 5.3. The only difference is that, now, the node size in the visualization corresponds to its influence over the information flow. Suppose the information can circulate only through friendship relationships. In that case, Ganesh is the most important node in the network, as he is the bridge between all three communities. Ganesh can be thought of as the gatekeeper of information between communities, allowing him to choose which data he wants to pass along and when. Another thing to note is that if Ganesh were removed from the network, it would be broken into three parts. The other two vital nodes are Ljubica and Jack, who connect their community with the rest of the network.

In the last part of this chapter, you will take advantage of centrality algorithms to find the most important or influential users. There are multiple variations of node influence measures. To calculate the influence over the information flow in the network you can use *betweenness centrality*. As mentioned, it has various applications in social network analysis, but it can also be used to predict congestions in a road network (Kirkley et al., 2018). The most famous node centrality algorithm is probably *PageRank*, which was developed to rank websites and use the ranking information to produce better search results (Brin & Page, 1998). The beauty of the PageRank algorithm is that it can be applied to other domains. For example, it has been used to rank research paper authors based on citations (Ying Ding et al., 2010). I've also found one example where PageRank is applied to evaluate user reputation on YouTube (Hanm Yo-Sub et al., 2009). Finally, it can also be utilized to analyze protein interaction networks (Iván & Grolmusz, 2011).

Now, we will complete some practical examples to learn how to utilize Cypher query language and graph algorithms to characterize and evaluate the community structure of the Twitter followers network, followed by identifying the most influential nodes. To follow along with the examples in this chapter, you must have a Neo4j database instance with Twitter network data imported, as described in chapter 3.

5.1.1 Node degree distribution

One of the fundamental characteristics of a network is the node degree distribution. With a directed network, you can split the degree distribution into *in-degree* and *out-degree* distribution. The node in-degree counts the number of incoming relationships, and the out-degree counts the number of outgoing connections per node.

First, you will examine the out-degree distribution of the followers network. If you want to evaluate any distribution quickly in Neo4j Browser, you can use the `apoc.agg` `.statistics` function from the Awesome Procedures on Cypher (APOC) library.

NOTE The APOC library contains around 450 procedures and functions to help you with various tasks, ranging from data integration to batching and more. While it is not automatically incorporated with Neo4j, I recommend you include it in all your Neo4j projects. You can check out the official documentation to get a sense of all the procedures it features at https://neo4j .com/docs/apoc/current/.

The `apoc.agg.statistics` function returns statistical values, such as mean, max, and percentile values of given values. Since you are only counting the number of relationships per node, you simplify the query by using the `count {}` function.

Listing 5.1 Evaluating the node out-degree distribution with the `apoc.agg.statistics` function

```
MATCH (u:User)
WITH u, count{ (u)-[:FOLLOWS]->() } AS outDegree
RETURN apoc.agg.statistics(outDegree)
```

Table 5.1 shows the final distribution.

Table 5.1   Out-degree distribution of the followers network

total	3,594
min	0
minNonZero	1.0
max	143
mean	6.924874791318865
0.5	2
0.99	57
0.75	8
0.9	21
0.95	32
stdev	11.94885358058576

There are 3,594 samples or nodes in the distribution. User nodes have, on average, around seven outgoing relationships. The `0.5` key represents the 50th percentile value, the `0.9` key represents the 90th percentile value, and so on. While the average value of outgoing relationships is almost 7, the median value is only 2, which indicates that 50% of nodes have two or fewer outgoing connections. Around 10% of users have more than 21 outgoing relationships.

You can always draw a histogram of out-degree distribution in your favorite visualization library if you are more visually oriented, like me. Figure 5.5 shows an example.

Visualizing charts is beyond the scope of this chapter, so I won't go into details of how I produced figure 5.5. However, Jupyter notebooks for chapters 9 and 10 contain code that draws histograms with the seaborn library in Python.

Interestingly, even a small subgraph of the Twitter network follows the power-law distribution, which is typical for real-world networks. I have limited the bin range to visualize only nodes with an out-degree of 60 or less, for chart readability. More than 1,000 nodes have zero outgoing connections, and most nodes have fewer than 10 links. You have previously observed that the highest out-degree is 143, and only 5% of nodes have the out-degree of greater than 32.

> ### Exercise 5.1
> Fetch the top five users with the highest out-degree. Use the `count {}` operator.

Now, you will repeat the same process to evaluate the in-degree distribution. First, you will use the `apoc.agg.statistics` function to evaluate the in-degree distribution in Neo4j Browser, as shown in listing 5.2.

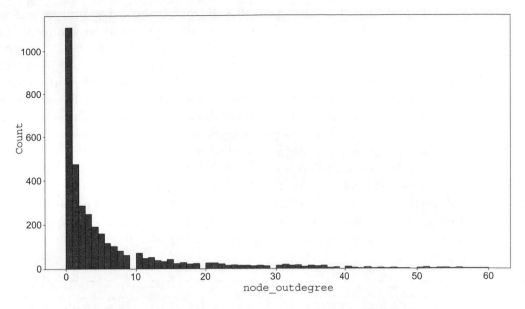

Figure 5.5 Out-degree distribution chart visualized with a seaborn histogram

Listing 5.2 Evaluating the node out-degree distribution with the `apoc.agg.statistics` function

```
MATCH (u:User)
WITH u, count{ (u)<-[:FOLLOWS]-() } AS inDegree
RETURN apoc.agg.statistics(inDegree)
```

Table 5.2 shows the final distribution.

Table 5.2 Out-degree distribution of the followers network

total	3594
min	0
minNonZero	1.0
max	540
mean	6.924874791318865
0.5	0
0.99	112
0.75	4
0.9	16
0.95	35
stdev	22.7640611678852

What immediately caught my eye is that the mean value is identical for out- and in-degree. This might make sense to you, as the total count of nodes and relationships is identical, so the mean values should be the same. More than half of the users have no incoming connections. While I have scraped the Twitter API for the follower relationships of all users, I have only included relationships between users who have either posted or were mentioned in the 12,000 scraped tweets. It looks like around half of the users don't have any followers included in this subgraph. One outlier has 540 incoming relationships (followers count), meaning one in seven users follow them.

Again, I'll show the in-degree distribution with the seaborn library (figure 5.6). Though I did not aim to get the power-law distribution of node in- and out-degrees, most real-world networks tend to exhibit such a distribution. However, when dealing with smaller subsets of a graph, the node degree distribution is highly dependent on the sampling method used to retrieve the dataset. As the data sample grows, its node degree distribution will increasingly resemble the overall graph degree distribution (figure 5.6).

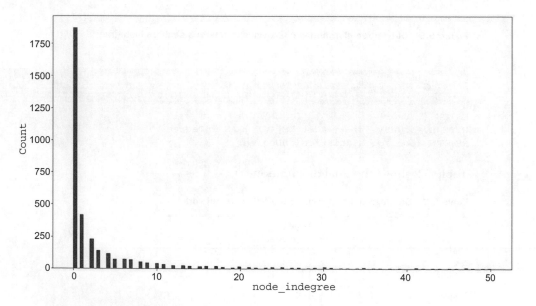

Figure 5.6   In-degree distribution chart visualized with a seaborn histogram

Exercise 5.2
Fetch the top five users with the highest in-degree (follower count). Use the `count{}` operator.

The solution to exercise 5.2 produces the output shown in table 5.3.

Table 5.3 Top five users with the highest in-degree

user	inDegree
"elonmusk"	540
"AndrewYNg"	301
"NASA"	267
"OpenAI"	265
"GoogleAI"	264

The highest in-degree users are pretty interesting. Elon Musk takes the crown. It seems that he is popular within the tech community, or at least in the given Twitter subgraph. In second place is none other than Andrew Ng. If you have dabbled with any machine learning, you have probably heard of him, as he is one of the most famous machine learning instructors.

Exercise 5.3

Remember, I've only included users who either published a tweet or were mentioned in one. Pick one of the top five users with the highest in-degree and examine the tweets they published or were mentioned in.

The solution Cypher statement to exercise 5.3 is shown in listing 5.3.

Listing 5.3 Examining mentions and published posts for NASA

```
MATCH (u:User)
WHERE u.username = "NASA"
OPTIONAL MATCH m=(u)<-[:MENTIONS]-()
OPTIONAL MATCH p=(u)-[:PUBLISH]->()
RETURN m,p
```

I've chosen to explore NASA's Twitter account. Note that I have used the OPTIONAL MATCH, as I don't know beforehand if NASA both published a tweet and was mentioned in one. Again, you could use a couple of variations of the Cypher statement to produce the same results, so don't worry if you got correct results but used a slightly different Cypher statement. The Cypher statement in listing 5.3 will produce the visualization shown in figure 5.7 in Neo4j Browser. NASA has published a single tweet and was mentioned in two other tweets in our dataset.

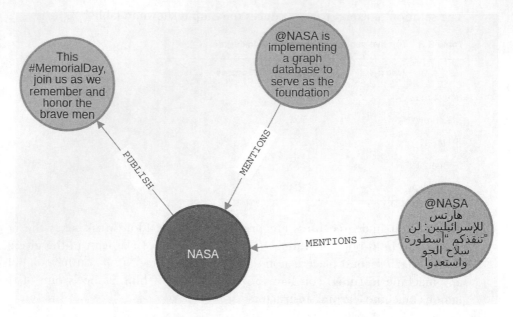

Figure 5.7   Network visualization of tweets published by or mentioning NASA

5.2   *Introduction to the Neo4j Graph Data Science library*

Before continuing with network characterization, you should get familiar with the Neo4j Graph Data Science library (GDS). The GDS is a plugin for Neo4j that features more than 50 graph algorithms, ranging from community detection and centrality to node-embedding algorithms and link prediction pipelines—and more. You can get an overview of all available graph algorithms in the official documentation (https://neo4j.com/docs/graph-data-science/current/).

Graph algorithms in the GDS library are executed on a *projected in-memory graph* structure separate from the graph stored in the database (figure 5.8). To execute graph algorithms with the GDS library, you must first project an in-memory graph. The projected graph is stored entirely in-memory, using an optimized data structure for scalable and parallel graph algorithm execution. You can create a projected in-memory graph using either *native projection* or *Cypher projection*.

Native projection is a bit more limited in selecting or filtering a specific subgraph you want to project, as you can only filter based on node labels and relationship types. However, it is the recommended way of projecting a graph as it is highly performant due to reading data directly from Neo4j storage.

The second available option for creating an in-memory graph is the Cypher projection. With it, you get all the flexibility of Cypher query language to select or filter any specific subgraph you might want to project. Of course, Cypher projection has a drawback, as it is slower than native projection and generally recommended only for the experimental or explorational phase of a project.

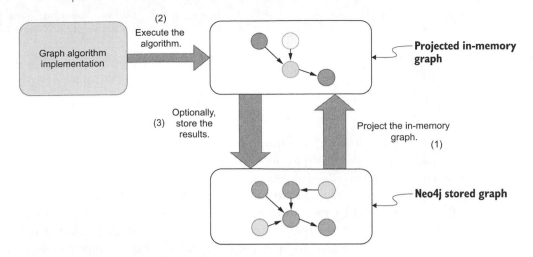

Figure 5.8 Graph Data Science library workflow

As the in-memory graph projection can be costly when dealing with large graphs, the GDS library also features a *graph catalog*. The graph catalog comes in handy when you want to execute multiple graph algorithms on the same projected graph. Instead of having to create an in-memory graph for each algorithm execution separately, you can create an in-memory graph once and then execute multiple graph algorithms on it. The projected graph can then be accessed via its name when executing graph algorithms, so the term *named graph* stuck with projected graphs stored in a graph catalog. Once the in-memory graph is created, you can execute graph algorithms on top of it.

Each algorithm has four modes of execution, depending on the use case:

- `stream`—Returns results as a stream of records and does not store results.
- `stats`—Returns a summary statistics of the result and does not store results.
- `mutate`—Writes the results back to the projected in-memory graph. This mode can only be used in combination with a named graph stored in a graph catalog. It is very useful when you want to use an output of one graph algorithm as an input to another.
- `write`—Writes the results back to the Neo4j database graph.

5.2.1 Graph catalog and native projection

Let's begin by reviewing a few examples covering network characterization and the GDS syntax and algorithm use cases. First off, you need to project an in-memory graph. You will use native projection to create an in-memory graph that consists of `User` nodes and `FOLLOWS` relationships. The native projection syntax is shown in the following listing.

Listing 5.4   Native projection syntax to create a named graph in the graph catalog

```
CALL gds.graph.project(
    graphName,
    nodeProjection,
    relationshipProjection,
    optional configuration
)
```

GDS procedures are executed using the `CALL` clause in combination with the procedure name. The procedure to store a named graph in the graph catalog with native projection is called `gds.graph.project()`. It contains three mandatory and one optional parameter. The first parameter is used to name the graph, under which it will be accessed when executing graph algorithms. The second parameter, called `nodeProjection`, defines the subset of nodes you want to project. Similarly, the `relationshipProjection` parameter specifies which relationships should be considered when creating an in-memory graph. An important thing to note is that a relationship will be skipped during projection if both adjacent nodes are not described in the `nodeProjection` parameter. In GDS terms, the starting node of the relationship is called the *source node* and the end node is called the *target node*.

To project the followers network, you need to only include `User` nodes and `FOLLOWS` relationships, with no additional configuration. The Cypher statement in listing 5.5 uses native projection to store an in-memory graph. The first parameter specifies its name, which will be used to access it when executing graph algorithms. The second parameter defines which nodes you want to include in the projection. When you only want to project a single type of node, you can define the desired node label as a string. Similarly, when you only want to project one type of relationship in the third parameter, you can specify the type as a string.

Listing 5.5   Projecting an in-memory graph consisting of `User` nodes and `FOLLOWS` relationships

```
CALL gds.graph.project('follower-network', 'User', 'FOLLOWS')
```

In later chapters, you will learn more about native projection and how to create an in-memory graph consisting of multiple node labels and relationship types. The GDS library also supports projecting node and relationship properties, which is useful when dealing with weighted networks.

5.3   *Network characterization*

Next, you will use the GDS library to characterize the Twitter follower network. These network characterization metrics provide a holistic view of the network's topology and can help in understanding the overall structure, efficiency of information flow, and level of interconnectedness among nodes in the network.

5.3.1 Weakly connected component algorithm

The first graph algorithm you will execute is the *weakly connected component* (WCC) algorithm. A WCC is a set of nodes within the graph, where a path exists between all nodes in the set if the direction of relationships is ignored. A WCC can be considered an "island" that cannot be reached from other graph components. While the algorithm identifies connected sets of nodes, its output can help you evaluate how disconnected the overall graph is.

Starting any graph analysis with a WCC algorithm is beneficial, as it offers an overview of the graph's structure, including connectivity and isolated parts. By identifying these disparate sections, you can concentrate further analysis on the most relevant components, simplifying the computational cost. Understanding the connectivity and how connected the overall graph is sets the stage for more detailed investigations, such as community detection or centrality analysis.

The WCC algorithm is probably a graph algorithm that should be executed as the first step of any graph analysis to evaluate graph connectivity. Figure 5.9 shows two WCCs. One component contains John, Alicia, and Amulya, and the other contains OpenAI, Google AI, NASA, and Andrew Ng.

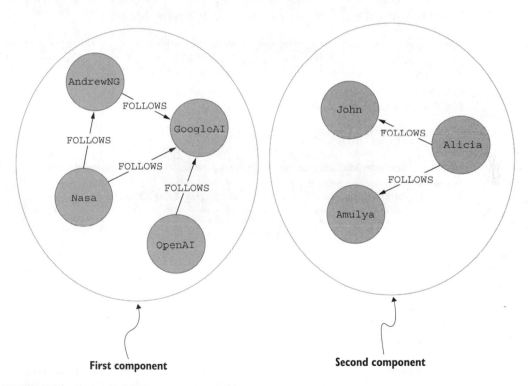

Figure 5.9   Network visualization of two WCCs

Nodes within a single WCC can reach all the other nodes if you ignore the relationship direction. For example, John can reach Alicia, even though the relationship is pointed in the other direction. Effectively, you could say the relationships are treated as undirected. The algorithm treats all nodes within the same community as being able to reach each other if a path exists between them, irrespective of the relationship's direction.

You will execute the WCC algorithm using the `write` mode. As mentioned, the `write` mode stores the results back to the Neo4j database but also provides summary statistics of the algorithm result. The syntax for graph algorithm procedures in GDS is shown in the following listing.

Listing 5.6   Graph algorithm procedure syntax

```
CALL gds.<algorithm>.<mode>(namedGraph, {optional configuration})
```

When using the `write` mode of an algorithm, you need to provide the mandatory `writeProperty` parameter, which specifies the name of the node property the algorithm results will be stored to. The procedure to execute the WCC algorithm is `gds.wcc`. You can execute the WCC algorithm on the followers network and store the results to Neo4j by using the Cypher statement in the following listing.

Listing 5.7   Executing the WCC algorithm on the follower network and storing the results as a `followerWcc` node property

```
CALL gds.wcc.write('follower-network', {writeProperty:'followerWcc'})
YIELD componentCount, componentDistribution
```

Table 5.4 shows the resulting statistics.

Table 5.4   Summary statistics for the WCC algorithm executed on the followers network

componentCount	componentDistribution

547	{ "p99":"3,
	  "min":"1,
	  "max":"2997,
	  "mean":"6.570383912248629,
	  "p90":"1,
	  "p50":"1,
	  "p999":"5,
	  "p95":"2,
	  "p75":"1 }

The `write` mode of the algorithm stores the results to the Neo4j database and provides the summary statistics shown in table 5.4. The node property that contains the algorithm results identifies the component ID to which the node belongs.

There are 547 disconnected components in the followers network, and the largest contains 2,997 members. Most real-world networks have a single connected component containing most of the nodes in the network and a couple of disconnected peripheral components. As the dataset you are analyzing is only a portion of a larger network, having a higher count of components is not unusual, due to many missing users and relationships that would otherwise connect various parts of the network if they were included. I've found one analysis on the Twitter network (Myers et al., 2014) where the authors analyzed a snapshot of the Twitter network from 2012 with 175 million users and 20 billion follow relationships. The analysis revealed that around 93% of the users belong in the largest WCC. Another analysis examined the Facebook graph (Ugander et al., 2011), where they learned that the largest WCC contains more than 99% of all nodes.

The `p90` result, or the 90th percentile of the component size, has a value of 1, which indicates that 90% of the components have only a single member. When a component contains only a single member, this means the node has no relationships.

Exercise 5.4
Count the number of members for the five largest WCCs. The component IDs are stored under the `followerWcc` property of the `User` nodes. Use the `followerWcc` property as a grouping key in combination with the `count()` function to count the number of members by component.

The solution to exercise 5.4 produces the output shown in table 5.5.

Table 5.5   Member count of the five largest WCCs

componentId	countOfMembers
0	2997
1293	5
1049	3
289	3
335	3

You can observe that there is a single component, which contains 85% of the nodes in the network. The component IDs are not deterministic, meaning you can get different values for the component IDs. However, the component member distribution should be identical.

The second-largest component contains only five members. You can visualize the second-largest component in Neo4j Browser with the Cypher statement in the following listing (see also figure 5.10). If you have different component IDs, make sure to change the component ID in the WHERE clause.

Listing 5.8   Retrieving User nodes that have no outgoing FOLLOWS relationships

```
MATCH p=(u:User)-[:FOLLOWS]->()
WHERE u.followerWcc = 1293
RETURN p
```

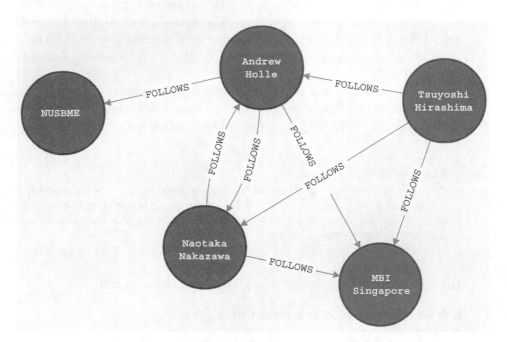

Figure 5.10   Network visualization of the second-largest WCC in the follower network

I've inspected the usernames shown in figure 5.10 on Twitter, and it seems they are some professors from Singapore and Kyoto universities. They follow each other but don't have any connections to the rest of the network in our small Twitter snapshot.

Exercise 5.5

Identify the number of WCCs that contain only one member. Remember, if a WCC contains only a single member, this effectively means that node has no incoming or outgoing relationships. Instead of using the followerWcc property to count those components, you can simply filter the User nodes with no FOLLOWS relationships and count them. The count will be identical to the number of WCCs with a single member.

5.3.2   *Strongly connected components algorithm*

A *strongly connected component* (SCC) is a subgraph of a directed graph in which a path exists between all its nodes. The only difference between the WCC and SCC algorithms is that the SCC algorithm considers relationship directions. Therefore, the SCC algorithm is only applicable to a directed graph. If the relationship direction is ignored, then you are dealing with WCCs.

Figure 5.11 shows four SCCs. The first component contains NASA, Andrew Ng, and Google AI. You can notice that although OpenAI can reach all the nodes in the first component, the path from Google AI to OpenAI is not possible, as the SCC algorithm does not ignore the relationship direction. Similarly, Amulya in the third component can be reached by Alicia and John, but a directed path from Amulya to either John or Alicia does not exist.

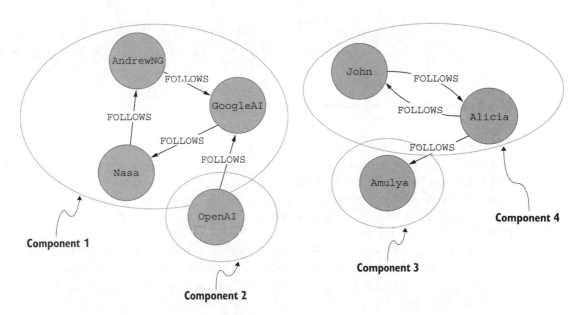

Figure 5.11   Network visualization of four SCCs

The SCC algorithm is useful when directed paths and reachability play an important role. For example, imagine a road network where the nodes represent intersections and relationships represent road connections. For example, many large city centers have a lot of one-way road connections. Using the SCC algorithm, you could evaluate the consequences of closing one or several road connections and how it would affect the reachability of places within the city.

Figure 5.12 visualizes a toy road network, where the nodes represent intersections and the relationships between them represent the road connections. For example, nodes A and B are connected in both directions, while the link between B and E

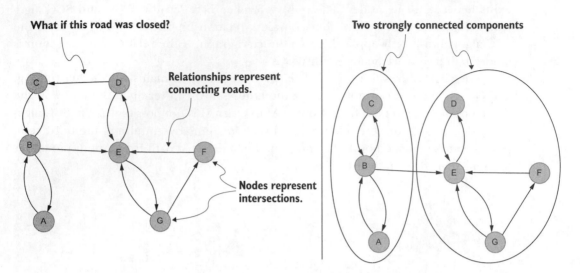

Figure 5.12   An example SCC use case in a road network

connects one way. Using the SCC algorithm, you can evaluate the reachability of nodes if a particular road is closed. For example, if the road between intersections D and C were to be closed due to maintenance, there would be no way to get from the right side of the network to the left. Specifically, you couldn't get from nodes D, E, F, or G to nodes A, B, or C. Therefore, nodes A, B, and C would form the first SCC, while D, E, F, and G form the second.

In the context of Twitter, the SCC can be applied to identify smaller well-connected groups of nodes. One research paper (Swati et al., 2016) claims you could use the SCC algorithm to identify groups of users for more precise marketing targeting. Another article (Efstathiades, 2016) used the SCC algorithm to suggest a movement of the user only following popular users while not making many connections with other unpopular users. The result is an increased number of SCCs over time.

Again, you will use the `write` mode of the algorithm to store the results back to the Neo4j database.

Listing 5.9   Executing the SCC algorithm on the follower network and storing the results as a `followerScc` node property

```
CALL gds.scc.write('follower-network', {writeProperty:'followerScc'})
YIELD componentCount, componentDistribution
```

Table 5.6 shows the resulting statistics.

Table 5.6 Summary statistics for the SCC algorithm executed on the followers network

componentCount	componentDistribution
2704	(cf { "min": 1, "p5": 1, "max": 796, "p999": 7, "p99": 2, "p1": 1, "p10": 1, "p90": 1, "p50": 1, "p25": 1, "p75": 1, "p95": 1, "mean": 1.3291420118343196 }

As expected, the count of SCCs is higher than the count of WCCs. There are 2,704 SCCs, and the largest one contains 796 members.

> **Exercise 5.6**
>
> Count the number of members for the five largest SCCs. The component IDs are stored under the `followerScc` property of the `User` nodes.

The solution to exercise 5.6 produces the output shown in table 5.7.

Table 5.7 Member count for the five largest SCCs

componentId	countOfMembers
0	796
380	20
407	7
36	6
212	4

Similarly, as with the WCC algorithm, the community IDs are not deterministic. You could get different community IDs but should get the same counts.

> **Exercise 5.7**
>
> Visualize the second-largest SCC in Neo4j Browser. A node can have relationships to nodes in other SCCs, so you have to apply a filter to ensure all the nodes are in the second-largest SCC.

The solution to exercise 5.4 produces the network visualization shown in figure 5.13 in Neo4j Browser. You can observe that this community is tightly knit, as there are many connections between the nodes in the group. Judging by the usernames, it seems they all come from the same part of the world. Unfortunately, I am not a language expert, so I have no idea which part of the world it is.

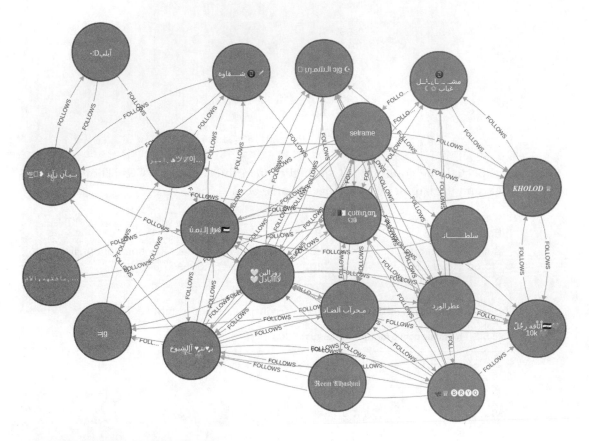

Figure 5.13   Network visualization of the second-largest SCC in the follower network

5.3.3   *Local clustering coefficient*

The *local clustering coefficient* (LCC) is a metric that quantifies how connected or close the neighbors of a particular node are. The LCC (figure 5.14) measures the average probability that two neighbors of a node are connected. Therefore, the value of the LCC ranges from 0 to 1. The LCC value of 0 indicates that the neighboring nodes have no connections between each other. On the other hand, the LCC value of 1 indicates that the network of neighbors forms a complete graph, where all the neighbors are connected.

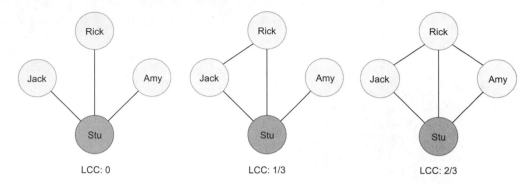

Figure 5.14 LCC values for an undirected graph

The LCC is more easily understood on an undirected graph. For example, in figure 5.14, Stu has three neighbors. When none of those neighbors have any connections to other neighbors, the LCC value is 0. Thus, Stu has the LCC value of 0 in the left example of figure 5.14. In the middle example, Stu has the LCC value of 1/3 or 0.33. Stu has three neighbors, so combinatorially, there are three possible relationships between them. As there is only one connection between Stu's neighbors in the middle example of figure 5.14, the LCC value for Stu is 1/3. The right-hand side example has two connections between Stu's neighbors; consequently, the LCC value for Stu is 2/3. If another relationship was created between Jack and Amy, then all the neighbors of the Stu node would form a complete graph, which would change Stu's LCC value to 1.

The LCC algorithm provides a metric to evaluate how strongly the neighbors of a node are connected. You can calculate the LCC value of a single node by dividing the number of existing links between neighbor nodes with the number of possible links between neighbor nodes. You can use the formula in figure 5.15 to calculate the LCC on a directed graph as well.

With a directed graph, the first difference is that a node has a neighboring node if it has at least a single connection to it. Even though Stu has four connections in figure 5.15, they only have three distinct neighbors. A neighbor of a node can have one incoming or outgoing connection to the original node or both. Only the count of distinct neighbors is important with the LCC algorithm. With a directed graph, each pair of neighbors can have up to two relationships between them, so the total possible number of connections between three neighbors is six. Again, you only need to count the number of existing connections between neighbors and divide it by the number of possible connections.

Unfortunately, the GDS library only supports the LCC algorithm for an undirected graph. However, as the directed LCC only counts the number of neighboring nodes and their links, you can easily implement the algorithm using only Cypher query language. Use the following Cypher statement to calculate the directed LCC value of each node, and store the results under the `lcc` node property.

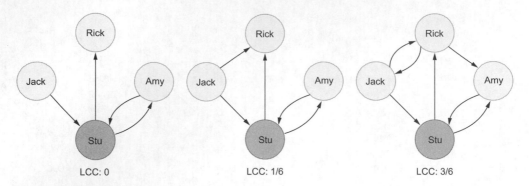

Figure 5.15   LCC values for a directed graph

```
MATCH (u:User)                          ⟵—| Matches all User nodes
OPTIONAL MATCH (u)-[:FOLLOWS]-(n)
WITH u,count(distinct n) AS neighbors_count    ⟵   Counts the number of their distinct neighbors
OPTIONAL MATCH (u)-[:FOLLOWS]-()-[r:FOLLOWS]-()-[:FOLLOWS]-(u)
WITH u, neighbors_count, count(distinct r) AS existing_links   ⟵   Counts the number of distinct links between neighbors
WITH u,
    CASE WHEN neighbors_count < 2 THEN 0 ELSE
      toFloat(existing_links) / (neighbors_count * (neighbors_count - 1))
      END AS lcc
SET u.lcc = lcc       ⟵—| Stores the LCC value under the lcc node property
```

Calculates the LCC value ⟶

You should already be familiar with most of the Cypher syntax in listing 5.10. You start by matching all the users in the database. Next, you count the number of distinct neighbors. As some User nodes don't have any FOLLOWS relationships, you must use the OPTIONAL MATCH clause. Using the MATCH clause would reduce the cardinality and effectively filter out all the User nodes that don't have any FOLLOWS relationships. If you remember from the WCCs example, there are around 500 User nodes that don't have any FOLLOWS relationships. Another small detail is that the Cypher pattern in the OPTIONAL MATCH does not provide a relationship direction. You want to count the number of distinct neighbors, irrespective of whether they have incoming, outgoing, or both types of relationships to the original node. As some neighbors can have both incoming and outgoing connections with the original User node, you need to use the distinct prefix within the count() function to get the correct result. The only variable missing before calculating the LCC is the count of existing links between neighbors. Again, you should use the OPTIONAL MATCH clause, as some neighbors might have zero connections, and you don't want to filter those out. I really like the Cypher syntax expressivity of defining the graph pattern that will count the number of links between neighboring nodes:

```
OPTIONAL MATCH (u)-[:FOLLOWS]-()-[r:FOLLOWS]-()-[:FOLLOWS]-(u)
```

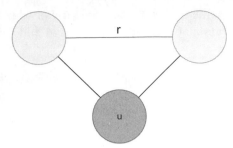

Figure 5.16   Visualized Cypher pattern to identify triangles

You can observe that I used the reference variable u twice in this pattern. Effectively, this graph pattern describes all triangles the u node participates in.

As you can see in figure 5.16, both the nodes must be adjacent to the node u, as described in the Cypher syntax. You are only interested in counting the r relationships between neighbors, so you combine the count() function and distinct prefix to fetch the count of existing links between neighbors. Similarly, as before, the FOLLOWS relationships in the specified graph pattern have no specified direction, as you want to consider all possible variations of relationship directions. Finally, you can use the LCC algorithm formula to calculate the LCC values for each node.

$$\frac{existing\ links}{neighbor\ count * (neighbor\ count - 1)}$$

The preceding equation can be used to calculate the directed LCC values. You take the count of existing links and divide it by the count of possible connections between neighbors, which is neighbors count times neighbors count minus 1. The formula does not work for nodes with a neighbor count of 0 or 1, as you would end up dividing by 0. By definition, the LCC value for nodes with less than 2 neighbors is undefined. However, I've come across some implementations where 0 is used instead of undefined for nodes with less than 2 neighbors, which is what I have also decided to use in this example. I've introduced the CASE statement to automatically assign the LCC value of 0 for nodes with less than 2 neighbors. If you have some experience with SQL query language, you will notice that the CASE statement is identical in Cypher. In any case, the Cypher syntax for the CASE clause is as follows:

```
CASE WHEN predicate THEN x ELSE y END
```

The predicate value should be a Boolean. You can then select the x value if the Boolean is true or the y value if the predicate is false.

Finally, you store the calculated LCC value under the `lcc` property of `User` nodes. Now that the LCC values are stored in the database, you can go ahead and calculate the average LCC.

> **Listing 5.11   Calculating the average LCC**

```
MATCH (u:User)
RETURN avg(u.lcc) AS average_lcc
```

The average LCC is 0.06. That's quite close to 0. One reason for such a small LCC value is that we only have a tiny snapshot of the Twitter network, so the information about followers is limited. Research on a more extensive Twitter network (Myers et al., 2014) demonstrates that the average LCC values are closer to between 0.15 and 0.20. It also seems that users on Twitter are less tightly knit than on Facebook (Ugander et al., 2011). That makes sense, as one typically connects with their friends and family on Facebook, which is a more strongly connected group of users. On the other hand, one study (Efsta-thiades et al., 2016) suggests Twitter users prefer to follow elite users or influencers rather than connecting with their family and real-life friends or neighbors as often.

5.4   *Identifying central nodes*

In the last part of this chapter, you will learn how to identify the most central nodes. The group of graph algorithms designed to identify the most central nodes is called *centrality algorithms*, with PageRank being the most famous one.

5.4.1   *PageRank algorithm*

PageRank was designed by Larry Page and Sergey Brin (1999) and helped make Google search what it is today. PageRank measures the transitive or directional influence of nodes. For example, the node degree quantifies the influence or importance of a node by considering only its direct neighbors. In contrast, PageRank also considers the indirect relationships with other nodes in the graph spanning over multiple hops. To put it into our Twitter subgraph context, if, for example, Elon Musk or Andrew Ng follows you, you gain more influence than if I follow you. PageRank evaluates the number of followers a particular node has as well as how influential those followers are.

PageRank was initially developed for ranking web pages' importance. The algorithm considers every relationship as a vote of influence (figure 5.17). I like to think that if a node is pointing to another node, it essentially states that the other node is important or influential.

You can then imagine how the votes flow throughout the network via directed relationships. Each node is initialized, with its score being equal to 1 divided by the number of nodes. Then, it passes its rank through its outgoing connections. The amount of influence passed through every relationship is equal to the node's influence divided by the number of outgoing links. After the first iteration, the node's rank is equal to the sum of incoming scores from other nodes. The algorithm then

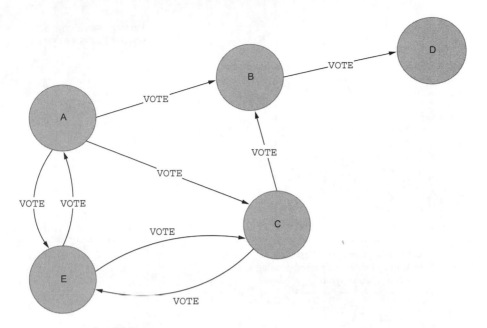

Figure 5.17   PageRank treats every relationship as a vote of influence.

iterates this process until it converges or hits a predefined number of iterations (figure 5.18).

However, the simplified PageRank calculation based on the network flow has a critical flaw. Node D in figure 5.17 has no outgoing links. A node without any outgoing connections is also known as a *dead end*. The presence of dead ends will cause the PageRank score of some or all nodes in the network to go down to zero, as it effectively leaks the rank score out of the network.

The PageRank algorithm introduces the *teleportation* ability to avoid rank leaking. Teleportation introduces a small probability of jumping to a random node instead of following the outgoing links. In the context of exploring web pages, imagine a web surfer traversing the internet. They might follow outgoing links from a web page to a web page or get bored and jump to a random page. The constant that defines the probability a surfer will follow an outgoing link is called the *damping factor*. Consequently, the probability that they will jump to a random page is 1 minus the damping factor. The typical value of the damping factor is 0.85, indicating a web surfer will jump to a random page about 15% of the time.

With the standard PageRank algorithm, the jump to a random node is uniformly distributed between all nodes in the network, meaning a bored surfer an equal chance of jumping to any node in the graph, including the one they are currently visiting. In this case, the intermediate node's rank after each iteration both sums the outgoing link's rank, as shown in figure 5.18, and adds the probability that a surfer will randomly jump to that node. The teleportation ability fixes the scenario where a dead-end node

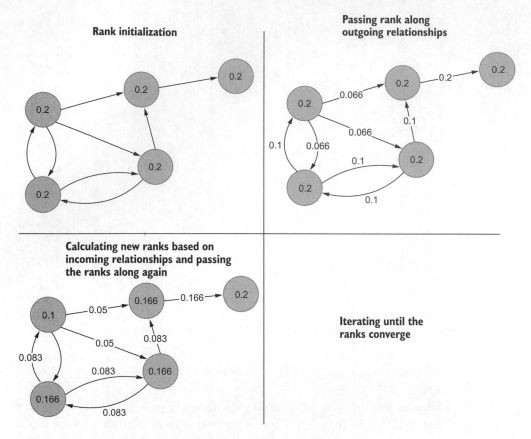

Figure 5.18   Simplified PageRank calculation based on network flow

leaks the whole network PageRank score, which would effectively be leaving all nodes at rank value zero. You can execute PageRank on the followers networks with the following Cypher statement.

Listing 5.12   Executing PageRank on the followers network

```
CALL gds.pageRank.write('follower-network',
  {writeProperty:'followerPageRank'})
```

The Cypher statement in listing 5.12 executes the PageRank algorithm on the projected follower network and stores the results back to the database as the `follower-PageRank` property of the `User` nodes.

Exercise 5.8

Retrieve the top five users with the highest PageRank score. The PageRank score is stored under the `followerPageRank` node property.

The solution to exercise 5.8 produces the output shown in table 5.8.

Table 5.8 **The most important nodes by PageRank score**

username	followerPageRank
"elonmusk"	20.381862706745217
"NASA"	8.653231888111382
"wmktech"	6.937989377788902
"Twitter"	6.937989377788902
"Wajdialkayal1"	6.551413750286345

Elon Musk is by far the most influential user in our Twitter subgraph. Interestingly, Andrew Ng, Google AI, and OpenAI were all among the first five positions given the incoming degree but have lost their places when using the PageRank score. Remember, PageRank evaluates the number of incoming connections as well as how influential the nodes behind the links are. Sometimes, a node with a high PageRank score only has a small number of influential connections. You can examine the top followers of each user in table 5.8 with the following Cypher statement.

Listing 5.13 **Examining the top five followers for the highest-ranking users**

```
MATCH (u:User)<-[:FOLLOWS]-(f)                    Matches the group of
WHERE u.username IN                               users using the IN clause
  ["elonmusk", "NASA", "wmktech", "Twitter", "Wajdialkayal1"]    <────
WITH u,f
ORDER BY f.followerPageRank DESC    <──    Orders the intermediate results by the
RETURN u.username AS user,                 followers PageRank score, descending
       round(u.followerPageRank, 2) AS pagerankScore,
       collect(f.username)[..5] AS topFiveFollowers    <──┐  Collects the top five
ORDER BY pagerankScore DESC                               │  followers grouped by
                                                          │  the original users
```

The Cypher statement in listing 5.13 begins by matching the top five users by their username property. Instead of using multiple OR predicates, you can use the IN operator to specify a list of possible values. Then, you use the WITH statement to order the results by the followers' PageRank score. Finally, you use the collect() function to produce an ordered list of followers by their PageRank score. The collect() function keeps the order of the input data. Because you first ordered the results in the WITH statement by the followers' PageRank score, the list result of the collect() function will contain an ordered list of followers by their PageRank score. Returning only the top five followers per user was achieved with *list slicing*. You may have come across list or array slicing if you have ever done any programming or SQL analysis. The list slicing syntax in Cypher is as follows:

```
array[from..to]
```

The square brackets syntax will extract the array elements from the start index `from` and up to (but excluding) the end index `to`. Cypher has a `round()` function that allows you to specify to round any number to the specified precision or decimal point. The results of the Cypher statement in listing 5.13 are shown in table 5.9.

Table 5.9   The most important nodes by PageRank score

user	pagerankScore	topFiveFollowers
"elonmusk"	20.38	["fchollet", "TheCuriousLuke", "DrLiMengYAN1", "douwekiela", "threadreaderapp"]
"NASA"	8.65	["BIBBIO2374449", "Lucian2drei", "NYTScience", "Cmcc-Climate", "abhibisht89"]
"wmktech"	6.94	["Wajdialkayal1", "alkayal_wajdi", "Websystemer", "Alkayal-Wajdi", "SwissCognitive"]
"Twitter"	6.66	["Lucian2drei", "Chuck_Moeller", "Omkar_Raii", "Sports-Center", "philipvollet"]
"Wajdialkayal1"	6.55	["wmktech", "Websystemer", "taylorwfarley", "RiM2ww", "saye2018"]

I was hoping that Elon or NASA would appear under top followers, but unfortunately, they don't follow anyone in our subgraph. The lack of follower relationships for Elon and NASA is not surprising, as they follow about 500 combined users but have more than 200 million followers themselves. If, for example, either Elon or NASA followed a user, their PageRank score would automatically be high because they would have one of the most influential nodes following them. A real-life analogy might be the following: imagine you just moved to Sweden and don't know anyone except the president of the country. Even though you only have one connection, that connection is very influential, which automatically gives you a lot of influence over the network.

The only exciting follower pattern that can be found in table 5.9 is that users wmktech and Wajdialkayal1 follow each other. They are both influential but also contribute to each other's importance by following one another.

5.4.2   *Personalized PageRank algorithm*

The Neo4j GDS library also supports the *personalized PageRank* variation. In the PageRank definition, a web surfer can get bored and randomly jump to other nodes. With the personalized PageRank algorithm, you can define which nodes the web surfer should jump to when they get bored. It can be said that by defining the `sourceNodes` to which the surfer is biased to jump, you are effectively inspecting the influence of nodes by looking through a particular node's or multiple nodes' point of view.

In this example, you will use the `stream` mode of the personalized PageRank algorithm. The `stream` mode returns the results of an algorithm as a stream of records.

The syntax of the personalized PageRank algorithm is almost identical to the Page-Rank algorithm, except you are also providing the `sourceNodes` parameter.

> **Listing 5.14 Running the personalized PageRank algorithm from the point of view of users who registered in 2016**

```
MATCH (u:User)
WHERE u.registeredAt.year = 2016
WITH collect(u) AS sourceNodes                    ◁─┐  Matches the source nodes
CALL gds.pageRank.stream('follower-network', {sourceNodes: sourceNodes})
YIELD nodeId, score                                ◁─┐  Executes the
RETURN gds.util.asNode(nodeId).username AS user, score   personalized
ORDER BY score DESC                                      PageRank algorithm
LIMIT 5;   ◁─┐  Uses the gds.util.asNode function to
              match the specific node by its internal ID
```

Matches the source nodes to be used in Personalized PageRank algorithm

First, you need to use the `MATCH` clause followed by the `collect()` function to produce a list of all users who registered in 2016. You can then input the collected users as the `sourceNode` parameter. By defining the `sourceNode` parameter, you are instructing the procedure to execute the personalized PageRank algorithm and use the provided nodes as the restart nodes when teleporting. The `stream` mode of the PageRank algorithms outputs two columns: `nodeId` and `score`. The `nodeId` represents the Neo4j *internal node id*, which the database automatically generates for every node in the database. You can use the `gds.util.asNode()` function to map the `nodeId` value to the actual node instance. The `score` column represents the PageRank score for a particular node.

The most important users from the point of view of users who registered in 2016 are Elon Musk followed by Andrew Ng, Ian Goodfellow, Hugging Face, and NASA. While Elon Musk and NASA are also present in the top five users by overall PageRank score, you can observe that the Andrew Ng, Ian Goodfellow, and Hugging Face accounts gained importance when determining PageRank score through the viewpoint of users who registered in 2016.

What would happen if you were to run personalized PageRank and use a node with no outgoing connections as the `sourceNodes` parameter? The following listing shows this process.

> **Listing 5.15 Running the personalized PageRank algorithm from the point of view of NASA**

```
MATCH (u:User)
WHERE u.username = "NASA"
WITH collect(u) AS sourceNodes
CALL gds.pageRank.stream('follower-network', {sourceNodes: sourceNodes})
YIELD nodeId, score
RETURN gds.util.asNode(nodeId).username AS user, score
ORDER BY score DESC
LIMIT 3;
```

Table 5.10 shows the PageRank scores for this example.

Table 5.10   The most important nodes by the PageRank score

user	score
"NASA"	0.15000000000000002
"ServerlessFan"	0
"dr_sr_simpson"	0

As there are no outgoing connections from the nodes specified in the `sourceNodes` parameter, the PageRank algorithm will keep on restarting at the selected source node, which will, in turn, leave all the other nodes with the PageRank score of 0. When running PageRank with default settings, all nodes with a PageRank score of 0.15 don't have any incoming relationships. They only get their importance by the web surfer randomly jumping to them, but they have no votes of significance from other nodes. With the personalized PageRank variation, you can also specify which nodes to jump to when bored, which, in turn, means some nodes will not even get the PageRank score of 0.15, as the surfer doesn't randomly jump to them.

> **Exercise 5.9**
>
> Execute the personalized PageRank algorithm, and use the `User` nodes who registered in the year 2019 as the `sourceNodes` parameter.

5.4.3   *Dropping the named graph*

Congratulations! You have now completed your first network analysis. After you have completed the planned graph algorithms execution sequence, it is recommended to drop the projected graph from memory. You can release the in-memory graph by using the `gds.graph.drop()` procedure.

Listing 5.16   Releasing the follower-network graph from memory

```
CALL gds.graph.drop('follower-network')
```

In the next chapter, you will learn how to infer monopartite networks based on indirect relationships. You will run many of the graph algorithms you learned in this chapter to solidify your skills in executing them and understanding their results.

5.5 Solutions to exercises

The solution to exercise 5.1 is as follows.

Listing 5.17 Fetching the users with the top five highest out-degrees

```
MATCH (u:User)
RETURN u.username AS user,
       count { (u)-[:FOLLOWS]->() } AS outDegree
ORDER BY outDegree DESC
LIMIT 5
```

The solution to exercise 5.2 is as follows.

Listing 5.18 Fetching the users with the top five highest in-degrees

```
MATCH (u:User)
RETURN u.username AS user,
       count{ (u)<-[:FOLLOWS]-() } AS inDegree
ORDER BY inDegree DESC
LIMIT 5
```

The solution to exercise 5.3 is as follows.

Listing 5.19 Examining mentions and published posts for NASA

```
MATCH (u:User)
WHERE u.username = "NASA"
OPTIONAL MATCH m=(u)<-[:MENTIONS]-()
OPTIONAL MATCH p=(u)-[:PUBLISH]->()
RETURN m,p
```

The solution to exercise 5.4 is as follows.

Listing 5.20 Counting the number of users for the five largest WCCs

```
MATCH (u:User)
WITH u.followerWcc AS componentId, count(*) AS countOfMembers
ORDER BY countOfMembers DESC
RETURN componentId, countOfMembers
LIMIT 5
```

The solution to exercise 5.5 is as follows.

Listing 5.21 Counting the number of WCCs that contain only one member

```
MATCH (u:User)
WHERE NOT EXISTS { (u)-[:FOLLOWS]-() }
RETURN count(*) AS countOfComponents
```

The solution to exercise 5.6 is as follows.

Listing 5.22   Counting the number of members for the five largest SCCs

```
MATCH (u:User)
WITH u.followerScc AS componentId, count(*) AS countOfMembers
ORDER BY countOfMembers DESC
RETURN componentId, countOfMembers
LIMIT 5
```

The solution to exercise 5.7 is as follows.

Listing 5.23   Visualizing the second-largest SCC in Neo4j Browser

```
MATCH p=(u1:User)-[:FOLLOWS]->(u2:User)
WHERE u1.followerScc = 380 AND u2.followerScc = 380
RETURN p
```

Make sure you correct the followerScc value if needed in the WHERE clause.

The solution to exercise 5.8 is as follows.

Listing 5.24   Retrieving the top five users with the highest PageRank score

```
MATCH (u:User)
RETURN u.username AS username, u.followerPageRank AS followerPageRank
ORDER BY followerPageRank DESC
LIMIT 5
```

The solution to exercise 5.9 is as follows.

Listing 5.25   Executing the personalized PageRank algorithm and using the User nodes who registered in the year 2019 as the sourceNodes parameter

```
MATCH (u:User)
WHERE u.registeredAt.year = 2019
WITH collect(u) AS sourceNodes
CALL gds.pageRank.stream('follower-network', {sourceNodes: sourceNodes})
YIELD nodeId, score
RETURN gds.util.asNode(nodeId).username AS user, score
ORDER BY score DESC
LIMIT 5
```

Summary

- Real-world networks follow the power-law distribution of node degree.
- For a directed network, the node degree can be split into in-degree, the count of incoming connections, and out-degree, which counts outgoing links.
- The Graph Data Science (GDS) library uses a projected in-memory graph to execute the graph algorithm on.
- Native projection is the better performing variation of projecting in-memory graphs.

- The `stream` mode of graph algorithms returns results as a stream of records and does not store results.
- The `stats` mode returns a summary statistics of the algorithm and does not store results.
- The `mutate` mode of a graph algorithm stores the results of the algorithm back to the projected in-memory graph.
- The `write` mode stores the results of the algorithm to the database.
- The weakly connected component (WCC) algorithm is used to identify disconnected parts or islands in the network.
- The WCC algorithm is often used early in an analysis to evaluate the connectedness and structure of a graph.
- A strongly connected component (SCC) is a subgraph of a directed graph in which a path exists between all nodes.
- The local clustering coefficient (LCC) examines how tightly knit the neighbors of a node are.
- The `CASE` clause can be used to specify generic conditional expressions.
- PageRank treats each relationship as a vote of influence and can be used to find the most influential nodes in the graph.
- PageRank has a damping factor parameter that specifies how often a random web surfer should follow an outgoing link as opposed to jumping to a random node.
- When running the PageRank algorithm with the default damping factor parameter of 0.85, nodes with no incoming relationships will have a PageRank score of 0.15.
- With the Personalized PageRank variation, you can specify which nodes the random surfer should teleport to, which gives you a view of the network from a specific point of view.
- After an analysis, make sure to release the projected graph from memory with the `gds.graph.drop` procedure.

Projecting
monopartite networks

6

This chapter covers

- Translating an indirect graph pattern into a direct relationship
- Using Cypher projection to project an in-memory graph
- Presenting self-loops
- Introducing weighted variations of degree and PageRank centrality algorithms

In the previous chapter, you performed a network analysis of the Twitter follower network. The decision to start with the follower network was straightforward. Most graph algorithms are designed to be executed on a monopartite network, where only a single node and relationship type are present. However, the Twitter social network schema contains multiple node types and relationships. Instead of adjusting graph algorithms to support multipartite networks (multiple node and relationship types), the general approach is to first project a monopartite network (single node and relationship type). I have briefly alluded to this concept in chapter 2, where I presented some options on how to infer monopartite projections on the Twitter social network.

Suppose you want to analyze how content spreads on Twitter and which users are the most influential content creators. Users can post content in the form of tweets. However, for a tweet to reach a wider audience and possibly go viral, it must be shared by other users with their audiences. On Twitter, sharing other people's content with your audience is called retweeting. So to understand which are the most influential content creators, you need to examine the retweeting behavior of the network. Many studies have been published using the retweet network, ranging from a network analysis of the European Parliament (Cherepnalkoski & Mozetič, 2015) to science- and health-related retweet clusters on Twitter during the COVID-19 pandemic (Durazzi et al., 2021). The most influential content creators on Twitter can be defined as users who publish the most retweeted content. However, you can take it up a notch and assume that it is not only the number of retweets that is important but also who is retweeting. For example, there is a large difference between a user like Andrew Ng, who is well respected in the machine learning world, sharing your content and someone who just joined the platform and has no audience doing the same. Therefore, Andrew Ng's retweet gives you more content influence than a user with no audience.

In general, centrality algorithms are a good fit for determining the most important or influential nodes in the network. Let's say you decide to use the PageRank algorithm, as you have already heard about it in the previous chapter. The PageRank algorithm is also a good match, as it considers both the number of incoming relationships and from which nodes they come to calculate the influence of a node in a network. To determine how you can utilize PageRank to identify the most influential content creators, you must consider the graph model you used to represent the retweet pattern in the Twitter social network.

In your Twitter social network schema, a user can publish a tweet as visualized on the right side of figure 6.1. However, when another user retweets a tweet, a new Tweet node is created with a RETWEETS relationship pointing to the original tweet. If you were to execute the PageRank algorithm on the network in figure 6.1, which node would be the most important? Remember that PageRank treats each relationship as a vote of confidence or influence. The influence then flows throughout the network. Please take a minute or two to think about which node in the network in figure 6.1 would be the most important based on the PageRank algorithm. For me, it is easier to start with the least influential nodes and work my way up to the most important ones.

Figure 6.2 visualizes the retweet pattern, where node sizes are scaled based on their PageRank score. The bigger the node is, the higher its PageRank score. User nodes have no incoming relationships, so their PageRank score is the lowest. Both the original tweet and the retweet have incoming relationships, so they are already more important than users. The retweet has a single incoming relationship, and the original tweet has two incoming connections. With the PageRank algorithm, both the count of incoming links as well as the importance of nodes linking to a particular node are considered when calculating the PageRank score. So it is not always

Retweet graph pattern

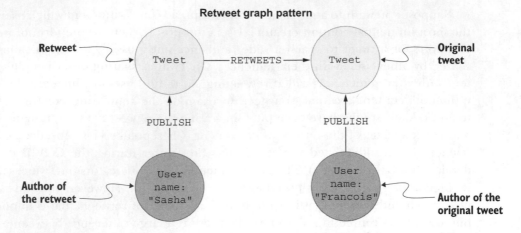

Figure 6.1   Graph model that represents a retweet pattern

given that a node with more incoming links will have a higher score. However, in the retweet network in figure 6.2, the original tweet draws influence from its author as well as the retweet and the retweet's author. On the other hand, the retweet node draws influence only from the retweet's author, which means the retweet will be less important than the original tweet.

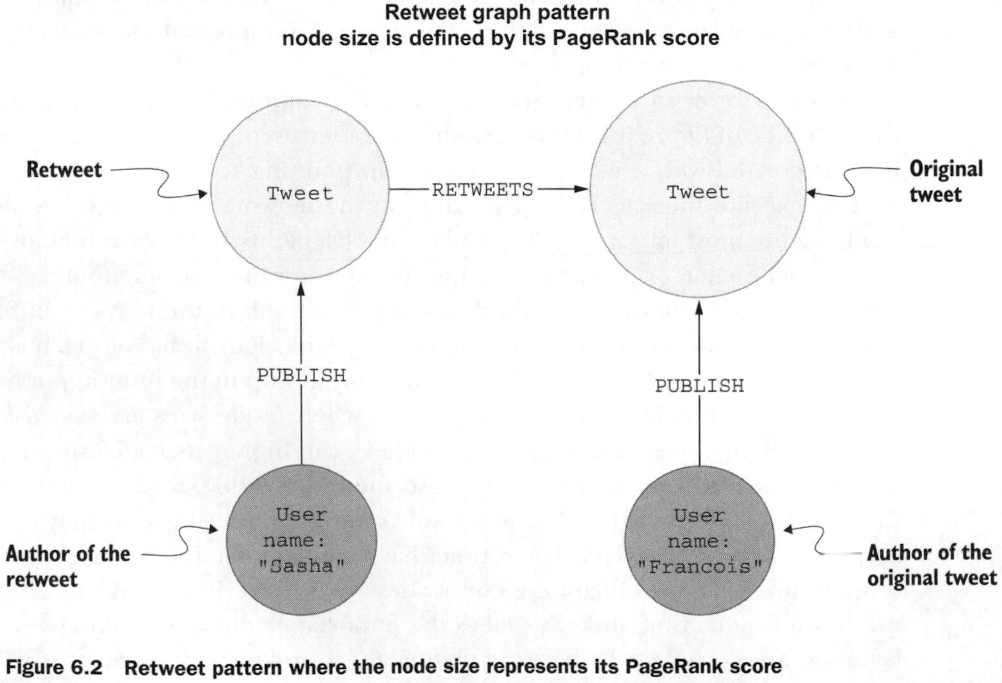

**Retweet graph pattern
node size is defined by its PageRank score**

Retweet ⟶   Tweet   ⟶ RETWEETS ⟶   Tweet   ⟵ **Original
tweet**

PUBLISH   PUBLISH

**Author of the
retweet** ⟶   User
name:
"Sasha"   User
name:
"Francois" ⟵ **Author of the
original tweet**

Figure 6.2   Retweet pattern where the node size represents its PageRank score

As visualized in figure 6.2, the influence flows from users to tweets and, optionally, through retweet relationships to the original content. In theory, the content with the highest retweet count will have the highest PageRank score. There are some exceptions, as the importance of tweets and retweets drops with a higher number of published tweets and retweets by a user; however, it is still a good approximation of which tweets were the most retweeted. You could then aggregate the importance of tweets by users and identify the most influential users. Unfortunately, this approach ignores one major item in your definition of influential content creators. Since users don't have any incoming relationships, the PageRank score is identical for all users, and the algorithm does not differentiate between important and unimportant users. Consequently, the PageRank score does not reflect whether influential users retweeted the content.

Interestingly, with network analysis, it is more frequent to adapt the dataset to fit the algorithm than the other way around. To determine which users are the most influential based on retweeting behavior, you must somehow model the influence flow between users. It turns out that the best way to model influence flow between users is to reduce the network where both users and tweets are present to a monopartite network where only users are considered. As a monopartite network contains only a single type of nodes, you need to somehow exclude Tweet nodes while preserving the information about the retweets. If a user retweets a post from another user, they increase or amplify the reach of the original tweet and, consequently, the author of the original tweet. You can represent how users amplify other users' content reach with a direct relationship. How you want to name the new *inferred relationship* depends on your domain and use case. In this example, I will name the new relationship type AMPLIFY, since it is used to represent how users amplify the reach of one another through retweets. The term *inferred relationship* means the relationship is not explicitly defined in data but is inferred or created based on some assumptions.

Figure 6.3 shows the concept of translating a graph pattern between two User nodes that spans over three relationships into a direct link between the two. On the left side of this visualization is the retweet pattern as it is stored in the database. However, since you want to evaluate how influential users are based on retweet patterns with the PageRank algorithm, you need to transform the indirect path between the two users into a direct relationship, as indicated on the right side of figure 6.3. The influence will flow between users using a direct relationship to model retweet behavior. Consequently, the PageRank algorithm will consider both the number of retweets as well as who retweeted the content in the final score when executed on the monopartite network, where the retweet pattern is modeled as a direct relationship.

You could easily describe this network transformation with a Cypher statement.

Listing 6.1 Describing the translation of the indirect retweet pattern to a direct AMPLIFY relationship

```
MATCH (s:User)-[:PUBLISH]->()-[:RETWEETS]->()<-[:PUBLISH]-(t:User)
CREATE (s)-[:AMPLIFY]->(t);
```

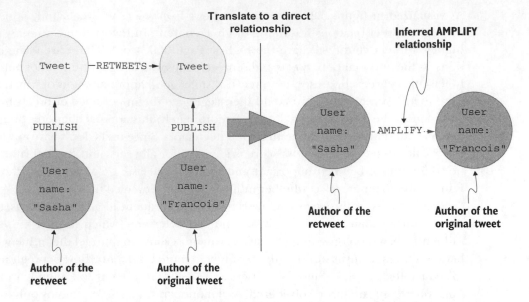

Figure 6.3   Translating an indirect retweet pattern into a direct `AMPLIFY` relationship

After you have transformed all the retweet patterns into a direct relationship, you end up with a monopartite network that contains only User nodes and AMPLIFY relationships (figure 6.4).

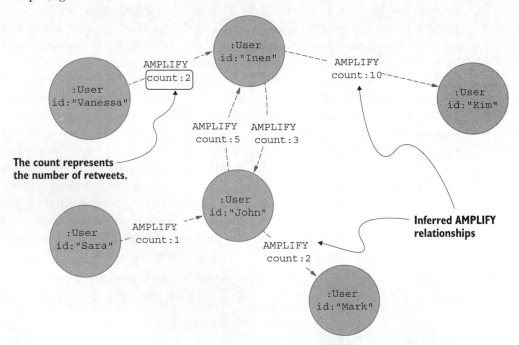

Figure 6.4   Projected monopartite network of `User` nodes and `AMPLIFY` relationships

Figure 6.4 visualizes a subgraph of the projected or inferred monopartite network that represents User nodes and AMPLIFY relationships, constructed based on the retweet pattern. Since a user can retweet posts from other users multiple times, you can store the count as the relationship property. Therefore, you can describe the network in figure 6.4 as directed and weighted. The same idea of a reduced monopartite network, where nodes represent only users and relationships represent the retweets between users, has been used by many researchers (Evkoski et al., 2020; Evkoski et al., 2021; Priyanta & Prayana Trisna, 2019).

The inferred amplify network could then be used to examine the users who produce the best (most sharable) content under the assumption that the retweet means that a user liked the content of the original tweet. I would imagine that if you want to express your disagreement with the tweet's content, you would quote the tweet and describe your dispute with the tweet. You defined that the quote and retweet should be stored under a different relationship type in the original graph schema. However, since there are no quotes in the dataset, you could assume that all the retweets are positive, meaning users agree with the original tweet's content.

You will learn more details and caveats of various approaches to inferring monopartite networks through practical examples. To follow the exercises in this chapter, you need to have the Twitter network imported into the Neo4j database, as described in chapter 3.

6.1 Translating an indirect multihop path into a direct relationship

You will begin by translating the multihop retweet relationship into a direct AMPLIFY relationship (figure 6.5). With Neo4j Graph Data Science (GDS), you could take two different approaches to accomplish this task.

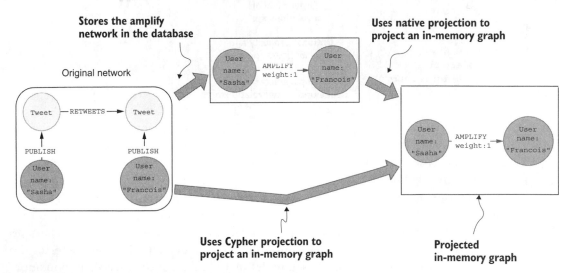

Figure 6.5 Two options to translate an indirect multihop path to a direct relationship in a projected graph

To project a monopartite retweet network with native projection, you must first materialize it in your Neo4j database. Native projection does not offer custom network transformations during graph loading. On the other hand, you can use Cypher projection to load a *virtual graph* into memory. In this context, a virtual graph is a graph that is not stored in the database and is constructed only at projection time. The ability to project custom transformations without storing them in the database is a nice feature that lets you explore various graph projections and analyze them while keeping the graph database clean. Cypher projection features all the expressivity of the Cypher query language to select, filter, and transform the graph to be projected. In the following subsection, you will learn how to use Cypher projection to avoid storing the monopartite retweet network in the database.

6.1.1   Cypher projection

Cypher projection, shown in the following listing, is a more flexible and expressive approach to projecting an in-memory graph. As you might deduce from the feature's name, you can use Cypher statements to define the nodes and relationships you want to load in the in-memory graph. The Cypher projection function is called `gds.graph` `.project` and has three mandatory and two optional parameters.

Listing 6.2   Cypher projection syntax

**Cypher statement to match
the desired graph pattern**

```
MATCH (sourceNode)-[relationship]->(targetNode)
RETURN gds.graph.project(
    'graph',
    sourceNode,
    targetNode,
    {dataConfig},
    {configuration}
) YIELD
    graphName,
    nodeCount,
    relationshipCount
```

Projected graph name

Source node of a relationship

Target node of a relationship

Optional property and type configuration map

Optional parameter map to define undirected relationships

You can think of Cypher projection as using Cypher statements to describe relationships of a projected graph, where each connection is defined with its source and target nodes. First, you must use the Cypher syntax to match the source and target nodes of the relationships you want to project. As mentioned, you can match existing relationships in the database or define virtual connections not materialized in the database. Once you have specified the source and target nodes of the desired relationships, you can use the `gds.graph.project` function in a WITH or RETURN clause to project a graph instead of having to use the CALL clause. The first parameter of the `gds.graph` `.project` function is used to define the name of the projected in-memory graph. On the other hand, the second and third parameters describe the source and target nodes of the projected relationship. The fourth parameter is optional and is used to specify node and relationship properties and their labels or types, if needed. By defining node labels and relationship types, you can efficiently filter them at algorithm runtime.

> **NOTE** Cypher projection is a more flexible and expressive approach to describing the graph you project. Essentially, it is a way of defining the projected graph using the node and relationship lists. As the relationship list is defined using Cypher statements, you can take full advantage of the expressiveness of Cypher Query Language to filter or transform the desired graph projection, without having to materialize it first in the database. However, there is a downside to this approach, as the performance of Cypher projection is worse than that of native projection. Because of its inferior performance, Cypher projection is not recommended for larger graphs or the production phase.

Next, you will use Cypher projection to load the retweet amplify network as an in-memory graph. You must prepare the relationship Cypher statement before using Cypher projection to load the in-memory graph and execute graph algorithms.

> **Exercise 6.1**
> Describe the retweet pattern in the `MATCH` statement. Return the user that retweeted another user under the `source` column and the user who was retweeted under the `target` column. Since a user can retweet another user multiple times, count the number of retweets and return the number of retweets under the `weight` column. Return only the first five rows of the result.

You can now use the Cypher statement used in exercise 6.1 as input to the `gds.graph` `.project` function to project an in-memory graph using Cypher projection.

Listing 6.3 Loading the amplify retweet network as an in-memory graph using Cypher projection

```
MATCH (source:User)-[:PUBLISH]->()-[:RETWEETS]->()<-[:PUBLISH]-(target:User)
WITH source, target, count(*) AS weight          ◁──── Matches the retweet pattern and
WITH gds.graph.project(                                counts the number of retweets
    'amplify',                                         between a pair of users
    source,
    target,
    {relationshipProperties:{weight:weight}}     ◁──── Projects an in-memory
) AS g                                                 graph using Cypher
RETURN g.graphName AS graph,                           projection
       g.nodeCount AS nodes,
       g.relationshipCount AS rels
```

The Cypher statement in listing 6.3 starts by matching the retweet pattern. The user who retweeted is specified as the `source` node, while the retweeted user is described as the `target` node. Next, you count the number of retweets between a single pair of users using the `count()` function. Now that the relationship list is prepared, you can project it using the `gds.graph.project` function. In this example, you provided the `source` and `target` nodes along with the relationship property `weight`, specified in the data configuration parameter. Check the documentation for a complete list of possible configuration keys: http://mng.bz/GyJO. The Cypher projection function will return the output shown in table 6.1.

Table 6.1   Cypher projection function output

graphName	nodeCount	relationshipCount
"amplify"	1828	2719

There are 1,828 nodes and 2,719 relationships in the projected in-memory `amplify` graph. The retweet amplification network can be described as a directed, weighted network.

6.2   Retweet network characterization

Next, you will perform a short network analysis of the retweet amplification network. This analysis aims to reinforce your experience with executing graph algorithms.

6.2.1   Degree centrality

First, you will evaluate the node degree distribution of the inferred network. In the previous chapter, you used a plain Cypher statement to calculate and visualize the node degree distribution. Here, the retweet amplification network is not materialized in the database, so you don't have the option of using a plain Cypher statement to calculate the node degree distribution. Instead, you can use the GDS degree centrality algorithm `gds.degree` to evaluate the node degree distribution

You can use the `stats` mode of the algorithm to examine the node degree distribution, as shown in the following listing. By default, the `gds.degree` centrality calculates the out-degree. Remember, the out-degree is the count of outgoing relationships a node has, while the in-degree counts the incoming links.

> **Listing 6.4   Evaluating the out-degree distribution of the inferred retweet amplification network**

```
CALL gds.degree.stats('amplify')
YIELD centralityDistribution
```

Table 6.2 shows the resulting distribution.

Table 6.2 Out-degree distribution of the retweet amplification network

Metric	Value
p99	18.00011444091797
min	0.0
max	146.00096893310547
mean	1.4874205599728507
p90	2.0000076293945312
p50	1.0
p999	61.00023651123047
p95	4.000022888183594
p75	1.0

On average, a node in the network has around 1.5 outgoing relationships. The pX values represent the percentile values; for example, p75 represents the 75th percentile value of 1.0, which means 75% of nodes have 1 or 0 outgoing relationships. You can deduce that the inferred retweet network is sparse.

Exercise 6.2

Use the degree centrality algorithm to calculate and return the top five nodes with the highest out-degree in the retweet amplification network. Use the `stream` mode of the algorithm to stream the results without storing them in the database or the projected graph. The `stream` mode of the `gds.degree` algorithm outputs `nodeId` and `score` columns. Use `gds.util.asNode` to map the node IDs to node instances and retrieve the `username` property for the top five nodes.

The solution to exercise 6.2 produces the output shown in table 6.3.

Table 6.3 The top five users by out-degree in the retweet amplification network

user	score
"textsla"	146.0
"godfrey_G_"	61.0
"iPythonistaBot"	48.0
"Beka "Bexx" Modebade"	36.0
"chidambara09"	33.0

The user textsla has retweeted posts from 146 different users. It wouldn't surprise me if most of the users on this list had automatic retweets in place for specific hashtags.

Since you are dealing with a weighted network, you can also evaluate the weighted out-degree distribution. Most of the GDS library graph algorithms support the algorithms' weighted variations by using the `relationshipWeightProperty` configuration parameter. You can evaluate the weighted out-degree distribution of the retweet amplification network with the following Cypher statement.

> **Listing 6.5   Evaluating the weighted out-degree distribution of the inferred retweet amplification network**

```
CALL gds.degree.stats('amplify', {relationshipWeightProperty:'weight'})
YIELD centralityDistribution
```

Table 6.4 shows the resulting distribution.

Table 6.4   Weighted out-degree distribution of the retweet amplification network

Metric	Value
p99	65.00048065185547
min	0.0
max	2,006.0078048706055
mean	4.715000173456038
p90	3.0000076293945312
p50	1.0
p999	670.0038986206055
p95	7.000022888183594
p75	1.0

Although the average weighted out-degree is 4.7, the 75th percentile is only 1 and the 90th percentile only raises to 3. It seems that there are a few outliers that raise the average of the whole population. For example, a single user has 2,006 retweets. Given that most of the retweets in this dataset happened in the three-day window, I would venture a guess that the highest retweeting users have some retweet automatization set up.

> **Exercise 6.3**
>
> Use the degree centrality algorithm to calculate and return the top five nodes with the highest weighted out-degree in the retweet amplification network. The solution is almost identical to exercise 6.2, except that you include the `relationshipWeight-Property` parameter to calculate the weighted out-degree.

The outgoing node degree can help you evaluate and identify users spreading or distributing content through the network the most.. On the other hand, you can use the in-degree distribution to identify users who produce the most sharable (and perhaps best?) content. The node degree centrality algorithm has an `orientation` parameter that allows you to evaluate in-degree, out-degree, or a combination of both. The `orientation` parameter has three possible inputs:

- `NATURAL`—Evaluates the out-degree (count of outgoing relationships)
- `REVERSE`—Evaluates the in-degree (count of incoming relationships)
- `UNDIRECTED`—Evaluates the sum of both the in- and out-degrees

Therefore, you can use the `orientation` parameter to evaluate the in-degree distribution by setting it to `REVERSE`.

> **Listing 6.6   Returns the top five users with the highest in-degree**

```
CALL gds.degree.stats('amplify', {orientation:'REVERSE'})
YIELD centralityDistribution
```

Table 6.5 shows the resulting distribution.

Table 6.5   In-degree distribution of the retweet amplification network

Metric	Value
p99	29.00011444091797
min	0.0
max	117.00048065185547
mean	1.4874205599728507
p90	3.0000076293945312
p50	0.0
p999	96.00048065185547
p95	7.000022888183594
p75	1.0

More than 50% of the users haven't been retweeted even once. In some way, it makes sense that there are fewer users who write content that is retweeted than users who do the retweeting. If you remember from the previous chapter as well, the in- and out-degree mean will always be identical, as the number of connections and users stays the same, and only the relationship direction is reversed. Interestingly, in this example, the 75th- and the 90th-percentile values are identical. It seems that the in-degree distribution is a bit more top-heavy than the out-degree. This would imply that several content creators consistently produce content that is being retweeted. Maybe that implies producing quality content, but we would have to investigate further. Perhaps, only their hashtag game is strong.

The solution of exercise 6.4 produces the output shown in table 6.6.

Table 6.6   Top five users by in-degree in the retweet amplification network

user	score
"Paula_Piccard"	117.0
"IainLJBrown"	96.0
"Eli_Krumova"	90.0
"Analytics_699"	69.0
"annargrs"	65.0

A total of 117 different users have retweeted Paula_Piccard. The difference between the first and fifth places is not as large as the out-degree distribution. You might assume they produce relevant and quality content, as they are often retweeted. You would have to scrape more tweets with the relevant hashtags for more accurate results.

You will now execute the weakly connected components (WCC) algorithm you learned in chapter 5 to consolidate your knowledge.

6.2.2   *Weakly connected components*

The WCC algorithm should be part of almost every network analysis. With it, you can evaluate how connected the network is and identify disconnected components.

> ### Exercise 6.6
> Evaluate the distribution of weakly connected component sizes with the `gds.wcc`
> `.stats` procedure.

Table 6.7 shows the statistics resulting from the WCC algorithm.

Table 6.7 Summary statistics for the WCC algorithm executed on the retweet amplification network

componentCount	componentDistribution
207	{ "p99": 28, "min": 1, "max": 1082, "mean": 8.830917874396135, "p90": 6, "p50": 2, "p999": 1082, "p95": 13, "p75": 3 }

The largest component consists of 1,082 members, which is around 60% of the total users in the retweet amplification network. As previously mentioned, most real-world networks have a single super component containing most of the network's nodes with a couple of smaller components on the side. What is strange to me is that minimum size components contain only a single member. With Cypher projection, you have filtered users who retweeted or were retweeted. My first thought was that there should be no components with only a single member. As this is an unexpected result, it is worth exploring. You can execute the following Cypher statement to examine sample components with a single member.

Listing 6.7 Examining sample components with a single member

**Collects nodes grouped
by component id**

**Executes the stream mode
of the WCC algorithm**

```
CALL gds.wcc.stream('amplify')
YIELD nodeId, componentId
WITH componentId, collect(nodeId) AS componentMembers,
    count(*) AS componentSize
WHERE componentSize = 1
WITH componentMembers[0] AS id
LIMIT 3
MATCH p=(n)-[:PUBLISH]->()-[:RETWEETS]-()
WHERE id(n)=id
RETURN p
```

**Filters components that
contain only a single member**

**Extracts the node ID
from the list for three
sample components**

**Matches their
retweets**

The Cypher statement in listing 6.7 starts by executing the `stream` mode of the WCC algorithm on the retweet amplification network. The `stream` mode of the WCC algorithm outputs the `nodeId` column, representing the internal node ID of the node, and the `componentId` column, which describes to which component the node belongs. In the next step of the Cypher statement, you aggregate by the `componentId` to calculate the component size and collect its members' node IDs. Afterward, you use the `WHERE` clause to filter components with only one member. As there should be only a single element in the `componentMembers` list of the single-member components, you can easily extract the only node ID using the square bracket syntax in combination with its index position. To not overwhelm the results visualization, you will only examine three components with a single member. The last thing you need to do is match the retweets pattern for the three specific node IDs. The Cypher statement in listing 6.7 will produce the visualization shown in figure 6.6 in Neo4j Browser.

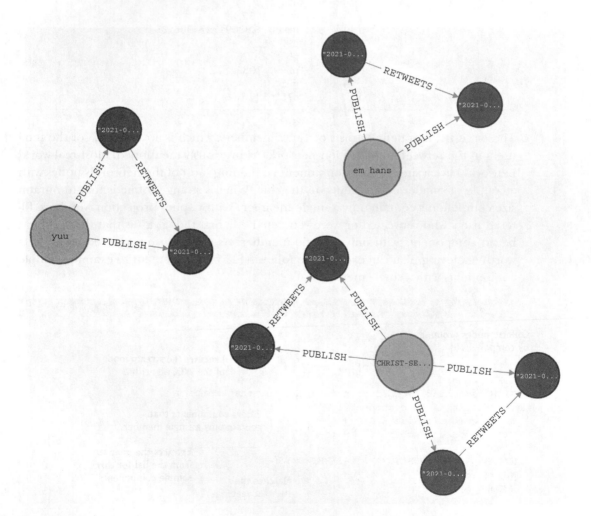

Figure 6.6   Components that contain a single member, where users retweeted themselves

On Twitter, a user can also retweet their posts. In graph theory, a *self-loop* is a relationship with the same start and end node. As mentioned, the WCC algorithm is helpful for identifying how connected the network is as well as identifying various unexpected patterns.

6.3 Identifying the most influential content creators

The main objective of the task in this chapter is to identify the most influential content creators on the available subset of the Twitter social network dataset. You will determine the most important content creators by following these two steps:

1 Ignore self-loops during projection.
2 Execute the weighted variant of the PageRank algorithm.

6.3.1 Excluding self-loops

I think it makes sense to exclude all the self-loops from the network before you execute the weighted PageRank algorithm. The self-loop can be translated as the node stating that it is influential. I think that retweeting your own tweets shouldn't increase your influence in the network. Unfortunately, there is no magic button to press that excludes self-loops, so you must project another in-memory graph using Cypher projection.

> **Exercise 6.7**
> Use Cypher projection to load the retweet amplification network into memory and exclude all self-loops. Essentially, you only need to change the relationship Cypher statement to filter out relationships that start and end at the same node. Name the new projected graph `amplify-noselfloops`.

6.3.2 Weighted PageRank variant

Next, you will execute the weighted PageRank algorithm to identify potential content influencers. Remember, the PageRank algorithm considers both the number of incoming connections and the nodes' importance that links to it. Instead of simply analyzing which user has the most retweets, you are also evaluating which other influential nodes in the network retweeted them.

The weighted variant of the PageRank algorithm also considers the relationship weight when calculating node importance. With the unweighted variant of PageRank, the node's importance is equally spread among its neighbors. On the other hand, with the weighted variant, each neighbor gets the share of importance related to the relationship weight (figure 6.7).

As previously mentioned, the weighted variant of the PageRank algorithm considers the relationship weight when it calculates how the influence spreads across the

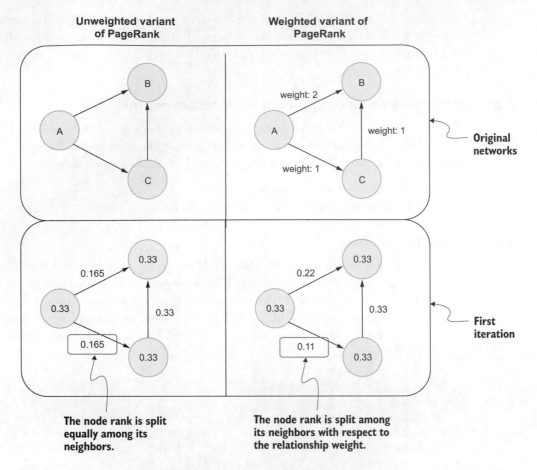

Figure 6.7   The difference between weighted and unweighted PageRank calculation in a single iteration

network. Figure 6.7 visualizes a simple network consisting of three nodes. The difference between the weighted and unweighted variants is demonstrated as to how node A spreads its influence. With the unweighted variant, nodes B and C get an equal share of importance from node A. In the weighted network, the relationship from node A to C has a weight of 1, and the connection from node A to B has a value of 2. In every iteration of the weighted PageRank algorithm, node B will receive two-thirds of node A's influence, and node C will receive only one-third. The equation to calculate the share of influence with the weighted PageRank algorithm is simply dividing the relationship weight by the sum of all outgoing relationship weights.

Now, you can execute the weighted PageRank algorithm on the retweet amplification network without self-loops. Similarly, as with degree centrality, you only need to include the `relationshipWeightProperty` parameter to execute the weighted variant of the algorithm. You must complete exercise 6.7 before executing the following Cypher statement.

Listing 6.8 Executing the PageRank algorithm on the retweet amplification network with no self-loops

Listing 6.8 Executing the PageRank algorithm on the retweet amplification network with no self-loops

```
CALL gds.pageRank.stream('amplify-noselfloops',
  {relationshipWeightProperty:'weight'})
YIELD nodeId, score
RETURN gds.util.asNode(nodeId).username AS user, score
ORDER BY score DESC
LIMIT 5
```

Table 6.8 shows the top five users for this example by PageRank score.

Table 6.8 Top five users by weighted PageRank score in the retweet amplification network with no self-loops

user	score
"Paula_Piccard"	8.270755243786214
"annargrs"	7.836125000000006
"psb_dc"	7.478576023152348
"IainLJBrown"	7.457764370226901
"Eli_Krumova"	6.95963977383344

The list of the top five users by weighted PageRank list is similar to the list of the top five users by in-degree. Of course, the Twitter subgraph you are analyzing is relatively tiny. While you haven't analyzed the tweet topics or hashtags, I've mentioned that I scraped the dataset by focusing on the natural language processing (NLP) and knowledge graph topics. So users in table 6.8 could be good candidates to follow on Twitter if you are interested in NLP or knowledge graph topic updates. Additionally, as a marketing strategy, you could try to contact and ask these users if they might be willing to share your content.

6.3.3 Dropping the projected in-memory graph

It is important to remember to release the projected in-memory graph once you are done with the analysis to free up memory for other analyses. At the moment, you should have two graphs loaded in memory. The following Cypher statement will drop all currently projected graphs.

Listing 6.9 Releasing all the projected graphs from memory

```
CALL gds.graph.list() YIELD graphName          ⟵──┐ Lists all projected graphs
CALL gds.graph.drop(graphName) YIELD nodeCount
RETURN 'dropped ' + graphName AS result        ⟵──┤ Releases each projected
                                                     graph from memory
```

6.4   *Solutions to exercises*

The solution to exercise 6.1 is as follows.

Listing 6.10   Counting the occurrence of the retweet pattern between users

```
MATCH (source:User)-[:PUBLISH]->()-[:RETWEETS]->()<-[:PUBLISH]-(target:User)
RETURN source, target, count(*) AS weight
LIMIT 5
```

The solution to exercise 6.2 is as follows.

Listing 6.11   Returns the users with the top five highest out-degrees

```
CALL gds.degree.stream('amplify')
YIELD nodeId, score
RETURN gds.util.asNode(nodeId).username AS user, score
ORDER BY score DESC
LIMIT 5
```

The solution to exercise 6.3 is as follows.

Listing 6.12   Returns the users with the top five highest weighted out-degrees

```
CALL gds.degree.stream('amplify',
  {relationshipWeightProperty:'weight'})
YIELD nodeId, score
RETURN gds.util.asNode(nodeId).username AS user, score
ORDER BY score DESC
LIMIT 5
```

The solution to exercise 6.4 is the following.

Listing 6.13   Returns the users with the top five highest weighted in-degrees

```
CALL gds.degree.stream('amplify', {orientation:'REVERSE'})
YIELD nodeId, score
RETURN gds.util.asNode(nodeId).username as user, score
ORDER BY score DESC
LIMIT 5
```

The solutions to exercise 6.5 are as follows.

Listing 6.14   Evaluates the weighted in-degree distribution

```
CALL gds.degree.stats('amplify', {orientation:'REVERSE',
  relationshipWeightProperty:'weight'})
YIELD centralityDistribution
```

Listing 6.15   Returns the users with the top five highest weighted in-degrees

```
CALL gds.degree.stream('amplify', {orientation:'REVERSE',
  relationshipWeightProperty:'weight'})
```

```
YIELD nodeId, score
RETURN gds.util.asNode(nodeId).username as user, score
ORDER BY score DESC
LIMIT 5
```

The solution to exercise 6.6 is as follows.

Listing 6.16 Evaluates the number and size of weakly connected components

```
CALL gds.wcc.stats('amplify')
YIELD componentCount, componentDistribution
```

The solution to exercise 6.7 is as follows.

Listing 6.17 Loads the amplify retweet network as an in-memory graph using Cypher projection and excluding self-loops

```
MATCH (source:User)-[:PUBLISH]->()-[:RETWEETS]->()<-[:PUBLISH]-(target:User)
WHERE NOT source = target
WITH source, target, count(*) AS weight
WITH gds.graph.project(
    'amplify-noselfloops',
    source,
    target,
    {relationshipProperties:{weight:weight}}
) AS g
RETURN g.graphName AS graph,
       g.nodeCount AS nodes,
       g.relationshipCount AS rels
```

Summary

- Inferring monopartite networks is a frequent step in graph analysis.
- Cypher projection can be used to project a virtual graph (nonexisting relationships in the database).
- Cypher projection is a more flexible but less performant option to project in-memory graphs.
- Cypher projection takes in a Cypher statement that defines the node and another Cypher statement that specifies the relationships that should be projected.
- The Cypher statement to define nodes with Cypher projection has the reserved columns id and labels.
- The Cypher statement to define relationships with Cypher projection has the reserved columns source, target, and type.
- The GDS library uses two directed relationships that point in the opposite direction to represent an undirected relationship.
- You can change the relationship direction or treat it as undirected during in-memory graph projection.
- The degree centrality distribution can be evaluated with the gds.degree.stats procedure.

- The weighted variant of PageRank considers the relationship weight when it calculates how the influence spreads over the graph.
- You can use weighted variants of the degree centrality and PageRank algorithms by defining the `relationshipWeightProperty` parameter.
- The parameters `nodeLabels` and `relationshipTypes` can be used to consider only a subset of the projected graph as an input to a graph algorithm.
- A self-loop is a relationship that has the same start and end node.

7

Inferring co-occurrence networks based on bipartite networks

This chapter covers

- Extracting hashtags from tweets with Cypher query language
- Calculating the Jaccard similarity coefficient
- Constructing and analyzing monopartite networks using the Jaccard similarity coefficient
- Using the label propagation algorithm to evaluate the community structure of a network
- Using PageRank to find the most important node within a community

In the previous chapter, you learned how to transform a custom graph pattern into direct relationships to use them as an input to graph algorithms like PageRank. In this chapter, you will focus on bipartite networks and how to project them into monopartite networks. Let's start with a quick refresher on bipartite networks.

A bipartite network contains two sets or types of nodes. For example, figure 7.1 shows the bipartite network of tweets on the left and their hashtags on the right. As you can observe, the relationships always points from one type of node to another. There are no direct connections between tweets or hashtags.

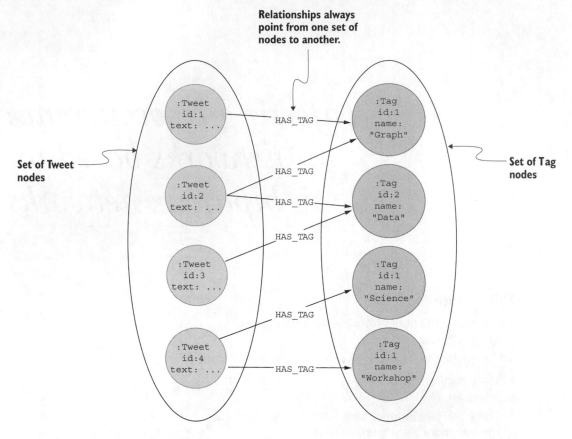

Figure 7.1   Bipartite network of tweets and hashtags

Imagine you work in a marketing analytics role for a company that deals with natural language processing (NLP) and knowledge graphs. Your boss decides it might be worthwhile to improve the hashtag strategy for the content published on Twitter. You have been assigned the task of identifying relevant hashtags to target the company's ideal customer as best as possible. Since the Twitter dataset you have used so far contains tweets about NLP and knowledge graphs, you can analyze the hashtags in the dataset to identify which the company should target.

Your first thought might be to use the PageRank algorithm to identify the most important hashtags. Remember, graph algorithms like PageRank expect monopartite networks as input or at least networks where the influence can flow throughout the connections. With a bipartite network, one type of node has only incoming relationships, and the other type has only outgoing connections. If you were to execute PageRank on the example bipartite network of tweets and hashtags, which nodes do you think would come out on top?

Since tweets don't have any incoming relationships, their PageRank score will equal the chance of a web surfer randomly landing on them. With the default value of the damping factor of 0.85, the PageRank score for nodes with no incoming connections is 0.15. On the other hand, hashtags have only incoming relationships. The influence flows from tweets to hashtags but does not flow further, as there are no outgoing connections from hashtags. In practice, the PageRank rank of hashtags would be equal to their count of incoming relationships (in-degree). However, the actual values of PageRank and in-degree would be different due to distinct score calculation techniques.

Remember, the goal is to determine the most important and relevant hashtags in the dataset. If the definition of hashtag importance is as simple as their frequency, then using the in-degree metric of the `Tag` nodes would suffice.

However, some of the hashtags in the dataset might not be relevant to the marketing targeting objective. You could completely miss other relevant hashtags by looking at only the most frequently mentioned hashtags, as you don't know whether the dataset is skewed toward a particular topic. Additionally, strategically combining hashtags could significantly improve the reach of content by targeting a wider audience instead of only using the most frequently mentioned ones. So your mission is to find important hashtags as well as other hashtags that could be used in combination to increase virality. A well-known technique used to identify communities of hashtags that are commonly used together is to examine how often pairs of hashtags co-occur in tweets. By analyzing how often pairs of hashtags co-occur in the same tweet, you build a co-occurrence network. The term *co-occurrence network* refers to a network construction method that analyzes relationships between various entities in a text. In the case of tweets and their hashtags, you can use the co-occurrence network method to analyze relationships between hashtags appearing in the text of a tweet.

Figure 7.2 shows the co-occurrence network of keywords in medical articles. Co-occurrence networks are constructed by connecting pairs of entities in the text using a set of criteria defining co-occurrences. The co-occurrence definition can vary from scenario to scenario. In this example, co-occurrence is defined as two keywords occurring in the same article. The more times a pair of keywords are present in the same article, the stronger the connection is between the two. A similar technique was used to analyze the scientific literature surrounding the COVID-19 research (Al-Zaman, 2021; Andersen et al., 2020). Additionally, researchers have also used the biomedical literature co-occurrence network to predict new links (Kastrin et al., 2014).

However, you are not limited to analyzing only the co-occurrence of keywords in a given text. In the *Game of Thrones* analysis (Beveridge et al., 2018), Andrew Beveridge popularized analyzing books through the lens of co-occurrence entity networks. The *Game of Thrones* book analysis consists of two steps. First, Beveridge identified all of the characters in the book. In the next step, he defined a co-occurrence event between a pair of characters if they appear within 15 words of one another. In this context, a co-occurrence event can be understood as an interaction between a pair of characters. In

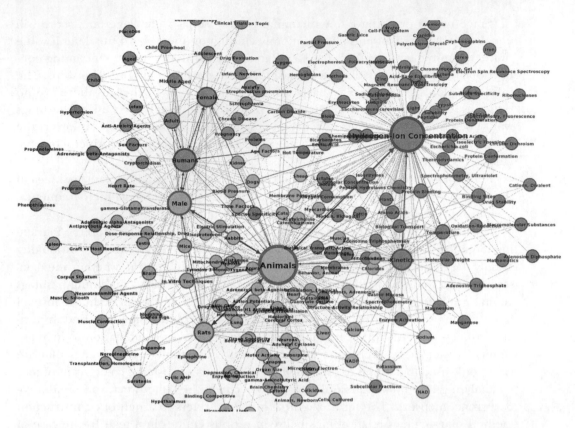

Figure 7.2   Co-occurrence network of medical keywords

my previous works, I have used this technique to construct a co-occurrence or interaction network between characters in the book *Harry Potter and the Philosopher's Stone*.

Just by looking at figure 7.3, you can evaluate which are the main characters in the first Harry Potter book and evaluate how they interact with each other. The node size is based on the node degree, so the more connections a node has, the bigger the node size is. It only makes sense that Harry Potter has the most interactions with other characters, as the book narrative is mostly written from his perspective.

The first two examples of the co-occurrence analysis demonstrate scenarios where keywords or entities are extracted from a text and then connected using an arbitrary co-occurrence event. The third example I've prepared is visualizing how the ingredients co-occur in various dishes or recipes. Again, the node size in figure 7.4 is based on the number of connections it has. In the center of the left-hand side community, you can observe eggs, flours, sugar, and milk. I would imagine that the dishes with those ingredients mostly fall under bread, pancakes, or sweets. For some reason, peanut butter is also frequently present in this community. You can observe main-dish types of ingredients on the right-hand side, including onions, tomato sauce, potatoes,

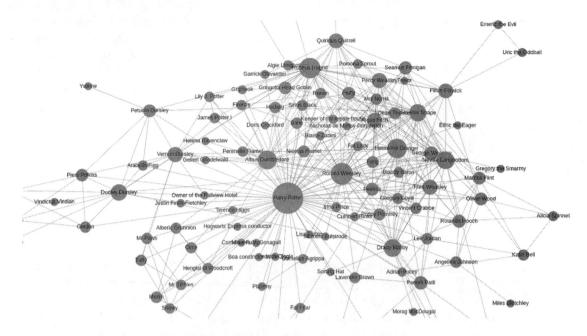

Figure 7.3 Co-occurrence network of characters in the first Harry Potter book

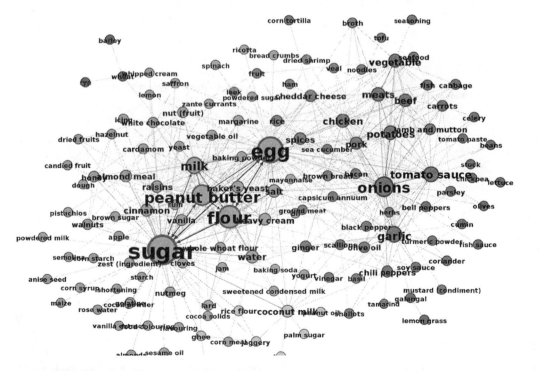

Figure 7.4 Co-occurrence network of ingredients in dishes

and meat. Interestingly, one research paper (Cooper, 2020) uses the ingredient co-occurrence network to analyze packaged food in the United States. Another research paper (Kular et al., 2011) uses the ingredient co-occurrence network to examine the relationships between cuisines and various cultures.

Let's now circle back to the task of identifying the most optimal strategy to use and combining various hashtags that will reach users with knowledge graphs and NLP interest. You can start with a hypothesis that if two hashtags co-occur within the same tweet, they are somehow related or fall under a similar topic. Based on that hypothesis, the co-occurrence network method would connect hashtags that might have the same or similar overall topic. The co-occurrence network can also help you produce various groups of hashtags that could be used together.

Figure 7.5 shows the process of constructing a co-occurrence network of hashtags based on the original bipartite network of tweets and hashtags. On the left-hand side of the visualization is the original bipartite network. A tweet can contain multiple hashtags. For example, tweet A has the #Growth and #Startup hashtags. In this example, the co-occurrence is defined as a pair of hashtags co-occurring in the same tweet. Hence, on the right-hand side of the visualization, where the co-occurrence network is visualized, there is a relationship between the #Finance and the #Startup hashtags, as they appear in the same tweet. If you look at tweet D, you'll notice it has three hashtags: #Data, #ML, and #NLP. Since the hashtags co-occur in the same tweet, there is a relationship between all three hashtags, as indicated on the right-hand side of figure 7.5.

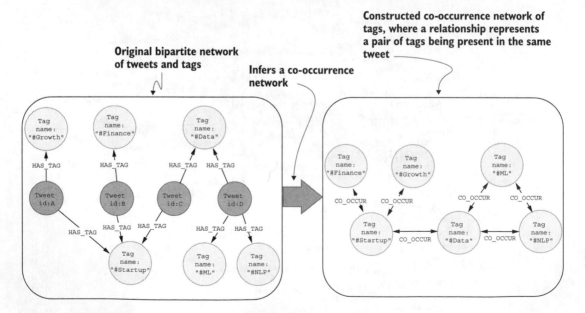

Figure 7.5   Constructing a co-occurrence network of tags based on whether they co-occur in the same tweet

This data transformation can be described with the following Cypher statement.

> **Listing 7.1 Describing the construction of a hashtag co-occurrence network with a Cypher statement**

```
MATCH (s:Tag)<-[:HAS_TAG]-(:Tweet)-[:HAS_TAG]->(t:Tag)
CREATE (s)-[:CO_OCCURRENCE]->(t);
```

Hashtags are used to index or define the topic of a tweet. By analyzing the co-occurrence network of hashtags, you learn which hashtags often overlap and potentially fall under the same overall topic. Constructing a Twitter hashtag co-occurrence network was used in multiple studies. For example, you could analyze how hashtags help drive virality. One study (Pervin, 2015) concluded that the popularity of a hashtag rises when it co-occurs with similar hashtags. On the other hand, the popularity of a hashtag drops if dissimilar hashtags accompany it. Social networks like Twitter are becoming increasingly relevant for spreading information about present social movements or events. Researchers have identified strategic combinations of hashtags that can be used to help gain visibility from different social circles, thus increasing the virality of certain social movements (Wang et al., 2016; Gleason, 2013). Another paper studies how the hashtag co-occurrence connections differ from their semantic similarity (Türker & Sulak, 2018). Finally, one exciting article (Vitale, 2018) uses the hashtag co-occurrence network to provide novel information and trends regarding smoking habits.

To find the most relevant groups of hashtags within the knowledge graph and natural language domain, you must first identify which hashtags are often used together and could potentially form a topic that reaches a specific audience of users. Here, you circle back to the previous hypothesis. If two hashtags frequently co-occur in the same tweet, you can assume they are related and fall under the same topic. To find communities or clusters of hashtags that form a topic, you can utilize community detection algorithms like the *label propagation algorithm* (LPA). The LPA is an algorithm to evaluate the community structure of a network. Most of the literature on the internet introduces the LPA as a semisupervised algorithm in which you can input initial communities for some nodes in the network. However, here you will use the unsupervised variant of the LPA, as you won't present any initial communities. The unsupervised variant of the LPA works as follows. First, it assigns a unique community label to each node. Then, it iterates over the network and updates each node label to the one most of its neighbors have. The idea behind this iteration is that a single community label can quickly become dominant in a densely connected group of nodes. Once the LPA reaches convergence, the algorithm stops, and the resulting node labels represent their communities.

Communities represent densely connected groups of nodes with sparser links between groups. For example, figure 7.6 shows two groups or communities of hashtags. The left community contains #Finance, #Growth, and #Startup hashtags. You could assign the left community as a more business-oriented topic. On the other side, the right community in figure 7.6 consists of #ML, #Data, and #NLP hashtags. Again, you could try to deduce the overall topic of the right community. In this example, something like a computer science or data science–oriented topic would fit.

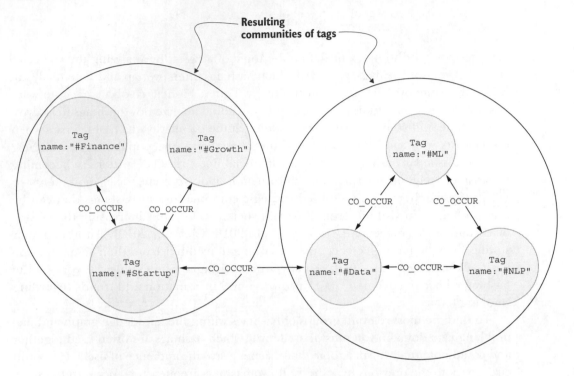

Figure 7.6   Identifying communities within the hashtag co-occurrence network

After you have identified communities of hashtags that form topics, you can use the PageRank algorithm to find the most central nodes within communities. Remember, we assume the co-occurrence between a pair of hashtags implies that they are somewhat related or similar. If you were to execute the PageRank algorithm on each community separately, you would identify the most central nodes of the communities. You can assume the most central nodes in the community are its representatives, as the PageRank algorithm treats every relationship as a vote. In the example of a hashtag co-occurrence network, it is a vote of similarity or relatedness. So the most similar hashtags to all the other hashtags in the community will rank the highest, which you can interpret as community representatives. To follow the exercises in this chapter, you need to have the Twitter network imported into the Neo4j database, as described in chapter 3.

7.1 *Extracting hashtags from tweets*

Before you can infer the hashtag co-occurrence network, you first must extract hashtags from the tweet's content. You will only extract hashtags from tweets that are not retweets, as the retweets have the same hashtags as the original tweets and would only skew the results. The process of extracting hashtags, shown in listing 7.2, is elementary text processing. You split the tweet text by the whitespace or newline characters to create a list of words. Then, you need to filter out words that start with a hashtag (#) sign. Once you have completed these two steps, you have successfully extracted hashtags from a tweet and can store them in the database.

Listing 7.2 Extracting hashtags from tweets that are not retweets

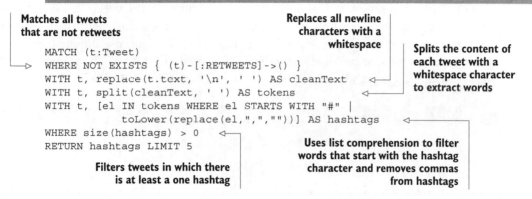

Matches all tweets that are not retweets

Replaces all newline characters with a whitespace

Splits the content of each tweet with a whitespace character to extract words

```
MATCH (t:Tweet)
WHERE NOT EXISTS { (t)-[:RETWEETS]->() }
WITH t, replace(t.text, '\n', ' ') AS cleanText
WITH t, split(cleanText, ' ') AS tokens
WITH t, [el IN tokens WHERE el STARTS WITH "#" |
          toLower(replace(el,",",""))] AS hashtags
WHERE size(hashtags) > 0
RETURN hashtags LIMIT 5
```

Filters tweets in which there is at least a one hashtag

Uses list comprehension to filter words that start with the hashtag character and removes commas from hashtags

Table 7.1 shows the extracted hashtags.

Table 7.1 Extracted hashtags

Hashtags
["#mindset", "#nlp", "#meditation", "#heartmath", "#bioresonance", "#mindcoaching", "#anxiety", "#hypnosis", "#mentalhealth"]
["#sql", "#code", "#datascience", "#ai", "#ml", "#machinelearning", "#iot", "#IIot", "#iotpl", "#python", "#rstats", "#cloud", "#cybersecurity"]
["#coaching", "#nlp", "#progressnotperfection", "#growthmindset", "#trainyourbrain", "#parentyourselffirst"]
["#acl2021nlp"]
["#medium", "#machinelearning", "#nlp", "#deeplearning", "#autocorrect", "#spellcheck", "#ai", "#tds", "#python"]

Interestingly, the NLP hashtag refers to *natural language processing* in the tech community, while the personal development community uses NLP as an acronym for *neurolinguistic programming*. While I was aiming to scrape only tweets around natural language processing and knowledge graph topics, it seems there are also some self-development tweets in the dataset. Having more diverse topics in your dataset is not a problem. It makes your analysis more interesting, as you will learn the driving hashtags behind more computer science–oriented topics, and you can later analyze self-help topics on your own.

Most marketing platforms allow you to specify keywords or hashtags and exclude undesired ones. Since your objective as a marketing analytics person is to design a targeting strategy on Twitter, you can also prepare a list of hashtags to be excluded. The company deals with NLP, so you would want to target the #nlp hashtag. You have learned that the #nlp hashtag is also popular in self-help topics, and since self-help topics are not relevant to the company, it makes sense to exclude the hashtags that fall under the self-help topics.

The Cypher statement in listing 7.2 starts by matching all the tweets that don't have an outgoing `RETWEETS` relationship. To create a list of words for each tweet, you use the combination of the `replace` and `split` functions. First, you use the `replace` function to replace all newline characters with whitespace characters. The syntax for the `replace` function is as follows.

Listing 7.3   `replace` function syntax

```
replace(string, search, replace)
```

`replace` is a basic function in most scripting languages and query language, so I hope it doesn't need any additional explanation. Similarly, `split` is also a very basic function and has the following syntax.

Listing 7.4   `split` function syntax

```
split(string, delimiter)
```

The input to the `split` function is a string and a delimiter character, while the output is a list of elements; again, a basic function available in most, if not all, programming languages. The last thing to do is to filter words that start with a hashtag (#) character. You can filter out hashtags from the list of words by using the *list comprehension* syntax, shown in the following listing. At first sight, it seems that the list comprehension function took some inspiration from the Python syntax.

Listing 7.5   List comprehension syntax

```
[element in list WHERE predicate | element]
```

The list comprehension syntax is wrapped by square brackets. The `element IN list` syntax is used to define a variable to reference an element in the list. Unlike Python, element manipulation and transformation can be defined right after the pipe | character instead of directly in the variable assignment. You have removed commas and lowercased the text in the element transformation part of the list comprehension syntax to not differentiate between #NLP and #nlp hashtags. You can also filter items in the list by using the WHERE clause.

Finally, you use the size() function to filter tweets with at least a single hashtag. The size() function returns the number of items in a list. In the previous chapter, you learned to use the size() function to access the node degree in an optimized way, but it can also be used to count the length of a list.

Before continuing with the co-occurrence analysis, you will extract hashtags and store them in the database. Every time you add a new node label in the database, it is advisable to identify the unique property of the node and define a unique constraint. With the hashtags, each node should represent a single hashtag, so you can simply define a unique constraint on the id property of Tag nodes.

Listing 7.6 Defining a unique constraint for `Tag` nodes on the `id` property

```
CREATE CONSTRAINT IF NOT EXISTS FOR (t:Tag) REQUIRE t.id IS UNIQUE;
```

Finally, you can execute the following Cypher statement to extract and store hashtags in the database.

Listing 7.7 Extracting hashtags and storing them in the database

```
MATCH (t:Tweet)
WHERE NOT EXISTS { (t)-[:RETWEETS]->() }
WITH t, replace(t.text, '\n', ' ') AS cleanText
WITH t, split(cleanText, ' ') AS tokens
WITH t, [el IN tokens WHERE el STARTS WITH "#" |
         toLower(replace(el, ",", " "))] AS hashtags
WHERE size(hashtags) > 0
UNWIND hashtags AS tag_id          ◁──┐  Transforming a list of
MERGE (tag:Tag {id: tag_id})          │  elements into individual rows
MERGE (t)-[:HAS_TAG]->(tag)           │  with the UNWIND clause
```

The Cypher statement in listing 7.7 introduces the UNWIND clause. The UNWIND clause is used to transform a list of elements into rows, similar to a FOR loop in various scripting languages. Essentially, you iterate over each element in the list and, in this case, merge a Tag node and connect it to the Tweet node. The UNWIND clause is always followed by the AS operator to assign a reference variable to the element value in the produced rows. The following Cypher statement demonstrates a simple usage of the UNWIND clause.

Listing 7.8 `UNWIND` clause syntax

```
UNWIND [1, 2, 3] AS i
RETURN i
```

Table 7.2 shows the elements displayed as rows.

Table 7.2   The UNWIND clause transforming a list of elements into rows

i
1
2
3

Exercise 7.1

Hashtags are now stored and connected to the `Tweet` nodes in the database. Before jumping to the co-occurrence analysis, investigate which hashtags appear in most tweets and retweets. Remember, you only stored hashtags for original tweets (not retweets) in the database. Therefore, first, match the original tweets in which the hashtags appeared. Next, count how many times those tweets were retweeted, and then return the top five hashtags by the sum of combined counts of original tweets and retweets. Since not all tweets are retweeted, use the `OPTIONAL MATCH` to count the number of retweets.

Table 7.3 shows the most popular hashtags.

Table 7.3   The most popular hashtags in tweets and retweets

hashtag	originalTweetsCount	retweetCount
#nlp	1,848	7,532
#ai	1,554	7,169
#machinelearning	1,474	7,007
#datascience	1,455	6,736
#bigdata	1,358	6,577

The most popular hashtags are #nlp, #ai, #machinelearning, and #datascience. Judging by the retweet count, they must frequently co-occur in the same tweets, as there are 12,000 tweets and retweets in total. Next, you will proceed with the co-occurrence part of the hashtag analysis.

7.2 Constructing the co-occurrence network

You can use Cypher query language to evaluate which hashtags most frequently co-occur.

> ### Exercise 7.2
> Evaluate which hashtags most frequently co-occur. Use the MATCH clause to define a graph pattern where two hashtags are present in the same tweet, and then use the count() function to count the number of tweets in which a pair of hashtags co-occur. Return only the top five most co-occurring pairs of hashtags.

The solution to exercise 7.2 is as follows.

Listing 7.9   Examining the top five most co-occurring pairs of hashtags

```
MATCH (h1:Tag)<-[:HAS_TAG]-()-[:HAS_TAG]->(h2:Tag)
WHERE id(h1) < id(h2)                              ◁─── Removing duplicates
WITH h1,h2,count(*) AS cooccurrences                    from the results
ORDER BY cooccurrences DESC LIMIT 5
RETURN h1.id AS tag1, h2.id AS tag2, cooccurrences
```

Table 7.4 shows the most frequently co-occurring pairs of hashtags.

Table 7.4   Top five most frequently co-occurring pairs of hashtags

tag1	tag2	cooccurrences
#ai	#nlp	1,507
#machinelearning	#nlp	1,428
#datascience	#nlp	1,410
#ai	#machinelearning	1,410
#datascience	#ai	1,405

Exercise 7.2 did not mention that you should, ideally, remove duplicates from the output, as you haven't learned how to do that yet. Since every hashtag will appear as the h1 variable as well as the h2 variable, the results will contain duplicates. The strategy of deduplicating results with the id(h1) < id(h2) is the most commonly used that I've seen in practice.

You could use a similar Cypher statement to project the co-occurrence network with Cypher projection. The resulting co-occurrence network based on the Cypher statement in listing 7.9 would look like figure 7.1.

Figure 7.7 shows a sample hashtag co-occurrence network, where the relationship weight represents the count of co-occurrences. You might wonder why there are two relationships between each pair of nodes in the opposite direction. If #NLP co-occurs with hashtag #AI, that directly implies that hashtag #AI also co-occurs with hashtag #NLP. In the context of graphs, you could say that the CO_OCCUR relationship is undirected, as the direction of the connection is not essential. However, the Graph Data Science (GDS) library has no concept of undirected relationships. A key concept behind an undirected relationship is that it allows traversals in both directions. You can replicate this functionality in a directed network by transforming a single undirected connection into two directed links that point in the opposite direction.

Co-occurrence network of hashtags

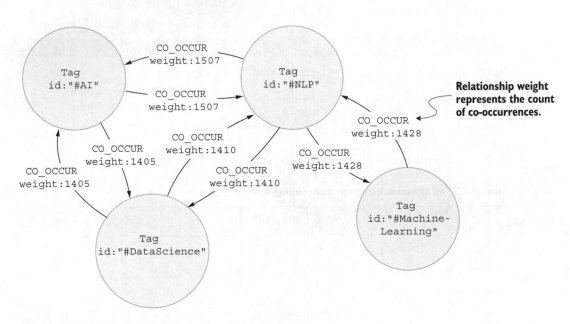

Figure 7.7 Sample weighted and undirected co-occurrence network

NOTE The GDS library has no notion of undirected relationships. When dealing with an undirected network in GDS, you represent each relationship in the network as two directed relationships that point in the opposite direction. In the node similarity algorithm example, the algorithm's output is an undirected network, where each undirected relationship is represented as two directed relationships, as shown in figure 7.8. The GDS library also allows transforming a single relationship into two relationships that point in the opposite direction during projection time.

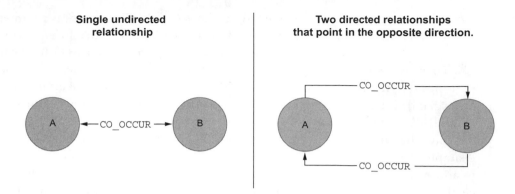

Figure 7.8   A single undirected relationship represented as two directed relationships that point in the opposite direction

7.2.1   *Jaccard similarity coefficient*

While there is nothing wrong with using the count of co-occurrences as the relationship weight, a more common approach is to use the *Jaccard similarity coefficient* to evaluate the similarity between nodes. The Jaccard similarity coefficient is simple to understand, as it only involves dividing the intersection by the union of two sets.

Figure 7.9 visualizes two baskets, where each basket contains a set of products. For example, basket A includes a couch, speakers, phone, and TV, while basket B contains a phone, TV, and headphones. If you want to calculate the Jaccard similarity coefficient between the two baskets, you first calculate the intersection and union of the two sets of products. Both baskets contain a phone and TV, the intersection of the two sets. There are five different products spread across both baskets, which is the union of the two sets. To calculate the Jaccard similarity coefficient, you simply divide the intersection (2) by the union (5) of the two sets, which results in 0.4. The added benefit of the Jaccard similarity coefficient is that it provides a metric that can be used to evaluate—in this example, how similar two baskets are based on their products.

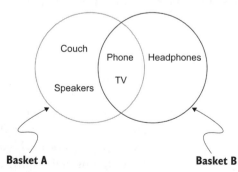

Figure 7.9   An example of two baskets with overlapping products

Jaccard similarity coefficient ranges from values 0 to 1. When there is no intersection of members between two sets, the Jaccard similarity coefficient equals 0. For example, let's say basket A contains a sandwich and juice, while basket B contains a TV. There is no intersection of items between baskets A and B, which consequently indicates that the Jaccard similarity coefficient between the two baskets is 0. On the other hand, the Jaccard similarity coefficient between two sets with identical members is 1. When two sets have the Jaccard similarity coefficient of 1, it implies the two sets have the same number of members, with identical members in both sets. In this example, both baskets A and B contain a sandwich and juice. However, if you were to add or remove any item from either basket, the Jaccard similarity would no longer be 1. The process of evaluating the hashtag overlap with the Jaccard similarity coefficient is shown in figure 7.10.

In a graph context, a typical input to the Jaccard similarity algorithm is a bipartite network consisting of two types or sets of nodes. The idea behind using the Jaccard similarity algorithm is to project a monopartite graph based on the bipartite input graph. Figure 7.10 shows the process to transform a network consisting of tweets and hashtags to a monopartite network of hashtags based on how many tweets they have in common. The process is the following:

1 For each hashtag, you first collect the set of tweets in which it appeared.
2 In the next step, you iterate over each pair of hashtags and calculate the Jaccard similarity coefficient by dividing the intersection of the two sets by their union.
3 Finally, you have the option to store the similarity coefficient between a pair of nodes in the form of a relationship.

The semantics of the inferred relationships depends on the domain. You could choose the CO_OCCUR type of relationships in the hashtag example. In the basket example, the inferred relationship could have a SIMILAR type.

The Jaccard similarity coefficient is a symmetric similarity metric. If node A is similar to node B, that directly implies node B is similar to node A. Like the preceding Cypher projection example, the resulting co-occurrence or similarity network will be undirected. Also, you can store the resulting Jaccard similarity coefficient between nodes as relationship properties.

7.2.2   *Node similarity algorithm*

Since the Jaccard similarity coefficient can be used to evaluate how similar a pair of nodes are, the GDS developers decided it made sense to name the algorithm the *node similarity algorithm*. The node similarity algorithm compares sets of nodes based on their neighbors using the Jaccard similarity coefficient or the overlap coefficient. A typical input is a bipartite network consisting of two types of nodes. Nodes with outgoing relationships are being compared, while their outgoing neighbors are used

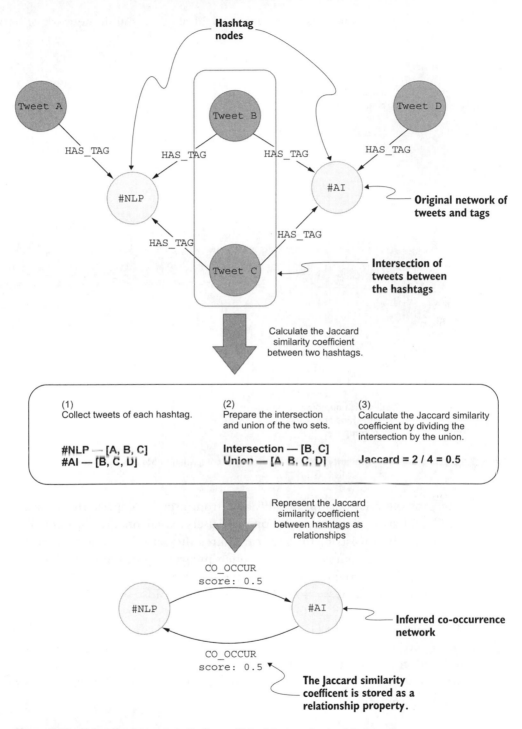

Figure 7.10   Using the Jaccard similarity coefficient to examine hashtag overlap

to construct the comparison set. Figure 7.11 shows a simple network of users and musical genres.

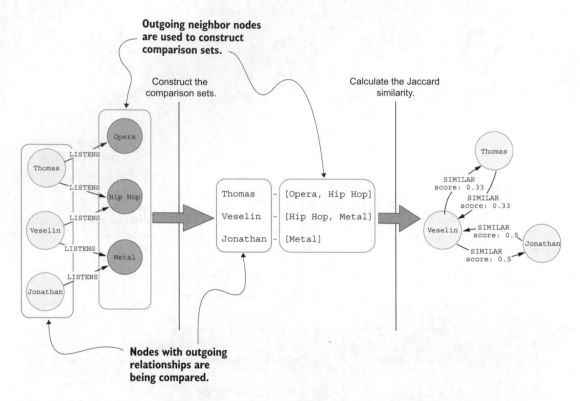

Figure 7.11   How the node similarity algorithm constructs comparison sets and evaluates similarity

The LISTENS relationships are directed from users to genres. In this scenario, the node similarity algorithm will compare users based on their outgoing neighborhood, which consists of the musical genres they are listening to. Realizing which nodes are being compared by the node similarity algorithm is crucial to executing the algorithm correctly. In our Twitter social network, the HAS_TAG relationships point from Tweet to Tag nodes. If you were to avoid reversing the direction of the relationship, you would effectively be comparing tweets based on how many tags they have in common. The GDS library allows reversing the relationship direction during projection, so you don't have to transform the underlying stored graph. When you want to transform the relationship direction during projection, you need to use the configuration map syntax to describe the projected relationships, as shown in the following listing.

Listing 7.10 Configuration map to describe the relationship type and its orientation

```
{ALIAS_OF_TYPE: {type:'RELATIONSHIP_TYPE',
                 orientation: 'NATURAL',
                 properties:['property1','property2']}}
```

Instead of simply specifying the relationship as a string, you need to construct a relationship configuration map. The ALIAS_OF_TYPE key specifies under which name the projected relationship will be available in the in-memory graph. The alias doesn't need be identical to relationship types stored in the database. Each alias key has a value that consists of a map describing which relationship types should be projected, their orientation, and optional properties. You can manipulate and transform the relationship direction with the orientation key. It has three possible values:

- NATURAL—Each relationship is projected the same way as it is stored in the database.
- REVERSE—Each relationship is reversed during graph projection.
- UNDIRECTED—Each relationship is projected in both natural and reverse orientation.

With the orientation configuration, you have the option to project the relationship as is, reverse its direction, or treat it as undirected. As mentioned, to treat a relationship as undirected, the engine simply duplicates the relationship in the opposite direction.

Moving on to the hashtag co-occurrence task, you need to project both Tweet and Tag nodes and include the HAS_TAG relationship with a reversed direction.

Listing 7.11 Projects Tweet and Tag nodes and includes reversed HAS_TAG relationships

```
CALL gds.graph.project(
    'tags',                             Projects multiple          Projects reversed
    ['Tweet', 'Tag'],                   node labels using          HAS_TAG
    {REVERSED_HAS_TAG: {orientation:'REVERSE', type:'HAS_TAG'}});   list syntax    relationships
```

Projected graph name

Listing 7.11 introduces two new native projection syntax options. First, you can specify multiple node labels to be projected using a list. In listing 7.11, you described both Tweet and Tag nodes to be projected. Second, you used the configuration map syntax to describe the projected relationships. The projected relationships will be available under the REVERSED_HAS_TAG alias and contain HAS_TAG connections with a reversed relationship direction.

Now that you have the network of tweets and hashtags projected, you can use the node similarity algorithm to infer a monopartite network. You can affect how dense or sparse the inferred network will be with topK and similarityCutoff parameters of the node similarity algorithm. The similarityCutoff parameter defines the threshold value of the Jaccard similarity coefficient between a pair of nodes that are still regarded as similar. For example, if the `similarityCutoff` is 0.5, then the relationships will be considered only between the pairs of nodes with a Jaccard similarity score of 0.5 or higher. On the other hand, the `topK` parameter specifies the limit on the number of similar relationships per node. As you can directly affect how many relationships should be stored with the `topK` and the `similarityCutoff` parameters, you consequently describe how sparse or dense the inferred co-occurrence network will be.

Defining how sparse or dense the inferred co-occurrence network between hashtags should be will directly correlate with how broad the communities of hashtags that form a topic will be. For example, if you use the `topK` value of 1, each node will have only a single outgoing relationship to its most similar neighbor. However, if you were to increase the `topK` value to 2, each node would have two outgoing relationships that specify which two nodes are the most similar to it.

Figure 7.12 shows a comparison of inferred co-occurrence networks if different `topK` values are used. As mentioned, the input to the node similarity algorithm is usually a bipartite network. In this example, you have a bipartite network of tweets and hashtags. The node similarity algorithm will then evaluate how similar the hashtags are based on the number of tweets they appear in together. Once the Jaccard similarity coefficient between pairs of hashtags is calculated, the algorithm will output the results as relationships between hashtags. You can observe a co-occurrence network with the `topK` value of 1 on the left-hand side of figure 7.12. Using the `topK` value of 1, each hashtag will have a single outgoing relationship, indicating its most similar hashtag. The resulting co-occurrence network on the left-hand side of figure 7.12 has eight nodes and eight relationships. For example, the #data hashtag is the most similar to the #datascience hashtag. Even though I previously stated that the Jaccard similarity coefficient is a symmetric similarity metric, the #datascience hashtag does not have a reverse relationship to the #data hashtag. Why is that so? The reason is that once you apply a `topK` filter to the node similarity algorithm, you lose the guarantee that all relationships will be symmetric. If you were to set the `topK` value to the number of the nodes in the inferred co-occurrence network, all relationships would be symmetric.

Returning to your scenario, once the co-occurrence network is created, the idea is to use an algorithm like the label propagation algorithm to find communities of tightly connected hashtags. A *community* is defined as a group of densely interconnected nodes that might have sparser connections with other groups. When using a lower `topK` value, there will be fewer connections in the inferred co-occurrence network. Consequently, the size of communities will be smaller, as there will be fewer densely interconnected nodes. Since the communities will be smaller, there will be more of them throughout the network. You defined that each community of hashtags will be regarded as a single topic. Therefore, by adjusting the `topK` value of the node similarity algorithm, you are essentially influencing how large the resulting communities of hashtags will be. The larger the community of hashtags is, the broader the resulting topic will be. When the communities of hashtags are larger,

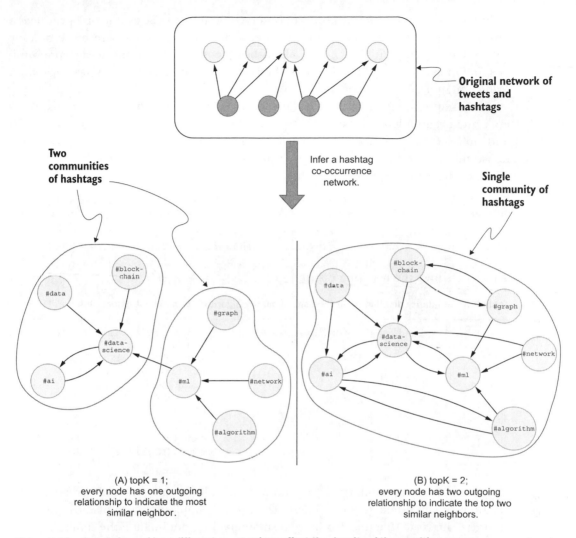

Figure 7.12   Comparison of how different `topK` values affect the density of the resulting co-occurrence network

you might produce a less-granular targeting strategy. On the other hand, using a smaller `topK` value would help you find smaller communities of hashtags and, consequently, devise a narrower marketing strategy.

In figure 7.12, you can observe that when using a `topK` value of 1, the community detection algorithm identified two communities in the resulting co-occurrence network. One community consists of #ai, #datascience, #data, and #blockchain hashtags, while the other community contains #ml, #graph, #network, #algorithm. When you use a higher `topK` value, the resulting co-occurrence network will be more interconnected, and consequently, a community detection algorithm will identify larger communities. A larger community of hashtags will result in broader topics, in your use case. On the right-hand side of figure 7.12, you can observe that using a `topK` value of 2 produces a more densely connected co-occurrence network. Since the nodes are more densely connected, a community detection algorithm identified larger and fewer communities. In figure 7.12, the algorithm identified only a single community of hashtags when using a higher `topK` value of 2.

Defining the `topK` parameter and the `similarityCutoff` parameter is a mix of science and art and depends on your use case. By default, the `topK` parameter value is 10 and the `similarityCutoff` is 1E-42, just slightly above zero. You can evaluate how dense the inferred network would be with default parameter values using the `stats` mode of the node similarity algorithm.

Listing 7.12   Evaluating the Jaccard coefficient distribution with default parameters

```
CALL gds.nodeSimilarity.stats('tags', {similarityMetric: 'JACCARD'})
YIELD nodesCompared, similarityPairs, similarityDistribution
```

Table 7.5 shows the resulting distribution.

Table 7.5   Similarity distribution of the node similarity algorithm with default parameters

nodesCompared	similarityPairs	similarityDistribution
2,093	13,402	{ "p1": 0.0005411244928836823, "max": 1.000007625669241, "p50": 0.4400005303323269, "p10": 0.0075757764279842238, "p75": 1.000007625669241, "p25": 0.11111116036772728, "mean": 0.4971548691088963, "stdDev": 0.39913025157864984 }

Executing the node similarity algorithm with default parameters would create 13,402 relationships between 2,093 hashtags. The average similarity score of those relationships is 0.49. Note that this distribution summary does not include the similarity score between all pairs of nodes but only for the top 10 similar neighbors of a node, as that is the default `topK` value. Interestingly, the median value (`p50`) is close to the average similarity value, and around 25% of relationships have the maximum possible similarity score of 1. When the similarity score is 1, a pair of hashtags are always together in a tweet. You can use the `similarityCutoff` parameter to exclude relationships between pairs of hashtags with a similarity score lower than the threshold.

Listing 7.13   Using the `similarityCutoff` parameter to define the similarity score threshold

```
CALL gds.nodeSimilarity.stats('tags',
  {similarityMetric: 'JACCARD', similarityCutoff:0.33})
YIELD nodesCompared, similarityPairs, similarityDistribution
```

Table 7.6 shows the resulting distribution.

Table 7.6 Similarity distribution of the node similarity algorithm using the `similarityCutoff` parameter

nodesCompared	similarityPairs	similarityDistribution
2,093	7,733	{ "p1": 0.3333320617675781, "max": 1.0000076256669241, "p50": 1.0000057220458984, "p10": 0.3636360168457031, "p75": 1.0000057220458984, "p25": 0.5000019073486328, "mean": 0.7893913483135638, "stdDev": 0.2606311318508915 }

You can observe that by setting the `similarityCutoff` value to 0.33, only 7,733 relationships would be created, instead of 13,402 with default parameter values. The 25th percentile value is 0.5, and interestingly, the median value is already the maximum score of 1. The average node degree of the resulting network would be around 4. As indicated by the similarity distribution, the relationships would be created between pairs of very similar or highly co-occurring hashtags, as the median value is already 1.0.

Exercise 7.3

Test out various combinations of the `topK` and `similarityCutoff` parameters using the `stats` mode of the node similarity algorithm, and evaluate how changing their values affects the density of the inferred network.

Unfortunately, there is no clear-cut solution to defining the `topK` and `similarityCutoff` parameters. This reminds me of the Goldilocks dilemma; they have to be just right. If you infer too dense a graph, further analysis of the inferred network might not produce valuable insights. The same applies if you infer too sparse a graph. As a beginner, you are advised to try various parameter configurations and inspect downstream results. Later, you could apply automatic hyperparameter optimization methods when you grasp the underlying data structure and how configuration values affect results.

With the hashtag co-occurrence example, you will use the `similarityCutoff` value of 0.25 and the `topK` value of 50. As you will execute other graph algorithms on the inferred co-occurrence network, you will use the `mutate` mode of the node similarity algorithm. The `mutate` mode stores the inferred network to the in-memory graph, which allows you to use the results of the node similarity algorithm as input to other graph algorithms, as shown in the following listing.

```
CALL gds.nodeSimilarity.mutate('tags',
  {topK:50, similarityCutoff:0.25,
    mutateRelationshipType:'CO_OCCURRENCE',
    mutateProperty:'score',
    similarityMetric: 'JACCARD'})
YIELD nodesCompared, relationshipsWritten
```

The inferred co-occurrence network of hashtags contains 2,093 nodes and 9,992 relationships.

7.3 *Characterization of the co-occurrence network*

Before moving on to the community detection part, you will consolidate your knowledge of characterizing a network using graph algorithms. Now that you are dealing with a monopartite graph, you can apply the same algorithms as in the previous chapters for network characterization.

7.3.1 *Node degree centrality*

You can use the node degree algorithm to further evaluate the node degree distribution of the inferred co-occurrence network. The thing is that the projected tags graph now contains Tweet and Tag nodes as well as REVERSE_HAS_TAG and CO_OCCURRENCE relationships. You can filter which nodes or relationships the algorithm should consider at the algorithm execution time with the nodeLabels and relationshipTypes parameters.

```
CALL gds.degree.stats('tags',
  {nodeLabels:['Tag'], relationshipTypes:['CO_OCCURRENCE']})
YIELD centralityDistribution
```

Table 7.7 shows the resulting distribution.

Table 7.7   Node degree distribution of the hashtag co-occurrence network

p99	21.00011444091797
min	0.0
max	40.00023651123047
mean	5.351917056393738
p90	13.000053405761719
p50	3.0000076293945312
p999	29.00011444091797
p95	17.00011444091797
p75	8.000053405761719

Both the `nodeLabels` and the `relationshipTypes` parameters expect a list as an input. The ability to filter nodes and relationships at algorithm execution time is a convenient feature that allows you to analyze various parts of the projected graph or analyze a newly inferred network.

The average node degree of the hashtag co-occurrence network is 5.3. Some of the hashtags have no `CO_OCCURRENCE` relationships, while at least 1 hashtag frequently co-occurs with 40 other hashtags. The `topK` parameter value of 50 did not affect the resulting network, as the highest degree is only 41.

7.3.2   *Weakly connected components*

The weakly connected component (WCC) algorithm does not need an introduction, as it was already presented in previous chapters. However, you should complete the two exercises in this section to consolidate your knowledge of executing and interpreting the results of the WCC algorithm.

> **Exercise 7.4**
> Execute the WCC algorithm on the hashtag co-occurrence network and store the results to the database as a node property `tcWcc`. Provide the `nodeLabels` and `relationshipTypes` parameters so that the algorithm will only consider the desired subset of the projected graph. Use the `write` mode of the algorithm to store the results to the database.

Table 7.8 shows the resulting statistics.

Table 7.8   Summary statistics for the WCC algorithm executed on the hashtag co-occurrence network

componentCount	componentDistribution
469	{ "p99": 19, "min": 1, "max": 491, "mean": 3.9808102345415777, "p90": 6, "p50": 2, "p999": 491, "p95": 11, "p75": 3 }

The `write` mode of the WCC algorithm also provides the high-level summary of the results, similar to the `stats` mode. There are 469 components in the hashtag co-occurrence network, and the largest contains 491 members, which is around 25% of the whole network. You can imagine you are dealing with quite a disconnected network, as most of the components have 10 or fewer members.

Exercise 7.5

Identify how many components have 10 or fewer members. First, you will need to count how many members are in each component based on their `tcWcc` property. After the first aggregation, you need to apply the filter and ignore components with more than 10 members. In the last step, you simply use the `count` function again to count the number of filtered components.

By completing exercise 7.5, you can observe that 445 components out of 467 have 10 or fewer members. One of the reasons the inferred network is so disconnected is because you are dealing with a tiny subset of the Twitter social network. I think adding more data would help to connect some of the components. On the other hand, hashtags like #meditation or #selfhelp will probably never frequently co-occur with AI or machine learning, and even if they do by some chance, they will never reach the similarity threshold where the co-occurrence relationship will be created between them.

7.4   *Community detection with the label propagation algorithm*

So far, you have only learned how to use the WCC and strongly connected components (SCC) algorithms to evaluate the community structure. In this last part of this chapter, you will learn how to use the label propagation algorithm (LPA) to find non-overlapping communities of hashtags. What is the difference between a community and a component? With the WCC algorithm, a component consists of nodes that can reach one another in the graph when ignoring the relationship direction. On the other hand, a community is defined as a group of densely interconnected nodes that might have sparser connections with other groups. Figure 7.13 shows a network that consists of only a single WCC.

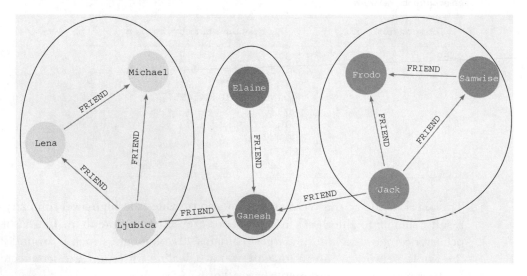

Figure 7.13   Example visualization of a network community structure

When you run a community detection algorithm like LPA on this network, the algorithm will identify groups of highly connected nodes. There are three communities in figure 7.13. For example, there is a community on the left-hand side where members are highly connected. Similarly, there is another community with densely connected nodes on the right-hand side of the visualization, while one of those nodes also has connections to the central community. You can execute the `mutate` mode of the label propagation algorithm with the following Cypher statement.

Listing 7.16 Executing the label propagation algorithm on the hashtag co-occurrence network and storing the results to the in-memory graph

```
CALL gds.labelPropagation.mutate('tags',
  {nodeLabels:['Tag'], relationshipTypes: ['CO_OCCURRENCE'],
   mutateProperty:'community'})
YIELD communityCount, communityDistribution;
```

As you can see, most of the graph algorithms follow the same syntax, which makes it easy to try out various graph algorithms. Again, you had to use the `nodeLabels` and the `relationshipTypes` parameters to select the hashtag co-occurrence network.

> **NOTE** The label propagation algorithm is a nondeterministic algorithm, which means it has the potential to yield different results, even when applied to the same dataset multiple times. This inherent nondeterminism arises from the algorithm's random nature of deciding the order in which nodes should update their labels. Therefore, such nondeterminism can result in variations across different outcomes.

If you want to evaluate the results with Cypher, you need to store the mutated `community` property from the in-memory graph to the Neo4j stored graph. You can store the node properties from the in-memory graph to the database with the `gds.graph.writeNodeProperties` procedure. Run the following Cypher statement to store the mutated `community` property from the in-memory graph to the database.

Listing 7.17 Writing the mutated in-memory graph node properties to the database

```
CALL gds.graph.writeNodeProperties('tags', ['community'])
YIELD propertiesWritten
```

The algorithm results are now available as the `community` node property of the `Tag` nodes. In the following listing, you will inspect the five largest communities and examine some of their members.

Listing 7.18 Inspecting the five largest communities of hashtags

```
MATCH (t:Tag)
RETURN t.community AS community,
       count(*) AS communitySize,
       collect(t.id)[..7] AS exampleMembers
ORDER BY communitySize DESC
LIMIT 5
```

Table 7.9 shows the resulting communities of hashtags.

Table 7.9   Top five largest communities of hashtags

community	communitySize	exampleMembers
15,809	43	["#mentalism", "#respect", "#special-needs", "#mondayvibes", "#goals", "#mindset", "#anxiety"]
15,828	42	["#auto_tagging", "#data_entry", "#itrules", "#writing-community", "#feg", "#crypto", "#tsa"]
17,537	35	["#programming", "#ml", "#iiot", "#iotpl", "#rstats", "#cybersecurity", "#serverless"]
16,093	34	["#nlpimpulse", "#iserlohn", "#zoom", "#selbstbild", "#selbstwert", "#spiegelbild", "#werte"]
16,271	31	["#artproject", "#nft", "#art", "#nfts", "#oculusquest", "#gaming", "#xrhub"]

The largest community of hashtags has 43 members. From the looks of it, the overall topic of the largest community is focused on mental health and personal growth. At first, I wasn't expecting these types of tweets in the dataset, but now I know that NLP can refer to both *natural language processing* and *neuro-linguistic programming*. The third- and fourth-largest communities are centered around computer science and software development. On the other hand, the fifth-largest community seems to revolve around nonfungible tokens (NFTs) and, interestingly, VR topics, like Oculus Quest, are also mentioned. You can remove the limit on the members as well as the limit of rows to further analyze the community structure.

Exercise 7.6

Identify the community of hashtags, where

- #nlp is a member
- #graph is a member

Table 7.10 shows the resulting communities.

Table 7.10   Communities where #nlp or #graph are members

15,699	["#graphdatabases", "#hcm", "#peopleanalytics", "#hranalytics", "#graphdatascience", "#twitch", "#graph", "#neo4j"]
17,533	["#datascience", "#ai", "#machinelearning", "#iot", "#python", "#nlp", "#100daysofcode", "#deeplearning", "#artificialintelligence", "#bigdata", "#robots"]

The results of exercise 7.6 provide recommendations for hashtags that you can use to devise a marketing strategy for your company. For example, suppose you want to target the natural language processing community. In that case, you should try to combine the #nlp hashtag with other relevant hashtags, like #datascience, #deeplearning, or #machinelearning, to reach a wider audience. On the other hand, you should exclude topics of hashtags that are not relevant, like the self-help domain, in this example. You could also explore other communities and search for other hashtags that might be relevant to your company.

7.5 Identifying community representatives with PageRank

Sometimes you get larger communities of hashtags from the label propagation algorithm. In the marketing strategy example, you might want to identify a few of the most central hashtags of a community to concentrate on, since it probably doesn't make sense to use 50 or more hashtags in your content.

You can run the PageRank algorithm to find representatives of communities. To find representatives with the PageRank algorithm, you need to execute it on each community separately. Unfortunately, you can't filter by mutated node properties at algorithm execution time. But you can use the *graph filtering* feature, shown in the following listing, which allows you to filter an existing in-memory graph by specifying node and relationship filters.

Listing 7.19 Subgraph projection syntax

```
CALL gds.graph.filter(
    graphName: String, -> name of the new projected graph
    fromGraphName: String, -> name of the existing projected graph
    nodeFilter: String, -> predicate used to filter nodes
    relationshipFilter: String -> predicate used to filter relationships
)
```

You can use the `nodeFilter` parameter to filter nodes based on node properties or labels. Similarly, you can use `relationshipFilter` parameter to filter relationships based on their properties and types. Filter predicates are Cypher predicates for either a node or a relationship. The filter predicate always needs to evaluate to `true` or `false`. Variable names within predicates are not arbitrarily chosen. A node predicate must refer to variable `n`, while the relationship predicate must refer to variable `r`.

The reason you have used the `mutate` mode of the label propagation algorithm is that you can now use the mutated properties for subgraph projections. If you had used the `write` mode directly, the label propagation algorithm results would not be available in the in-memory graph, so you wouldn't be able to filter on them.

For example, the community with the #ml hashtag contains 35 members. Instead of manually evaluating which are the most important within the group, you can use the PageRank algorithm to identify the representatives of the group. The following Cypher statement projects a subgraph that contains only the community of hashtags in which the #ml hashtag is a member.

Listing 7.20   Projecting a subgraph that contains only the largest community of hashtags

```
MATCH (h:Tag {id:"#ml"})                        Filtering nodes in a
WITH h.community AS communityId                  specific community
CALL gds.graph.filter(
  'ml-community',
  'tags',                                        A wildcard operator can be
  'n.community = $communityId',                  used when you don't want
  '*',                                           to apply any filters.
  { parameters: { communityId: communityId } })
YIELD graphName, fromGraphName, nodeCount, relationshipCount
RETURN graphName, fromGraphName, nodeCount, relationshipCount
```

**Any parameters used in the subgraph projection from outer operations
need to passed through the parameters configuration value.**

The fifth parameter is the configuration map, where you can define any parameters calculated before the subgraph projection procedure. In the Cypher statement in listing 7.20, you first match the #ml hashtag node and retrieve its `community` property. The `community` property is then passed to the subgraph projection procedure as a parameter. Finally, you can execute the PageRank algorithm on the newly projected `ml-community` in-memory graph to identify its representatives.

Listing 7.21   Identifying representatives of the largest community with the PageRank algorithm

```
CALL gds.pageRank.stream('ml-community')
YIELD nodeId, score
RETURN gds.util.asNode(nodeId).id AS tag, score
ORDER BY score DESC
LIMIT 5
```

Table 7.11 shows the resulting communities.

Table 7.11   Top five representatives of the largest community of hashtags

tag	score
#serverless	1.9529458990718058
#iiot	1.8179378938658664
#usa?	1.6916560123489326
#coders	1.4975137459724255
#frenchtech	1.4975137459724253

Interestingly, the most central hashtags in the same community as the #ml are #serverless, #iiot, and, unexpectedly, #usa. It might be that some internet of things (IoT) event was taking place in the United States during the window the tweets were scraped. On the other hand, it is not surprising that #ml coappears in tweets that talk about serverless or IoT technologies. You must also realize that you are dealing with a tiny sample of tweets. The results would probably change if you increased the number of tweets in your analysis, as you wouldn't be so dependent on what was going on during the three-day windows during which most of the tweets were created. Since the results of the community detection algorithm are nondeterministic, you might get results different from table 7.11.

> **Exercise 7.7**
>
> Find representatives of other communities. You need to use the subgraph projection feature to filter relevant nodes and then use the PageRank algorithm to find its representatives.

Congratulations! You have learned how to infer a co-occurrence network and analyze its community structure. The most crucial step in analyzing the hashtag co-occurrence network was the definition of the `topK` and `similarityCutoff` parameters of the node similarity algorithm. As discussed, the `topK` and the `similarityCutoff` parameters will directly affect how dense the inferred co-occurrence network will be. Consequently, the density of the co-occurrence network will correlate with how large the identified communities will be, which in the hashtag co-occurrence example means how broad the resulting topics will be. I recommend you test out various configurations of the two parameters and examine how they affect the resulting hashtag communities.

7.5.1 Dropping the projected in-memory graphs

It is important to remember to release the projected in-memory graph once you are done with the analysis to free up memory for other analysis. The following Cypher statement will drop all currently projected graphs.

Listing 7.22 Releasing all projected graphs from memory

```
CALL gds.graph.list() YIELD graphName        ◁──┐ Listing all
CALL gds.graph.drop(graphName) YIELD nodeCount   │ projected graphs
RETURN 'dropped ' + graphName        ◁──┐
                                        │ Releasing each projected
                                        │ graph from memory
```

7.6 Solutions to exercises

The solution to exercise 7.1 is as follows.

Listing 7.23 Retrieving the top five hashtags by the sum of the combined tweet and retweet count

```
MATCH (h:Tag)<-[:HAS_TAG]-(t:Tweet)
OPTIONAL MATCH (t)<-[r:RETWEETS]-()
RETURN h.id AS hashtag,
       count(distinct t) AS originalTweetsCount,
       count(r) AS retweetCount
```

```
ORDER BY retweetCount + originalTweetsCount DESC
LIMIT 5
```

The solution to exercise 7.2 is as follows.

Listing 7.24 Examining the top five most co-occurring pairs of hashtags

```
MATCH (h1:Tag)<-[:HAS_TAG]-()-[:HAS_TAG]->(h2:Tag)        ⟵┐  Removing
WHERE id(h1) < id(h2)                                        │  duplicates from
WITH h1,h2,count(*) AS cooccurrences                         │  the results
ORDER BY cooccurrences DESC LIMIT 5
RETURN h1.id AS tag1, h2.id AS tag2, cooccurrences
```

The solution to exercise 7.4 is as follows.

Listing 7.25 Executing the WCC algorithm on the hashtag co-occurrence network and storing the results to the database

```
CALL gds.wcc.write('tags',
  {writeProperty:'tcWcc',
   nodeLabels: ['Tag'], relationshipTypes: ['CO_OCCURRENCE']})
YIELD componentCount, componentDistribution;
```

The solution to exercise 7.5 is as follows.

Listing 7.26 Identifying how many components have 10 or fewer members

```
MATCH (t:Tag)
WITH t.tcWcc AS componentId, count(*) AS componentSize
WHERE componentSize <= 10
RETURN count(*) AS count
```

The solution to exercise 7.6 is as follows.

Listing 7.27 Identifying the members that are in the same community as the #nlp hashtag

```
MATCH (t:Tag)
WHERE t.id IN ['#nlp', '#graph']
WITH distinct t.community AS target_community
MATCH (o:Tag)
WHERE o.community = target_community
RETURN target_community, collect(o.id) as members
```

Summary

- Inferring monopartite networks is a frequent step in graph analysis.
- The Jaccard similarity coefficient can be calculated by dividing the intersection by the union of two sets.
- The GDS library uses two directed relationships that point in the opposite direction to represent an undirected relationship.

- The Jaccard similarity coefficient can be calculated with the `gds.nodeSimilarity` algorithm in GDS.
- The `similarityCutoff` parameter of the node similarity algorithm is used to define the threshold value of the similarity between a pair of nodes still regarded as similar.
- The `similarityCutoff` parameter of the node similarity algorithm is used to specify the limit on the number of similar relationships per node.
- The `stats` mode of the node similarity algorithm can be used to evaluate the density of the inferred similarity network.
- Cypher implements basic text functions, like the `replace` and `split` functions.
- Cypher syntax offers a list comprehension syntax, which is useful for filtering or transforming elements in a list.
- The `UNWIND` clause is used to transform a list of elements into rows, similar to a `for` loop in various scripting languages.
- You can change the relationship direction or treat it as undirected during in-memory graph projection.
- The GDS library uses two directed relationships that point in opposite directions to represent an undirected relationship.
- Parameters `nodeLabels` and `relationshipTypes` can be used to consider only a subset of the projected graph as an input to a graph algorithm.
- The label propagation algorithm is used to evaluate the community structure of a network.
- The label propagation algorithm is not deterministic, meaning the algorithm output may vary between different executions.
- Communities represent densely connected groups of nodes with sparser links between groups.
- You can use the graph filtering feature to project a new graph that contains a subset of an existing in-memory graph.
- PageRank can be used to find representatives of communities in a co-occurrence network.

Constructing
a nearest neighbor
similarity network

This chapter covers

- Manually extracting node features
- Presenting network motifs and graphlets
- Introducing betweenness and closeness centralities
- Constructing a monopartite network based on pairwise cosine similarities
- Using the community detection algorithm to complete a user segmentation task

This chapter will describe constructing a similarity network based on node properties or features. Like a typical machine learning preprocessing workflow, each data point or node is represented as a vector. In the machine learning context, a vector is a list of one or more numerical values. When dealing with graphs, there are generally two approaches you could take to describe a node as a vector. You could manually produce a set of features that describes a node, or you could use various graph algorithms to produce vectors representing a node in the network. In this chapter, you will manually create representations of nodes to describe their roles in the network and then use those representations to construct an inferred similarity network.

Figure 8.1 shows the process of extracting node features from the follower network. There are multiple approaches to describing a node as a vector. In this chapter, you will manually identify and extract relevant features that will be used to construct a similarity network. After that, you will evaluate how similar the nodes are based on the extracted features. The most common metric to evaluate the similarity between two vectors is *cosine similarity*. Cosine similarity is defined as the cosine of the angle between two vectors. You will calculate cosine similarity between pairs of nodes and store the relationship between nodes deemed similar. As in the last chapter, you will define the similarity threshold of when a relationship should be created. Notice that nodes connected in the original network are not necessarily connected in the inferred similarity network.

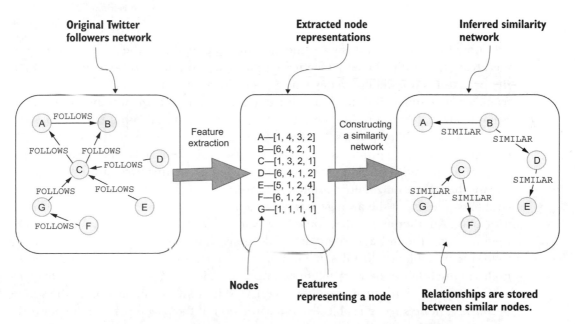

Figure 8.1   Extracting node representations and constructing a similarity network based on them

Cosine similarity is defined as the cosine of the angle between two vectors, as visualized in figure 8.2. The measure ranges between –1 and 1. When a pair of vectors has an identical direction, meaning the angle between the vectors is 0, the cosine similarity is 1. On the other hand, when the two vectors have opposite directions, the cosine similarity is –1. In practice, you deem two vectors similar when their cosine similarity is close to 1.

Imagine you work as an analyst at Twitter. Your supervisor gives you the task of identifying the types of users on the platform but doesn't tell you exactly what to look for or how to group users. There are several features in the dataset you could use to describe a user. For example, you know how often and what hashtags they use in their tweets or retweets. You are also aware of who they follow or mention on the platform.

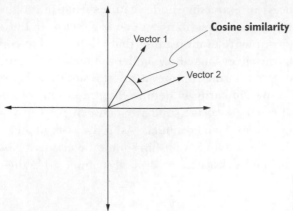

Figure 8.2 Cosine similarity is measured as the cosine of the angle between two vectors.

Additionally, you also have some timeline information about when a user or a tweet was created. As with all manual feature engineering, you first must decide which metrics or features you will use to describe a node. Since you have a small subset of tweets from a small time window, it doesn't make sense to analyze whether users have become inactive by not posting or retweeting anymore. On the other hand, exploring features that would help you split users by content creators versus those who primarily only retweet might be interesting. For example, you could take the total count of tweets and the ratio between retweets and all tweets as the first two features.

Another interesting metric could be the average time it takes a user to retweet. You could assume that if the average retweet time is minimal, you are most likely dealing with a bot. Another metric that could help you identify bots is inspecting whether multiple users post identical content at similar times. Since you have information about followers available, exploring some metrics that encapsulate the position and roles of nodes in the follower network might be worth considering. You will learn how to characterize a node's immediate neighborhood as well as investigate its role in the whole network. A node's *role* is a subjective interpretation of the part it plays in the network. For example, you can use the betweenness centrality algorithm to evaluate which nodes act as bridges between various communities or parts of the network. Similarly, you can use closeness centrality to evaluate how close a node is to all the other nodes in the network. Assuming most, if not all, information on Twitter is spread through follower relationships, you could identify nodes that can disseminate information through the network the fastest due to their position in the network.

After the feature extraction process, you will construct a similarity network between users based on pairwise cosine similarity between their feature vectors. You will then use a community detection algorithm like the label propagation algorithm, introduced in the previous chapter, to identify various segments of users. Since the relationships connect similar nodes, the community detection algorithm will identify groups of nodes that are densely interconnected in the inferred similarity network. The identified groups of users can be interpreted as user segmentation based on the manually extracted features. In a business environment, the task of grouping individuals based on specific characteristics is known as *user segmentation*, while in a technical setting, it is referred to as *unsupervised clustering* or *community detection*.

Figure 8.3 shows the process of using a community detection algorithm on the inferred similarity network to identify groups of users that can be interpreted as segments. The density of the inferred similarity network will directly correlate with the size of communities. You cannot predefine how many segments or clusters you want to identify with this approach; however, you can influence the size of clusters by tuning the density of the inferred similarity network.

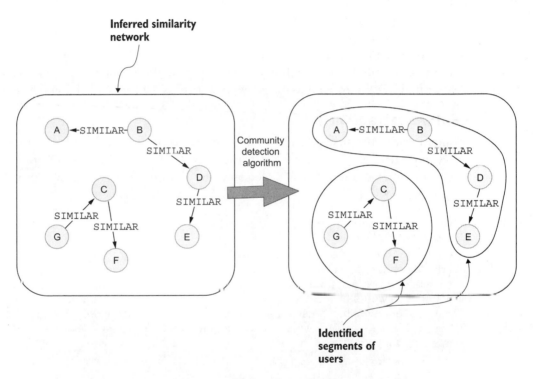

Figure 8.3 Using a community detection algorithm to identify segments of users

Several research papers (for example, Tinati & Carr, 2012; Beguerisse-Díaz et al., 2014) focus on defining user roles on the Twitter network. Although extracted features vary from paper to paper, and one can use multiple community detection or clustering techniques to group users together, the underlying idea seems to be always identical. The first part involves identifying and extracting relevant features that describe a user. The feature extraction is done manually, allowing the analyst to explain all the features and their relevance. For example, if you use a model that automatically transforms nodes into vectors, it is hard to explain what those vectors mean. Finally, researchers then use various community detection or clustering techniques to group users into segments.

You could use the approach of constructing a nearest neighbor graph and evaluating its community structure to identify specific groups or clusters in many other domains. For example, you could use this technique to segment users to create personalized services (Voulodimos et al., 2011) or cluster customers to improve market forecasting and planning research (Kashwan & Velu, 2013). You could also use a similar approach to cluster research papers by examining the relevance of specific sentence structures in their abstracts (Fukuda & Tomiura, 2018). While the feature extraction might look very different in different analyses, ranging from employing simple statistics to extracting network features or even document embeddings, the input to the analysis will always be a vector representing each data point. Next, plenty of algorithms are available to group data points based on their vector representations, and I am not here to argue which is best and why. Instead, I want to give you an example of using a graph-based approach to unsupervised clustering, where the number of final clusters or communities is not predefined. To follow the exercises in this chapter, you need to have the Twitter network imported into the Neo4j database, as described in chapter 3.

8.1   *Feature extraction*

As mentioned, the first step in the user segmentation process is feature extraction. Every node feature will be stored as its property. First, you will use your Cypher knowledge to extract the number of tweets and the ratio between retweets and tweets for each user.

> ### Exercise 8.1
> Calculate the number of tweets for each user and store it as the `tweetCount` property. Make sure to include those users that have zero published tweets. Additionally, calculate the ratio between retweets and tweets for each user. Specifically, divide the count of retweets by the sum of retweets plus tweets, and store it as the `retweetRatio` property. When a user has no retweets or tweets, use a default value of zero. You can use a single or two Cypher statements to calculate both features, whatever is easier for you.

Next, you will evaluate the distribution of how long it takes on average for a user to retweet a tweet after it has been published. You could hypothesize that if a user retweets a lot almost instantly, it is likely a bot. The following listing introduces the `duration.between()` function, which is used to calculate the duration between two datetimes.

Listing 8.1   **Evaluating the distribution of average duration between a retweet and tweet created dates**

Uses the duration.between() function to calculate the duration between two datetimes

```
MATCH (u:User)-[:PUBLISH]-(retweet)-[:RETWEETS]->(tweet)
WITH u, toInteger(duration.between(
  tweet.createdAt, retweet.createdAt).minutes) AS retweetDelay
```

```
WITH u, avg(retweetDelay) AS averageRetweetDelay
RETURN apoc.agg.statistics(averageRetweetDelay,
  [0.05, 0.10, 0.25, 0.5, 0.9]) AS result
```

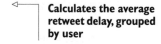

Calculates the average retweet delay, grouped by user

The `duration` temporal type behaves like an object and has multiple methods to extract the duration in years, days, minutes, and more. You can review all the available methods in the documentation: http://mng.bz/NVnd.

The results of the Cypher statement in listing 8.1 are shown in table 8.1.

Table 8.1　Distribution of average time between retweet and original tweet per user

`total`	1,385
`min`	0.0
`minNonZero`	0.05769228935241699
`0.1`	2.583343267440796
`max`	1,439
`0.05`	1.0000073909759521
`mean`	372.21522092560997
`0.25`	22.00012183189392
`0.5`	206.00097632408142
`0.9`	1,057.0078122615814
`stdev`	410.56837279615803

You can observe that you have information for only 1,385 users, slightly less than 40% of all users. Five percent of users retweet within a minute, and 10% of users retweet within 2.5 minutes. You could use a combination of retweets and average time to retweet to identify bots. If a user consistently retweets within a minute or two, you are likely dealing with a bot. You can observe that, otherwise, the average time to retweet is around 6 hours, which makes sense for a normal human being who is not constantly looking at their Twitter feed.

Exercise 8.2

Calculate the average duration in minutes between tweet and retweet per user and store it as a `timeToRetweet` property. Use the mean value of 372 minutes for users that have never retweeted (have missing values).

Another feature that might indicate bots is whether multiple users are posting identical content.

Exercise 8.3
Inspect pairs of tweets with identical content that are not retweets. The content is available in the `text` property. Additionally, ignore occurrences when a single author posts multiple tweets with the same content.

By solving exercise 8.3, you can observe that there are only five tweets that all have identical content. Since this feature is present with only 5 users, only 1 per 1,000 users, you will ignore it.

8.1.1   Motifs and graphlets

Next, you will focus on encoding a user's role in the follower network. Nodes with similar roles do not have to be next to one another in the network. For example, you could say users with a large following have a role in producing certain types of content. There could be multiple users with a large following, and they don't have to follow one another or be close in the network, but they still hold a similar role. In this example, you are effectively examining only the direct neighborhood of a node. You can encode a node's local neighborhood by counting its *graphlets*. A graphlet is a position of a node in a distinctly connected subgraph consisting of k nodes. You might already be familiar with two-node graphlets, although you have probably never heard that name before.

Figure 8.4 shows all the two-node directed graphlets. A two-node directed graphlet consists of two nodes and has directed relationships. There are three possible variations of directed relations between two nodes. When you are counting graphlets, you are essentially counting how many times a node is present in that graph pattern.

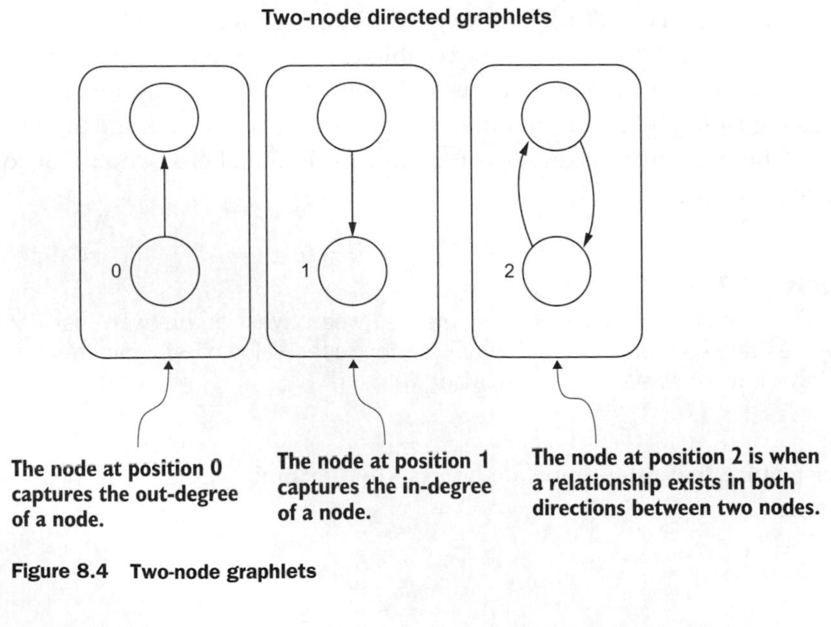

Two-node directed graphlets

The node at position 0 captures the out-degree of a node.

The node at position 1 captures the in-degree of a node.

The node at position 2 is when a relationship exists in both directions between two nodes.

Figure 8.4   Two-node graphlets

Figure 8.5 presents a visual representation of the count of two-node graphlets for node A. As shown in figure 8.4, a graphlet with a node at position 0 has an outgoing connection. So if you want to count the graphlet at position zero for node A, you count the number of outgoing connections, which is 2 in the example in figure 8.5. Similarly, by evaluating its incoming degree, you can count the graphlets at position 1 for node A. Finally, with a directed graph, you can have relationships in both directions between two nodes, as shown on the right side of figure 8.5. In some social networks, two users can be regarded as friends when they follow one another. In figure 8.5, only nodes A and D follow one another.

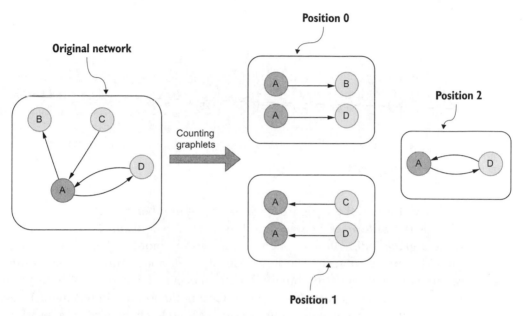

Figure 8.5   Counting two-node graphlets

Exercise 8.4

Calculate the incoming and outgoing degrees for all the users in the follower network, and store the results under the `inDegree` and `outDegree` properties. Additionally, count how many friends (graphlet two) patterns are present for each user and store the output as the `friendCount` property.

Next, you will look at three-node graphlets and calculate some of them to encode a node's local neighborhood. Figure 8.6 shows all the 30 variations of directed three-node graphlets. It would be a nice exercise in Cypher to calculate all of them; however, you will only calculate the three visualized graphlets in figure 8.6.

Three-node graphlets

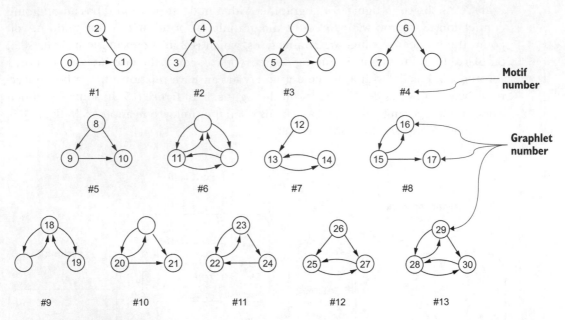

Figure 8.6   Three-node graphlets

You may also notice that figure 8.6 shows motif numbers as well as graphlet numbers. What is the difference between the two? A *motif* is a distinctly connected subgraph, while a *graphlet* describes a node's position in the motif. For example, if you look at motif 1, you can observe that it consists of three nodes and two relationships. With motifs, you only count how often this pattern occurs in a network. On the other hand, you can observe there are three options for a node position in this motif 1; therefore, there are three graphlets available. Motifs are used to characterize a network structure (Kim et al., 2011), while graphlets come in handy when you want to describe a local neighborhood of a node (Pržulj et al., 2004).

While you may not ordinarily find scenarios in which people focus solely on calculating graphlet or motif counts, it's essential not to overlook their significance. Many algorithms, in fact, use them as key components in deriving representations of individual nodes (Rossi et al., 2017) or even entire graphs (Dutta et al., 2020; Gorrec et al., 2022).

Exercise 8.5
Calculate graphlets 5, 8, and 11 shown in figure 8.6 for each user in the follower network and store them as node properties. Store graphlet 5 under the `graphlet5` node property and so on. I recommend you use a separate Cypher statement for each graphlet calculation.

8.1.2 Betweenness centrality

You have used graphlets to encode the local neighborhood of a node; however, you have not yet extracted any features that would describe a user's position in the global network. You will start by executing the betweenness centrality algorithm to extract a feature that describes how often a user acts as a bridge between various communities. The *betweenness centrality* algorithm assumes all information travels along the shortest paths between nodes. The more often a node lies on those shortest paths, the higher its betweenness centrality rank.

Figure 8.7 visualizes a Marvel network of characters, where relationships appear between characters that appeared in the same comic book. Both the size of the node

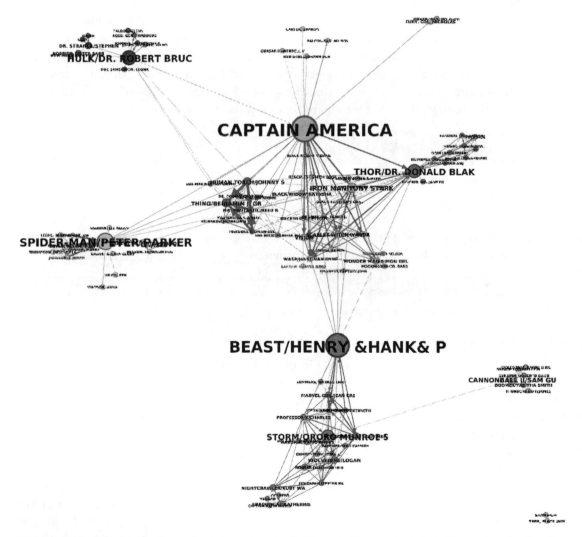

Figure 8.7 Sample visualization of the betweenness centrality rank (Source: Sanhueza. Licensed under CC BY 3.0 license)

and the size of the character name are calculated using betweenness centrality. The higher the betweenness centrality rank is, the larger the node and caption size is. You can observe that nodes that connect different communities are the largest. For example, Captain America is at the center of the network and acts as a bridge between the central community and all other communities. Another excellent example of betweenness centrality is the Beast character, who is the only link between the central and the bottom communities in figure 8.7. If he were to be removed from the network, the network would be split into two separate components. Therefore, the Beast character acts as a bridge between the bottom community and the rest of the network. Acting as a bridge also gives a node influence over the information flow between the two communities.

Before executing the betweenness centrality algorithm on the follower network, you must project an in-memory graph, as shown in listing 8.2. You will use the same projected graph to execute graph algorithms and then construct the nearest neighbor graph. For that reason, you also need to include all the previously calculated node features in the projection. Completing exercises 8.1 through 8.5 is a requirement to execute the following Cypher statement that projects an in-memory graph.

> **Listing 8.2 Projecting the in-memory graph that describes the follower network and includes all the precalculated node features**

```
CALL gds.graph.project('knnExample','User', 'FOLLOWS',
 {nodeProperties:['tweetCount', 'retweetRatio', 'timeToRetweet', 'inDegree',
 'outDegree', 'friendCount', 'graphlet5', 'graphlet8', 'graphlet11']})
```

Now, you can execute the betweenness centrality algorithm. You will use the `mutate` mode to store the results back to the projected graph in the following listing.

> **Listing 8.3 Mutating the betweenness centrality algorithm**

```
CALL gds.betweenness.mutate('knnExample', {mutateProperty:'betweenness'})
```

8.1.3 Closeness centrality

Closeness centrality is a measure that indicates how close a node is to all the other nodes in the network. The algorithm starts by calculating the shortest paths from a node to all the other nodes in the network. Once the shortest paths are calculated, the algorithm sums the distance to all the other nodes. By default, it returns an inverse of the distance sum so that a higher score means that a node has a higher closeness centrality rank. One can interpret closeness as the potential ability to reach all the other nodes as quickly as possible.

Figure 8.8 shows the same Marvel network as figure 8.7. The difference is that here, the node and the caption size are calculated by the closeness centrality algorithm instead of the betweenness centrality algorithm. You can observe that the largest nodes are in the center of the network, which makes sense, as they can reach all the other nodes the fastest. On the other hand, characters on the outskirts of the network

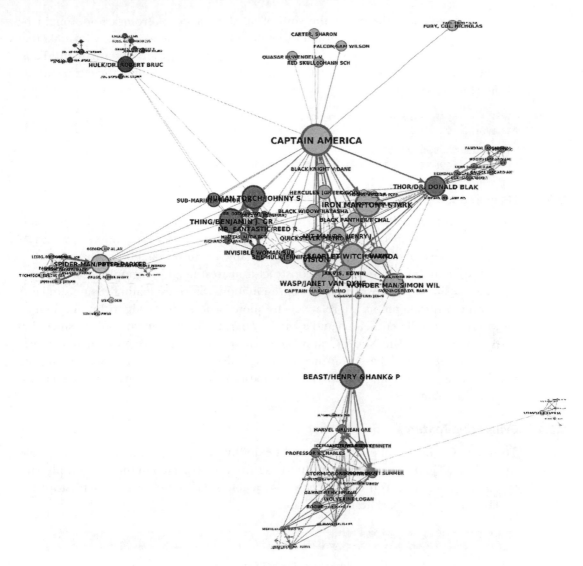

Figure 8.8 Sample visualization of closeness centrality rank

have a minimal closeness centrality rank. Captain America is in such a privileged position that he leads in both categories of centralities. On the other hand, for example, Iron Man is trailing far behind Spider-Man and Beast by the betweenness centrality. However, he is in front of them when looking at the closeness centrality rank, due to his position in the center of the network.

The first variant of closeness centrality might be unreliable on disconnected graphs. Remember, the algorithm tries to find the shortest path to all the other nodes in the graph. If the original variant is used on disconnected graphs, the shortest path might not exist, and therefore, the sum of all shortest paths from a node might be infinite. In practice, there are several variations of the closeness centrality formula that deal with disconnected graphs. In this example, you will use the Wasserman and Faust variation of the formula (Wasserman & Faust, 1994). You can execute the `mutate` mode of the closeness centrality algorithm with the following Cypher statement.

Listing 8.4   Mutating the closeness centrality algorithm

```
CALL gds.closeness.mutate('knnExample',
  {mutateProperty:'closeness', useWassermanFaust: true})
```

8.2   Constructing the nearest neighbor graph

You have completed the first step of the user segmentation process by manually extracting the features. The second step is to group or cluster users into segments. As mentioned, several different methods are available to cluster data points based on vector representations. Here, you will construct a nearest neighbor graph based on pairwise cosine similarity between vector representations. Since evaluating cosine similarity between many data points is a relatively frequent process, some algorithm implementations do an intelligent search and avoid comparing all pairs of data points, since that doesn't scale well. The Neo4j Graph Data Science (GDS) library implements an efficient similarity search based on the cosine similarity metric. Before constructing the nearest neighbor graph, it is advisable to explore the distributions and correlations between the features.

8.2.1   Evaluating features

To utilize Cypher's full expressivity and flexibility to analyze features, you must store the `closeness` and `betweenness` properties from the projected in-memory graph back to the stored graph. You can use the `gds.graph.writeNodeProperties` to store the mutated properties back to the database.

Listing 8.5   Storing the mutated properties to the database

```
CALL gds.graph.writeNodeProperties('knnExample',
  ['betweenness', 'closeness'])
```

You will start by examining which node features correlate the most. The GDS library offers a `gds.similarity.pearson(vector1, vector2)` function that calculates the correlation between two vectors. You will compare all pairs of features and identify the ones that correlate most. Many clustering techniques are influenced by feature collinearity, which can skew results. *Feature collinearity* is a phenomenon during which one feature highly correlates with another one. You can use the following Cypher statement to identify the most correlating features.

Listing 8.6 Identifying the five most frequently correlating pairs of features

```
WITH ['tweetCount', 'retweetRatio', 'timeToRetweet', 'friendCount',
      'inDegree', 'outDegree', 'graphlet5', 'graphlet8',
      'graphlet11', 'closeness', 'betweenness'] AS features
MATCH (u:User)
UNWIND features as feature1
UNWIND features as feature2
WITH feature1,
     feature2,
     collect(u[feature1]) as vector1,
     collect(u[feature2]) as vector2

WHERE feature1 < feature2
RETURN feature1,
       feature2,
       gds.similarity.pearson(vector1, vector2) AS correlation
ORDER BY correlation DESC LIMIT 5
```

Uses two UNWINDs to compare each feature to all the others

Avoids comparing a feature with itself and removes duplicates

Calculates the correlation

Table 8.2 shows the resulting pairs.

Table 8.2 The top five correlating pairs of features

feature1	feature2	correlation
friendCount	graphlet5	0.8173954540589915
graphlet8	outDegree	0.7867637411832583
graphlet11	graphlet5	0.7795975711131173
friendCount	graphlet11	0.6578582639591071
betweenness	friendCount	0.6370096424048863

It appears that some of the features are highly correlated. For example, the `friend-Count` highly correlates with `graphlet5`, `graphlet11`, and `betweenness` features. Also, the `graphlet8` variable correlates with the outgoing degree. To remove some of the highly correlated pairs of features, you will ignore the `friendCount`, `graphlet8`, and `graphlet5` features from your segmentation process.

Next, you will quickly evaluate the distributions of the remaining features. You can use the following Cypher statement to calculate basic distribution statistics.

Listing 8.7 Mutating the hashtag co-occurrence network to the in-memory graph

```
WITH ['tweetCount', 'retweetRatio', 'timeToRetweet','inDegree',
      'outDegree', 'graphlet11', 'closeness', 'betweenness'] AS features
MATCH (u:User)
UNWIND features as feature
WITH feature,
     apoc.agg.statistics(u[feature],
                         [0.5,0.75,0.9,0.95,0.99]) as stats
```

```
RETURN feature,
       round(stats.min,2) as min,
       round(stats.max,2) as max,
       round(stats.mean,2) as mean,
       round(stats.stdev,2) as stdev,
       round(stats.`0.5`,2) as p50,
       round(stats.`0.75`,2) as p75,
       round(stats.`0.9`,2) as p90,
       round(stats.`0.95`,2) as p95,
       round(stats.`0.99`,2) as p99
```

Table 8.3 shows the resulting distribution.

Table 8.3   Feature distribution

feature	min	max	mean	stdev	p50	p75	p90	p95	p99
"tweetCount"	0.0	754.0	0.96	13.74	0.0	1.0	1.0	2.0	6.0
"retweetRatio"	0.0	1.0	0.37	0.48	0.0	1.0	1.0	1.0	1.0
"timeToRetweet"	0.0	1439.0	372.08	254.87	372.0	372.0	613.0	944.0	1353.01
"inDegree"	0.0	540.0	6.92	22.76	0.0	4.0	16.0	35.0	112.0
"outDegree"	0.0	143.0	6.92	11.95	2.0	8.0	21.0	32.0	57.0
"graphlet11"	0.0	75.0	0.2	1.88	0.0	0.0	0.0	0.0	4.0
"closeness"	0.0	0.25	0.04	0.06	0.0	0.11	0.13	0.14	0.15
"betweenness"	0.0	199788.66	2385.97	10885.16	0.0	17.57	4075.66	11850.37	48312.5

Interestingly, the first thing I noticed is that more than 95% of users have a graphlet11 count of 0. Some might say you could drop the graphlet11 feature due to its low variance; however, you will keep it in this example. The closeness centrality scores range from 0.0 to 0.25 with an average of 0.04. On the other hand, the betweenness centrality is not normalized, so the scores are much higher, as it ranges from 0.0 to nearly 200,000.

Normalization in the context of machine learning refers to the process of transforming the range of features or variables in data. It's a crucial preprocessing step in many machine learning algorithms. Normalization makes the features more comparable by changing their scale to a standard range, typically between 0 and 1 or –1 and 1. While you do not need to normalize features if you are using the cosine similarity metric to infer a similarity network, you must be careful if you are using any other metrics. For example, with Euclidean distance, which is simply the distance between two points, a normalization would definitely affect the results.

8.2.2   *Inferring the similarity network*

You have preprocessed and evaluated the node features. Everything is ready to continue with the user segmentation process. To run the community detection algorithm and identify user segments, you must first infer a similarity network based on a pairwise cosine similarity metric between user vectors. The Neo4j GDS library offers an efficient cosine similarity search with the `gds.knn` algorithm. The `gds.knn` algorithm is used to construct a nearest neighbor similarity graph and should not be confused with more mainstream kNN classification or regression models.

Similarly, as in the previous chapter, you can affect how dense or sparse the inferred similarity network will be with the `topK` and `similarityCutoff` parameters. In this example, if you infer a denser network, the resulting communities will be larger; therefore, the user segmentation process will output fewer segments or groups of users. On the other hand, if you infer a sparser similarity network, the segmentation will be more granular. There is no right or wrong way to define the `topK` and `similarityCutoff` parameters—it always depends on your task. In this example, you will use the `topK` value of 65 and leave the `similarityCutoff` at the default value.

Since you need to execute a community detection algorithm on the output of the `gds.knn` algorithm, you will use the `mutate` mode to store the results to the projected graph. The `gds.knn` algorithm creates new relationships between users that pass the similarity threshold defined with the `topK` and `similarityCutoff` parameters. Run the following Cypher statement to execute the `mutate` mode of the `gds.knn` algorithm.

Listing 8.8 Mutating the user similarity network to the in-memory graph

```
CALL gds.knn.mutate('knnExample', {
    nodeProperties:['tweetCount', 'retweetRatio', 'timeToRetweet','inDegree',
        'outDegree', 'graphlet11', 'closeness', 'betweenness'],
    mutateRelationshipType:'SIMILAR',
    mutateProperty:'score',
    topK:65
})
```

8.3 User segmentation with the community detection algorithm

The last step in the user segmentation process is to execute a community detection algorithm to identify groups or segments of users. So far, you have used the label propagation algorithm to evaluate the community structure of a network. In this chapter, you will instead use the Louvain algorithm. The Louvain algorithm has a task identical to the label propagation algorithm to group densely connected nodes into groups or communities. However, it uses slightly different underlying mathematics to achieve this. If you are interested in mathematics, you can read the article in which the Louvain algorithm was proposed (Blondel et al., 2008). Run the following Cypher statement to `mutate` the results of the Louvain algorithm to the projected in-memory graph.

Listing 8.9 Storing the mutated property `userSegmentation` to the database

```
CALL gds.louvain.mutate('knnExample',
    {relationshipTypes:['SIMILAR'], mutateProperty:'userSegmentation'})
```

In the `communityCount` output, there are 22 identified communities.

> **NOTE** Like label propagation, the Louvain method is not deterministic. Therefore, you can get different results on every run, due to the stochastic nature of the algorithm.

To further investigate, you must store the mutated `userSegmentation` property to analyze the segmentation with Cypher.

Listing 8.10   Mutating the hashtag co-occurrence network to the in-memory graph

```
CALL gds.graph.writeNodeProperties('knnExample', ['userSegmentation'])
```

Finally, you can evaluate the user segmentation results. Use the following Cypher statement to evaluate average feature values for the five largest user segments.

Listing 8.11   Evaluating the user segmentation results

```
MATCH (u:User)
RETURN u.userSegmentation as community,
       count(*) AS memberCount,
       round(avg(u.tweetCount), 2) AS tweetCount,
       round(avg(u.retweetRatio), 2) AS retweetRatio,
       round(avg(u.timeToRetweet), 2) AS timeToRetweet,
       round(avg(u.inDegree), 2) AS inDegree,
       round(avg(u.outDegree), 2) AS outDegree,
       round(avg(u.graphlet11), 2) AS graphlet11,
       round(avg(u.betweenness), 2) AS betweenness,
       round(avg(u.closeness), 2) AS closeness
ORDER BY memberCount DESC
LIMIT 5
```

Table 8.4 shows the resulting user segmentation.

Table 8.4   User segmentation results

community	memberCount	tweetCount	retweetRatio	timeToRetweet	inDegree	outDegree	graphlet11	betweenness	closeness
270	217	3.5	0.007	385.3	15.28	19.12	1.09	10283.99	0.08
84	197	1.0	0.001	375.43	0.0	0.0	0.0	0.0	0.0
725	179	0.92	0.2	376.72	19.13	7.82	0.78	4692.19	0.12
737	156	0.0	0.0	372.0	0.0	0.03	0.0	0.0	0.0
381	145	0.0	1.0	35.68	2.5	4.43	0.55	845.37	0.04

The largest segment contains 217 members, and its members have, on average, 3.5 tweets. They do almost no retweeting, since their retweet ratio is 0.07. On the other hand, they have, on average, 15 followers and follow 19 other users. Judging by their high betweenness score, they act as bridges between various communities. On the other hand, the fourth-largest community seems to contain inactive and isolated users, at least from our dataset point of view. They don't have any tweets or retweets and don't follow anyone or have any followers.

You can remove the LIMIT clause from the Cypher statement in listing 8.11 to evaluate all 22 segments. Additionally, you can play around with various topK and similarityCutoff values of the gds.knn algorithm to evaluate how its values affect user segmentation.

Exercise 8.6

In chapter 7, you used the PageRank algorithm to identify representatives of hashtag communities. Apply the same technique to identify segment representatives. First, use the graph filtering procedure to filter only users in the largest segment. After that, use the PageRank algorithm on the newly filtered projection to identify its representatives.

Congratulations! You have learned how to manually extract node features and complete a user segmentation process based on them with the help of the k-nearest neighbor graph and community detection algorithms.

8.4 Solutions to exercises

The solution to exercise 8.1 is as follows.

Listing 8.12 Calculating the tweet count and retweet ratio for each user

```
MATCH (u:User)
OPTIONAL MATCH (u)-[:PUBLISH]->(tweet)
WHERE NOT EXISTS { (tweet)-[:RETWEETS]->() }
WITH u, count(tweet) AS tweetCount
OPTIONAL MATCH (u)-[:PUBLISH]->(retweet)
WHERE EXISTS { (retweet)-[:RETWEETS]->() }
WITH u, tweetCount, count(retweet) AS retweetCount
WITH u, tweetCount,
  CASE WHEN tweetCount + retweetCount = 0 THEN 0
    ELSE toFloat(retweetCount) / (tweetCount + retweetCount)
      END AS retweetRatio
SET u.tweetCount = tweetCount,
    u.retweetRatio = retweetRatio
```

The solution to exercise 8.2 is as follows.

Listing 8.13 Calculating the average time to retweet per user and storing it

```
MATCH (u:User)
OPTIONAL MATCH (u)-[:PUBLISH]-(retweet)-[:RETWEETS]->(tweet)
```

```
WITH u, toInteger(duration.between(
  tweet.createdAt, retweet.createdAt).minutes) AS retweetDelay
WITH u, avg(retweetDelay) AS averageRetweetDelay
SET u.timeToRetweet = coalesce(averageRetweetDelay, 372)
```

The solution to exercise 8.3 is as follows.

Listing 8.14   Inspecting pairs of tweets with identical content that are not retweets

```
MATCH (t1:Tweet), (t2:Tweet)
WHERE NOT EXISTS { (t1)-[:RETWEETS]->() }
  AND NOT EXISTS { (t2)-[:RETWEETS]->() }
  AND id(t1) < id(t2)
  AND NOT EXISTS { (t1)<-[:PUBLISH]-()-[:PUBLISH]->(t2) }
  AND t1.text = t2.text
RETURN t1, t2 LIMIT 5
```

The solution to exercise 8.4 is as follows.

Listing 8.15   Calculating the two-node graphlets and storing them as node properties

```
MATCH (u:User)
WITH u,
     count{ (u)<-[:FOLLOWS]-() } AS inDegree,
     count{ (u)-[:FOLLOWS]->() } AS outDegree,
     count{ (u)-[:FOLLOWS]->()-[:FOLLOWS]->(u) } AS friendCount
SET u.inDegree = inDegree,
    u.outDegree = outDegree,
    u.friendCount = friendCount
```

The solution to exercise 8.5 is as follows.

Listing 8.16   Calculating and storing the count of graphlet 5

```
MATCH (u:User)
OPTIONAL MATCH p=(u)-[:FOLLOWS]->()-[:FOLLOWS]->()-[:FOLLOWS]->(u)
WITH u, count(p) AS graphlet5
SET u.graphlet5 = graphlet5
```

Listing 8.17   Calculating and storing the count of graphlet 8

```
MATCH (u:User)
OPTIONAL MATCH p=(u)-[:FOLLOWS]->()-[:FOLLOWS]->()<-[:FOLLOWS]-(u)
WITH u, count(p) AS graphlet8
SET u.graphlet8 = graphlet8
```

Listing 8.18   Calculating and storing the count of graphlet 11

```
MATCH (u:User)
OPTIONAL MATCH (u)-[:FOLLOWS]->(other1)-[:FOLLOWS]->(other2)-[:FOLLOWS]->(u),
               (u)<-[:FOLLOWS]-(other1)<-[:FOLLOWS]-(other2)<-[:FOLLOWS]-(u)
```

```
WHERE id(other1) < id(other2)
WITH u, count(other1) AS graphlet11
SET u.graphlet11 = graphlet11;
```

The solution to exercise 8.6 is as follows.

Listing 8.19 Filtering a subgraph that contains only the largest community of hashtags

```
CALL gds.graph.filter('largestSegment', 'knnExample',
 'n.userSegmentation=270', '*')
```

Listing 8.20 Identifying representatives of the community with the PageRank algorithm

```
CALL gds.pageRank.stream('largestSegment',
  {relationshipTypes:['SIMILAR'], relationshipWeightProperty:'score'})
YIELD nodeId, score
RETURN gds.util.asNode(nodeId).username AS user, score
ORDER BY score DESC
LIMIT 5
```

Summary

- A node's role in a network can be described with various local neighborhood and global features.
- Nodes with a similar role in the network don't need to be close in the network.
- Motifs are used to characterize a network structure.
- Graphlets are used to encode a node's direct neighborhood.
- Betweenness centrality is used to identify nodes that act as bridges between various communities.
- Closeness centrality identifies nodes that have the potential to share information to all the other nodes the fastest.
- A nearest neighbor graph is constructed by evaluating one of the vector similarity measures.
- The most common vector similarity measure used is cosine similarity.
- Cosine similarity is measured by the cosine of the angle between two vectors.
- Feature collinearity is a phenomenon that occurs when one feature highly correlates with another one.
- The gds.graph.writeNodeProperties procedure can be used to store the node properties from the in-memory graph to the database.
- The Louvain algorithm is very similar to label propagation but uses different underlying mathematics.
- The Louvain algorithm is not deterministic, meaning it can produce different results on each execution.
- PageRank can be used to find representative nodes in the inferred similarity network.

Part 3

Graph machine learning

In this exciting journey of exploring graph data science, you have witnessed the power of graphs, learned about graph algorithms, and discovered how to use them in various scenarios. Now, it's time to build on that foundation and dive into predictive analytics, where you will learn how to predict missing node properties and future relationships by training machine learning models. In chapter 9, your journey begins with a dive into the world of node embeddings. Here, you'll learn how to represent nodes as a vector while allowing the representation to retain network information. The vector representations of nodes will then be used to build a node classification model. Progressing to chapter 10, you'll be introduced to link prediction, a critical task in numerous fields, from social network analysis to recommendation systems. You will learn how to calculate network features, which will be used to train and evaluate a link prediction model. Chapter 11 introduces you to the techniques of knowledge graph completion, a link prediction task executed on a heterogeneous graph. You will delve into knowledge graph embeddings, which are used to capture the complex structure of heterogeneous graphs. Lastly, as a bonus, chapter 12 guides you in applying natural language processing techniques, such as named entity recognition and relationship extraction, to construct a graph.

Node embeddings and classification

This chapter covers

- Introducing node embedding models
- Presenting the difference between transductive and inductive models
- Examining the difference between structural roles and homophily-based embeddings
- Introducing the node2vec algorithm
- Using node2vec embeddings in a downstream machine learning task

In the previous chapter, you used a vector to represent each node in the network. The vectors were handcrafted based on the features you deemed essential. In this chapter, you will learn how to automatically generate node representation vectors using a *node embedding model*. Node embedding models fall under the dimensionality reduction category.

An example of feature engineering and dimensionality reduction is the body mass index (BMI). BMI is commonly used to define obesity. To precisely characterize obesity, you could look at a person's height and weight, and measure their fat percentage, muscle content, and waist circumference. In this case, you would be dealing with five input features to predict obesity. Instead of having to measure all five features before an observation can be made, the doctors came up with a BMI.

Figure 9.1 visualizes a BMI scale used to evaluate a person's body type. For example, if the BMI is 35 or greater, the BMI scale would regard that person as extremely obese. BMI is calculated by dividing a person's weight in kilograms by their height in square meters and is a rough estimate of body fat. Instead of using five input features, a single embedded feature is a good representation of the expected output. It is a good approximation but by no means a perfect descriptor of obesity. For example, a rugby player would be considered obese given the BMI, but they probably have more muscle than fat. An embedding model reduces the dimensionality of input features while retaining a strong correlation to a given problem. An added bonus of using an embedding model is that you can collect less data for training and validating the model. In the case of BMI, you can avoid potentially costly measurements by only comparing the height and weight ratios.

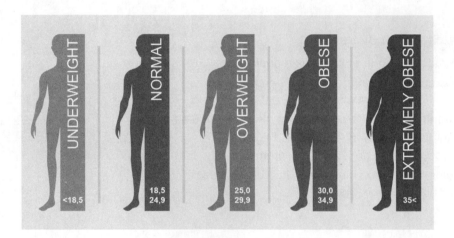

Figure 9.1   Body mass index chart

Every graph can be represented as an *adjacency matrix*. An adjacency matrix is a square matrix in which the elements indicate whether pairs of nodes are connected. Such a matrix can be regarded as a *high-dimensional representation* of the network.

Figure 9.2 visualizes an adjacency matrix representing a graph with four nodes, A, B, C, and D. Each element in the adjacency matrix indicates whether the pair of nodes is connected. For example, the element in column C and row D has a value of 1, which indicates that a relationship between nodes C and D is present in the graph. If the value of the element in the matrix is 0, then a relationship between the pair of nodes does not exist.

Now, imagine you have a graph with a million nodes. In an adjacency matrix, each node would be represented with a row in the matrix that has a million elements. In

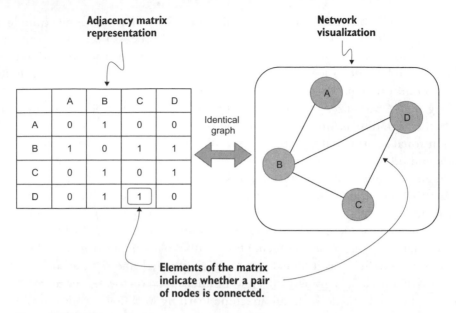

Figure 9.2 Adjacency matrix

other words, each node can be described with a vector that has a million elements. Therefore, an adjacency matrix is regarded as a high-dimensional network representation, as it grows with the number of nodes in the graph.

Suppose you want to train a machine learning model and, somehow, use the network structure information as an input feature. Let's say you use an adjacency matrix as an input. There are a couple of problems with this approach:

- There are too many input features.
- Machine learning models are dependent on the size of the graph.
- Overfitting can become a problem.

If you add or remove a single node from the graph, the size of the adjacency matrix changes and your model is no longer functional, as there is a different number of input features. Using the adjacency matrix as an input to your model could also cause overfitting. In practice, you often want to embed a node's local representation to compare nodes with similar neighborhood topology, instead of using all relationships between nodes as a feature input. Node embedding techniques try to solve these issues by learning lower-dimensional node representation for any given network. The learned node representations or embeddings should automatically encode the network structure so that the similarity in the embedding space approximates the similarity in the network. A key message is that the node representations are learned instead of manually engineered. The doctors reduced the dimensionality in the BMI example by a manual formula. The node embedding techniques aim to remove painstaking manual feature engineering and provide the best possible node representations by treating the embedding process as a separate machine learning step. The node embedding step is an unsupervised process because it learns to represent nodes without using labeled training data. Node embedding models use techniques based on deep learning and nonlinear dimensionality reduction to achieve this (Hamilton et al., 2018).

Figure 9.3 visualizes the node embedding process. The node embedding model takes the high-dimensional representation of a graph as an input and outputs a lower-dimensional representation. In the example of a graph with a million nodes, each node can be represented with a vector of a million elements. Suppose you execute a node embedding model on this graph. With most node embedding models, you can define the embedding dimension. The *embedding dimension* is the number of elements in the embedding matrix that describe a node. For example, you could set the embedding dimension to be 256. In that case, each node would be described with a vector that contains 256 elements. Reducing the number of elements from a million to 256 is incredibly beneficial, as it allows you to efficiently describe the network topology or position of a node in a graph with a lower-dimensional vector. Lower-dimensional vectors can be used in a downstream machine learning workflow, or they can be used to infer a similarity network using the nearest neighbor graph algorithm.

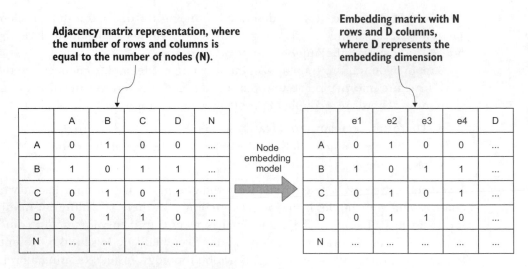

Figure 9.3   Adjacency matrix

9.1   *Node embedding models*

Node embedding models aim to produce lower-dimensional representations of nodes, while preserving network structure information. These lower-dimensional representations can then be used as feature inputs for various machine learning tasks, such as node classification, link prediction, and community detection, thereby simplifying the computational complexity and potentially improving the performance of models.

9.1.1 Homophily vs. structural roles approach

What does *network structure information* mean exactly? A common approach is to represent nodes in the embedding space so that neighboring nodes in the graph are close in the embedding space.

Figure 9.4 shows the so-called community-based approach to node embeddings. Neighboring nodes in the graph are also close in the embedding space. Therefore, nodes that belong to the same community should be close in the embedding space. This approach is designed under the node *homophily* assumption that connected nodes tend to be similar or have similar labels in a downstream machine learning workflow.

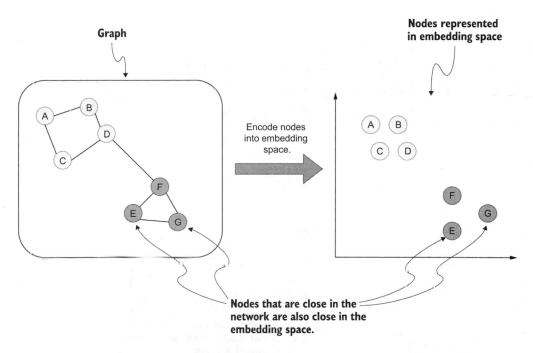

Figure 9.4 Homophily approach to node embedding

For example, you and your friends probably have similar interests. Suppose you wanted to predict a friend's interest. In that case, you could encode their position in the friendship network with a homophily-based node embedding model and train a supervised model based on training examples to predict or recommend their interests. If the hypothesis that a person and their friends have similar interests is valid, the trained model should perform relatively well. One node embedding algorithm you could use in this example is the fast random projection (FastRP) algorithm (Chen et al., 2019). Another approach is to encode nodes in the embedding space so that nodes with a similar network role are close in the embedding space.

You were briefly introduced to node roles in the previous chapter. Figure 9.5 visualizes the node embedding process, where the nodes are encoded close in the embedding space based on their network *structural roles*. In figure 9.5, both nodes D and F act as bridges between the two communities. One can assume they have similar network roles, and therefore, they are encoded close in the embedding space. You could use the structural role embedding approach to analyze roles of researchers in coauthorship. For example, you could use the structural role approach to node embedding to analyze roles of researchers in a coauthorship network or, perhaps, determine roles of routers on the internet network. For instance, the role eXtraction (RolX) algorithm (Henderson et al., 2012) is a node embedding algorithm that encodes nodes with a network structural role close in the embedding space.

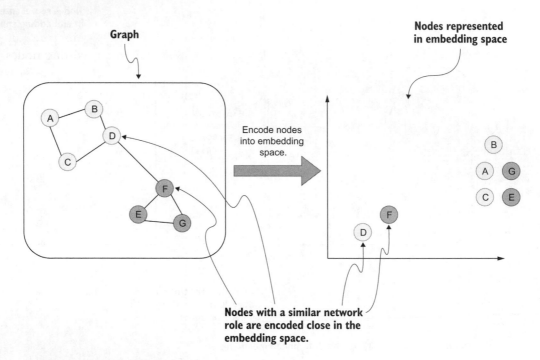

Figure 9.5 Structural roles approach to node embedding

Which design of the node embedding models you want to use depends on the downstream task you need to complete. Some algorithms, like node2vec (Grover & Leskovec, 2016), can also produce a combination of the two embedding designs as the output.

9.1.2 Inductive vs. transductive embedding models

Some node embedding models have a significant limitation. A typical process of using a node embedding model in a machine learning workflow involves calculating the embeddings and feeding them, for example, into a classification machine learning model. However, the difference between *inductive* and *transductive* node embedding models is in their ability to encode new unseen nodes during training.

When dealing with a *transductive* node embedding algorithm, you cannot calculate embeddings for nodes not seen during the initial embedding calculation. You can consider transductive models as creating a vocabulary during initial computation, where the key of the vocabulary represents a node and its value represents the embedding. If a node was not seen during the initial computation, it is not present in the vocabulary; hence, you cannot simply retrieve the embeddings for the new unseen nodes. If you want to calculate the embeddings for the new nodes, you must calculate the embeddings for the whole graph, meaning all the previously observed nodes as well as the new nodes. Since the embeddings might change for existing nodes, you must also retrain the classification model.

On the other hand, *inductive* node embedding models can calculate embeddings for unseen nodes during the initial computation. For example, you can train a model based on the initial computation of node embeddings. When a new node is introduced, you can calculate the embedding for the new node without recalculating embeddings for the whole graph. Likewise, you don't need to retrain the classification model for every new node. Encoding previously unseen nodes is a great advantage when dealing with growing or multiple separate graphs. For instance, you could train a classification model on a single graph and then use it to predict node labels for nodes of different separate graphs. To learn more about inductive models, I recommend reading up on the GraphSAGE model (Hamilton et al., 2017).

9.2 Node classification task

Now, it is time to start with a practical example. Imagine you are working at Twitch as a data scientist. Twitch is a streaming platform that makes it possible for anyone to start streaming their content to the world. In addition, other users can interact with streamers through the chat interface.

Every day, new users join the platform who decide they want to start streaming. Your manager wants you to identify the language of the new streams. Since the platform is worldwide, streamers likely use around 30 to 50 languages. Let's assume converting audio to text and running language-detection algorithms is not feasible for whatever reason. One of the reasons could be that many streamers on Twitch play video games, and therefore, audio from video games could distort language detection.

What other way could you predict the languages of new streamers? You have information about users who chat in particular streams. One could hypothesize that users mostly chat in a single language. Therefore, if a user chats in two streams, it is likely that both streams are in the same language. For example, if a user is chatting in a

Japanese stream and then switches a stream and interacts with the new streamer through chat, the new stream is likely in Japanese. There might be some exceptions with the English language, as for the most part, many people on the internet have at least a basic understanding of English. Remember, this is only an assumption that still needs to be validated.

Figure 9.6 visualizes the process of extracting network information to predict the new streamers' languages. Raw data has the structure of a bipartite `(:User)-[:CHATTED]→` `(:Stream)` graph. The first step in the process is to project a monopartite graph where the nodes represent streams, and the relationships represent their shared audience. The schema of the projected monopartite graph can be represented with the following Cypher statement: `(:Stream)-[:SHARED_AUDIENCE]-(:Stream)`. The monopartite graph is undirected, so if stream A shares the audience with stream B, it is automatically implied that stream B also shares the audience with stream A. In addition, you can add the count of shared audiences between streamers as a relationship weight. Suppose that extracting raw data and transforming it into a monopartite graph can be done by a data engineer on your team. The data engineer can take an approach similar to what you learned in chapter 7 to project a monopartite graph. Your job is now to train a prediction model and evaluate its results.

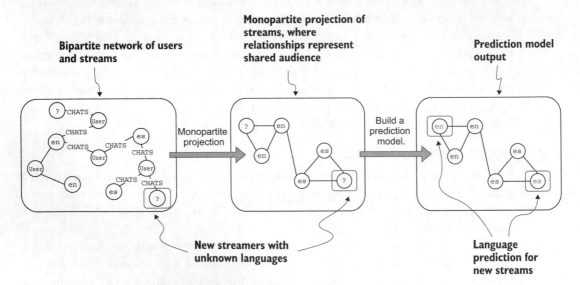

Figure 9.6   The process of predicting the language for new streams

The idea is to prepare a Jupyter notebook that can be used once a day to predict the languages of new streamers. Remember, if streams are close in the shared audience network, they likely have the same language. Therefore, you will use a node embedding model that uses a homophily-based approach to encoding nodes in the embedding space. One of the simplest and most broadly used node embedding models is node2vec, which you will use in this example. Once the node embeddings are calculated, you will use them for training a random forest classification model based on training examples of streams for which you already know the language. In the last step of the process, you will evaluate the predictions with a standard classification report and confusion matrix.

To follow the examples, you need to have a Jupyter notebook environment ready and access to a Neo4j database. The database should be empty before starting this chapter. You will use the scikit-learn Python library to split the data, train the model, and evaluate the results, so make sure you have it installed. The notebook with all the code in this chapter is also available on GitHub (https://github.com/tomasonjo/graphs-network-science).

9.2.1 Defining a connection to a Neo4j database

Start by opening a new Jupyter notebook, or download the filled-in notebook from the GitHub link in the previous paragraph. You will need to have the following three Python libraries installed to follow the code examples:

- Neo4j
- pandas
- scikit-learn

You can install all three libraries with pip or the Conda package manager.

First, you need to define the connection to the Neo4j database.

> **Listing 9.1 Defining the connection to Neo4j**

```
from neo4j import GraphDatabase

url = 'bolt://localhost:7687'
username = 'neo4j'
password = 'letmein'

driver = GraphDatabase.driver(url, auth=(username, password))
```

Listing 9.1 imports the `GraphDatabase` object from the `neo4j` library. To establish the connection with the Neo4j database, you need to fill in and optionally change the credentials. Once the credentials are defined, pass them to the `driver` method of the `GraphDatabase` object. The driver allows you to spawn sessions in which you can execute arbitrary Cypher statements.

Next, you will define a function that takes a Cypher statement as parameter and returns the results as a pandas dataframe, as shown in the following listing. The pandas dataframe is a convenient data structure that can be used to filter, transform, or easily integrate with other Python libraries.

Listing 9.2   Defining a function that executes an arbitrary Cypher statement and returns a pandas dataframe

```
def run_query(query):
    with driver.session() as session:
        result = session.run(query)
        return result.to_df()
```

9.2.2 *Importing a Twitch dataset*

Now that the environment is ready, you can circle back to the specified task. Remember, the data engineer on your team was kind enough to extract the information about the streams and chatters as well as perform the monopartite projection. They prepared two CSV files with relevant information. The first CSV file contains information about nodes in the network, as shown in table 9.1.

Table 9.1   Node CSV structure

id	language
129004176	en
50597026	fr
102845970	ko

The node CSV contains information about stream IDs and their language. In this example, you have the language information for all the streams so that you can evaluate the classification model accuracy of the test data. It is good practice to define unique constraints on the unique properties of nodes to speed up the import. You will start by defining the unique constraint on the id property of the Stream nodes.

Listing 9.3   Defining a constraint on Stream nodes

```
run_query("""
CREATE CONSTRAINT IF NOT EXISTS FOR (s:Stream) REQUIRE s.id IS UNIQUE;
""")
```

Since you are working in a Python environment, you need to execute Cypher statements via the run_query function, which is defined in listing 9.2. The function returns the output in a pandas dataframe format. Here, however, you are not interested in the result of the Cypher statement, so you don't have to assign the output to a new variable.

Now, you can go ahead and import the information about the Twitch streams and their languages. The CSV is available on GitHub, so you can utilize the LOAD CSV clause to retrieve and import the CSV information into the database, as shown in the following listing.

Listing 9.4   Importing nodes

```
run_query("""
LOAD CSV WITH HEADERS FROM "https://bit.ly/3JjgKgZ" AS row
MERGE (s:Stream {id: row.id})
SET s.language = row.language
""")
```

The relationship CSV file contains information about shared audiences between streams and their count, as shown in table 9.2.

Table 9.2   Relationship CSV structure

source	target	weight
129004176	26490481	524
26490481	213749122	54
129004176	125387632	4591

The relationship CSV contains three columns. The `source` and `target` columns contain the stream IDs that have a shared audience, while the `weight` column indicates how many shared users chatted in both streams. You can import the relationship information with the following Cypher statement.

Listing 9.5   Importing relationships

```
run_query("""
LOAD CSV WITH HEADERS FROM "https://bit.ly/3S9Uyd8" AS row
CALL{
    WITH row
    MATCH (s:Stream {id:row.source})
    MATCH (t:Stream {id:row.target})
    MERGE (s)-[r:SHARED_AUDIENCE]->(t)
    SET r.weight = toInteger(row.weight)
} IN TRANSACTIONS
""")
```

Exercise 9.1

Inspect how many, if any, `Stream` nodes have no incoming or outgoing relationships.

Luckily, there are no isolated nodes in the dataset. An *isolated node* is a node that has no incoming or outgoing relationships. When extracting node features from a dataset, always pay special attention to isolated nodes. For example, if there were some `Stream` nodes without any relationships, that would be a case of missing data. If you waited a few days, hopefully, someone would chat in their stream, and you would create new relationships for that stream so that it would not be isolated anymore. On the other hand, isolated `Stream` nodes can have any language. Since most node embedding algorithms encode isolated nodes identically, you would introduce noise to your classification model by including isolated nodes. Therefore, you would want to exclude all isolated nodes from the training and test datasets.

On the other hand, if you are dealing with isolated nodes and the relationships are not missing, meaning that no new relationships will be formed in the future, you can include isolated nodes in your workflow. For example, imagine you were to predict a person's net worth based on their network role and position. Suppose a person has no relationships and, therefore, no network influence. In that case, encoding isolated nodes could provide a vital signal to the machine learning model that predicts net worth. Always remember that most node embedding models encode isolated nodes identically. So if isolated nodes all belong to a single class, then considering them would make sense. However, if isolated nodes belong to various classes, then it would make sense to remove them from the model to remove noise.

9.3   *The node2vec algorithm*

Now that the graph is constructed, it is your job to encode nodes in the embedding space to be able to train the language prediction model based on the network position of the nodes. As mentioned, you will use the node2vec algorithm (Grover & Leskovec, 2016) for this task. The node2vec algorithm is transductive and can be fine-tuned to capture either homophily- or role-based embeddings.

9.3.1   *The word2vec algorithm*

The node2vec algorithm is heavily inspired by the word2vec (Mikolov et al., 2013) skip-gram model. Therefore, to properly understand node2vec, you must first understand how the word2vec algorithm works. Word2vec is a shallow, two-layer neural network that is trained to reconstruct linguistic contexts of words. The objective of the word2vec model is to produce word representation (vectors) given a text corpus. Word representations are positioned in the embedding space such that words that share common contexts in the text corpus are located close to one another in the embedding space. There are two main models used within the context of word2vec:

- Continuous bag-of-words (CBOW)
- Skip-gram model

Node2vec is inspired by the skip-gram model, so you will skip the CBOW implementation explanation. The skip-gram model predicts the context for a given word. The context is defined as the words adjacent to the input term.

Figure 9.7 visualizes how training pairs of words are collected in a skip-gram model. Remember, the objective of the skip-gram model is to predict context words or words that frequently co-appear with a target word. The algorithm creates training pairs for every word in the text corpus by combining the particular word with its adjacent words. For example, in the third row of figure 9.7, you can observe that the word

Input text   **Training samples**

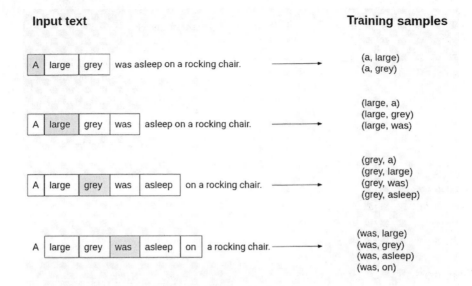

Figure 9.7 **The process of predicting the language for new streams**

grey is highlighted and defined as the target word. The algorithm collects training samples by observing its adjacent or neighboring words, representing the context in which the word appears. In this example, two words to the left and the right of the highlighted word are considered when constructing the training pair samples. The maximum distance between words in the context window with the target word in the center is defined as the *window size*. The training pairs are then fed into a shallow, two-layer neural network.

Figure 9.8 visualizes the word2vec neural network architecture. Don't worry if you have never seen or worked with neural networks. You simply need to know that during the training of this neural network, the input is a *one-hot-encoded* vector representing the input word, and the output is also a one-hot-encoded vector representing the context word.

Most machine learning models cannot work directly with categorical values. Therefore, one-hot encoding is commonly applied to convert categorical values into numerical ones. For example, you can see that all the distinct categories in figure 9.9 transformed into columns through the one-hot-encoding process. There are only three distinct categories in figure 9.9, so there are three columns in the one-hot-encoding output. Then, you can see that the category `Blue` is encoded as 1 under the `Blue` column and 0 under all other columns. Essentially, the numerical representation of the category `Blue` is [1,0,0]. Likewise, the numerical representation of `Yellow` is [0,0,1]. As you can observe, the one-hot-encoded vectors will have a single 1 under the column of the category they belong to, while the other elements of the vectors are 0. Consequently, the one-hot-encoding technique assures that the Euclidean distance

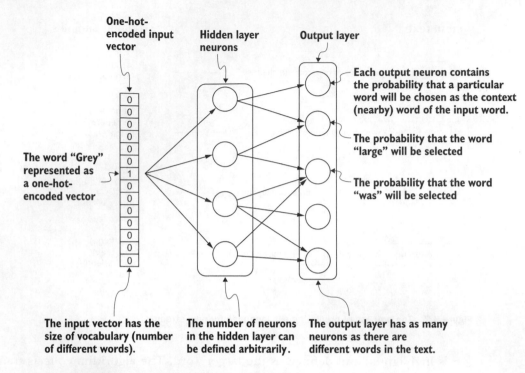

Figure 9.8   Word2vec shallow neural network architecture

between all classes is identical. While this is a straightforward technique, it is quite popular, as it allows the simple transformation of categorical values into numerical ones, which can then be fed into machine learning models.

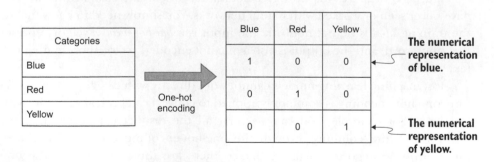

Figure 9.9   One-hot-encoding technique transforming categorical values into numerical values

After the training step of the skip-gram model is finished, the neurons in the output layer represent the probability a word will be associated with the target word. Word2vec uses a trick where we aren't interested in the output vector of the neural network but have the goal of learning the weights of the hidden layer. The weights of the hidden layer are actually the word embedding we are trying to learn. The number of neurons in the hidden layer will determine the *embedding dimension* or the size of the vector representing each word in the vocabulary. Note that the neural network does not consider the offset of the context word, so it does not differentiate between directly adjacent context words to the input and those more distant in the context window or even if the context word precedes or follows the target term. Consequently, the window size parameter has a significant influence on the results of the word embedding. For example, one study (Levy, 2014) found that larger context window size tends to capture more topic or domain information. In contrast, smaller windows tend to capture more information about the word itself (e.g., what other words are functionally similar).

9.3.2   *Random walks*

So what does word2vec have to do with node embeddings? The node2vec algorithm uses the skip-gram model under the hood; however, since you are not working with a text corpus in a graph, how do you define the training data? The answer is quite clever. Node2vec uses *random walks* to generate a corpus of "sentences" from a given network. Metaphorically, a random walk can be thought of as a drunk person traversing the graph. Of course, you can never be sure of an intoxicated person's next step, but one thing is certain. A drunk person traversing the graph can only hop onto a neighboring node.

The node2vec algorithm uses random walks to produce the sentences, which can be used as input to the word2vec model. In figure 9.10, the random walk starts at node A and traverses to node H via nodes C, B, and F. The random walk length is decided arbitrarily and can be changed with the *walk length* parameter. Each node in the random walk is treated as a word in the sentence, where the size of the sentence is defined with the walk length parameter. Random walks start from all the nodes in the graph to make sure to capture all the nodes in the sentences. These sentences are then passed to the word2vec skip-gram model as training examples. That is the gist of the node2vec algorithm.

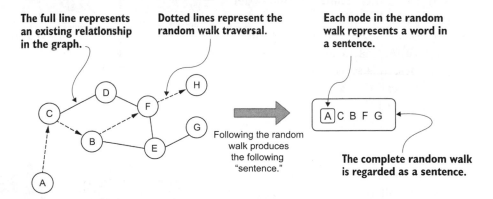

Figure 9.10   Using random walks to produce sentences

However, the node2vec algorithm implements second-order biased random walks. A step in the first-order random walk only depends on its current state.

Imagine you somehow wound up at node A in figure 9.11. Because the first-order random walk only looks at its current state, the algorithm doesn't know which node it was at in the previous step. Therefore, the probability of returning to a previous node or any other node is equal. There is no advanced math concept behind the calculation of probability. Node A has four neighbors, so the chance of traversing to any of them is 25% (1/4).

Suppose your graph is weighted, meaning each relationship has a property that stores its weight. In that case, those weights will be included in the calculation of the traversal probability.

In a weighted graph, the chance of traversing a particular connection is its weight divided by the sum of all neighboring weights. For example, the probability of traversing from node A to node E in figure 9.12 is 2 divided by 8 (25%) and the probability of traversing from node A to node D is 37.5%.

On the other hand, second-order walks consider both the current as well as the previous state. To put it simply, when the algorithm calculates the traversal probabilities, it also considers where it was at the previous step.

In figure 9.13, the walk just traversed from node D to node A in the previous step and is now evaluating its next move. The likelihood of backtracking the walk and immediately revisiting a node in the walk is controlled by the return parameter p. If the value of return parameter p is

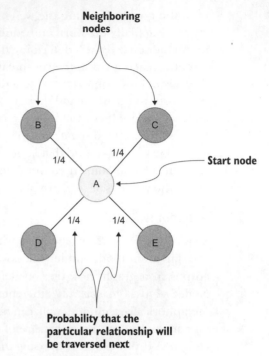

Figure 9.11   First-order random walks

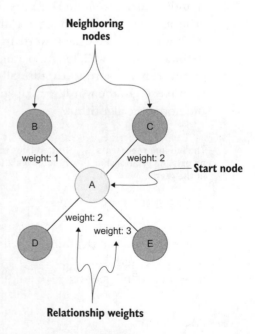

Figure 9.12   First-order weighted random walks

low, then the chance of revisiting node D is higher, keeping the random walk closer to the starting node of the walk. Conversely, setting a high value to parameter p ensures lower chances of revisiting node D and avoids two-hop redundancy in sampling. A higher value of parameter p also encourages moderate graph exploration.

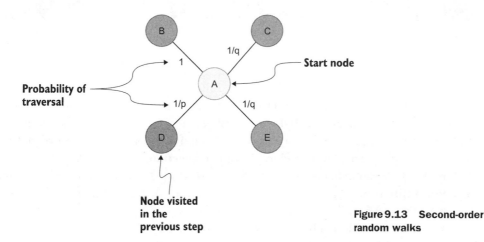

Figure 9.13   Second-order random walks

The inOut parameter q allows the traversal calculation to differentiate between inward and outward nodes. Setting a high value for parameter q ($q > 1$) biases the random walk to move toward nodes closer to the node in the previous step. Looking at figure 9.13, if you set a high value for parameter q, the random walk from node A is more biased toward node B. Such walks obtain a local view of the underlying graph with respect to the starting node in the walk and approximate breadth-first search. In contrast, if the value of q is low ($q < 1$), the walk is more inclined to visit nodes further away from node D. In figure 9.13, nodes C and E are further away, since they are not neighbors of the node in the previous step. This strategy encourages outward exploration and approximates depth-first search.

Authors of the node2vec algorithm claim approximating depth-first search will produce more community- or homophily-based node embeddings. On the other hand, the breadth-first search strategy for random walks encourages structural role embeddings.

9.3.3   Calculate node2vec embeddings

Now that you have a theoretical understanding of node embeddings and the node2vec algorithm, you will use it in a practical example. As mentioned, your task as a data scientist at Twitch is to predict the languages of new streamers based on shared audiences or chatters between different streams. The graph is already constructed, so you only need to execute the node2vec algorithm and train a classification model. As always, you first must project an in-memory graph. Relationships represent shared audiences between streams. When stream A shares an audience with stream B, that directly implies that stream B also shares an audience with stream A. Therefore, you can treat the relationships as undirected. Additionally, you know how many users were shared between a pair of streams, which you can represent as a relationship weight. Execute the following query to project an undirected weighted network of shared audiences between streams.

Listing 9.6   Projecting the in-memory graph of streams and their shared audience in-memory

```
run_query("""
CALL gds.graph.project("twitch", "Stream",
  {SHARED_AUDIENCE: {orientation: "UNDIRECTED", properties:["weight"]}})
""")
```

The Cypher statement in listing 9.6 projects an in-memory graph named `twitch`. To treat relationships as undirected, you must set the `orientation` parameter value to `UNDIRECTED`. The `properties` parameter of relationships can be used to define the relationship properties to be included in the projection.

Finally, you can execute the node2vec algorithm. There are multiple parameters you could fine-tune to get the best results. However, hyperparameter optimization is not in the scope of this chapter. You will use a `embeddingDimension` parameter value of 8, which means that each node will be represented with a vector of eight elements. Next, you will define the `inOutFactor` parameter to be 0.5, which encourages more depth-first search walks and produces homophily-based embeddings. In this example, you are not interested in the structural roles of nodes and only want to encode how close they are in the graph. All the other parameters will be left at default values. Execute the following Cypher statement to execute the node2vec algorithm and store the results to the database.

Listing 9.7   Calculating node2vec embeddings and storing them to the database

```
data = run_query("""
CALL gds.beta.node2vec.write('twitch',
  {embeddingDimension:8, relationshipWeightProperty:'weight',
   inOutFactor:0.5, writeProperty:'node2vec'})
""")
```

9.3.4 *Evaluating node embeddings*

Before you train the language classification model, you will evaluate the embedding results. You will start by examining the cosine and Euclidean distance of embeddings of pairs of nodes where a relationship is present. The cosine and Euclidean distance distribution can be calculated with Cypher and then visualized with the seaborn library.

Listing 9.8   Evaluating the cosine and Euclidean distance of embeddings of connected nodes

```
import matplotlib.pyplot as plt
import seaborn as sns
```

```
plt.rcParams["figure.figsize"] = [16, 9]

df = run_query("""
MATCH (c1:Stream)-[:SHARED_AUDIENCE]->(c2:Stream)
RETURN gds.similarity.euclideanDistance(
    c1.node2vec, c2.node2vec) AS distance, 'Euclidean' as metric
UNION
MATCH (c1:Stream)-[:SHARED_AUDIENCE]->(c2:Stream)
RETURN gds.similarity.cosine(
    c1.node2vec, c2.node2vec) AS distance, 'cosine' as metric
"""
)

sns.displot(
    data=df,
    x="distance",
    col="metric",
    common_bins=False,
    facet_kws=dict(sharex=False),
    height=7,
)
```

The code in listing 9.8 produces the visualization in figure 9.14, which shows the distribution of cosine and Euclidean distance of embeddings between pairs of nodes where a relationship is present. With Euclidean distance, the lower the value is, the more similar or close the nodes are in the embedding space. You can observe that the top of the distribution is slightly lower than 1. Most of the nodes are very similar based on Euclidean distance; however, there are some pairs of nodes where the distance is slightly larger. On the other hand, with cosine similarity, two nodes are very close in the embedding space when the value is close to 1. Similarly, most pairs of

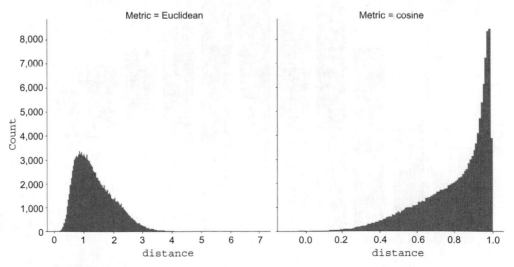

Figure 9.14 Distribution of cosine and Euclidean distance of embeddings between pairs of nodes where a relationship is present

nodes where the relationship is present have a cosine similarity close to 1. So what happens when a pair of nodes have a relationship but their cosine similarity of embeddings is, for example, less than 0.5? Using the following code, you can investigate the dependence of cosine similarity between pairs of connected nodes based on their combined degree values.

> **Listing 9.9   Evaluating the dependence of cosine similarity to the combined node degree values**

```
df = run_query("""
MATCH (c1:Stream)-[:SHARED_AUDIENCE]->(c2:Stream)
WITH c1, c2, gds.similarity.cosine(
        c1.node2vec, c2.node2vec) AS cosineSimilarity,
    count{ (c1)-[:SHARED_AUDIENCE]-() } AS degree1,
    count{ (c2)-[:SHARED_AUDIENCE]-() } AS degree2
RETURN round(cosineSimilarity,1) AS cosineSimilarity,
    avg(degree1 + degree2) AS avgDegree
ORDER BY cosineSimilarity
"""
)

sns.barplot(data=df, x="cosineSimilarity", y="avgDegree", color="blue")
```

The code in listing 9.9 produces the visualization in figure 9.15, where you can clearly see that the more connections a node has, on average, the less similar it is to its neighbors. That makes sense in a way. Imagine if you only had one friend; you might be almost identical to them in several meaningful ways. However, when you have 100

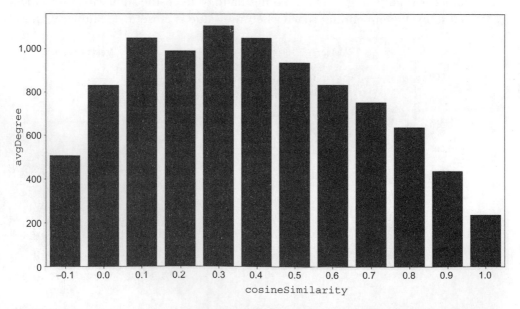

Figure 9.15   Distribution of average cosine similarity of connected nodes based on the combined node degree values

friends, you can't be identical to all of them. You can pick some attributes from each friend that you share, but it is practically impossible to be identical to all of them, unless they are also all identical.

You have also specified the relationship weight to calculate the node2vec embeddings. The higher the relationship weight is, the more biased the random walk is to traverse it. You can examine how the cosine similarity of connected nodes is dependent on the relationship weight with the following code.

Listing 9.10   Evaluating the dependence of cosine similarity of connected nodes to the relationship weight

```
df = run_query("""
MATCH (c1:Stream)-[r:SHARED_AUDIENCE]->(c2:Stream)
WITH c1, c2, gds.similarity.cosine(
    c1.node2vec, c2.node2vec) AS cosineSimilarity,
    r.weight AS weight
RETURN round(cosineSimilarity,1) AS cosineSimilarity,
    avg(weight) AS avgWeight
ORDER BY cosineSimilarity
"""
)
sns.barplot(data=df, x="cosineSimilarity", y="avgWeight", color="blue")
```

The code in listing 9.10 produces the visualization in figure 9.16, which shows the distributions of Euclidean and cosine similarities between a connected pair of nodes.

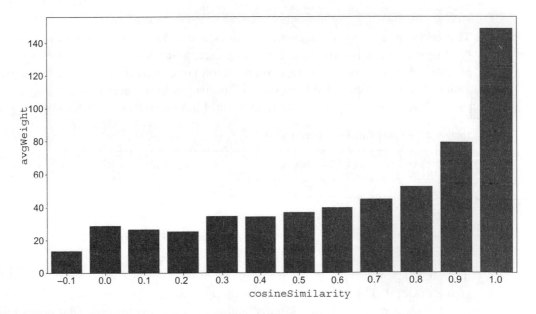

Figure 9.16   The distribution of average cosine similarity of connected nodes based on the combined node degree values

Again, you can distinctly observe the dependence of the cosine similarity of connected nodes to the relationship weight. The higher the relationship weight is, the more likely the random walk is to traverse it. Consequently, the more often a pair of nodes appear closely in the random walk, the more likely their embeddings are to be more similar. When a relationship weight is lower, the random walk is biased not to traverse it. Therefore, you can observe some examples where the embeddings are not similar at all, even when there is a relationship between a pair of nodes. One would assume that the pair of nodes are not connected when the cosine distance of their embeddings is close to zero. However, it might simply be the case that the random walk is biased in a way to avoid traversing the relationship between the two nodes.

9.3.5 *Training a classification model*

In the final section of this chapter, you will train a classification model to predict the languages of new streamers. First, you must retrieve the relevant data from the database and make the required preprocessing.

Listing 9.11 Retrieving and preprocessing relevant data for classification training

```
data = run_query("""
MATCH (s:Stream)
RETURN s.id AS streamId, s.language AS language, s.node2vec AS embedding
"""
)
data['output'] = pd.factorize(data['language'])[0]   ←——┐ Encodes languages to be
                                                         represented as integers
```

The code in listing 9.11 begins by retrieving the data from the database. A simple Cypher statement returns stream ID, language, and node embeddings. Since the languages are represented as strings, you need to map or encode them as integers. You can easily encode categorical values, such as languages, to integers with the `pd.factorize` method. After this step, the dataframe should have the structure shown in table 9.3.

Table 9.3 Pandas dataframe structure

streamId	language	embedding	output
129004176	en	[-0.952458918094635,...]	0
50597026	fr	[-0.25458356738090515,...]	1
102845970	ko	[-1.3528306484222412,...]	2

In table 9.3, you can observe that the `pd.factorize` method encoded the English language under 0. The French language is mapped to 1 and so on.

The `embedding` column contains vectors or lists representing each data point. So the input to the classification model will be the `embedding` model, and you will train it to predict the integer under the output column. In this example, you will use the random forest classifier from the scikit-learn library. As with all machine learning training, you must split your data into training and test sets. You will use the train_test_split to produce the train and test portions of the dataset. Execute the following code to train a random forest classification model to predict languages of new streams.

Listing 9.12 Splitting the dataset and training the random forest model classifier based on the training portion of the dataset

```
from sklearn.model_selection import train_test_split
from sklearn.ensemble import RandomForestClassifier

X = data['embedding'].to_list()
y = data['output'].to_list()

X_train, X_test, y_train, y_test = train_test_split(X, y, test_size = 0.2,
  random_state=0)

rfc = RandomForestClassifier()
rfc.fit(X_train, y_train)
```

9.3.6 *Evaluating predictions*

The last thing you will do in this chapter is evaluate the model on the test data. You will begin by examining the *classification report*. A classification report is used to measure the quality of predictions from a machine learning model. Execute the following code to produce the classification report.

Listing 9.13 Producing the classification report

```
from sklearn.metrics import classification_report

y_pred = rfc.predict(X_test)
print(classification_report(y_test,y_pred))
```

The code in listing 9.13 produces the report in figure 9.17, where you can observe that you are dealing with an unbalanced dataset, as there are 384 test data points for the English language and only 54 examples of French streams. Additionally, the language mapped under number 9 is Italian and has only 19 test data points. When dealing with unbalanced datasets, it makes sense to examine the F1 score. Both the F1 score and the weighted F1 score are 0.91, which is a great result. The hypothesis that chatters usually chat in streams that share the same language is valid.

Finally, you will produce the *confusion matrix*. The confusion matrix can help you evaluate actual versus predicted classes of data points. Execute the following code to visualize the confusion matrix.

	precision	recall	f1-score	support	
0	0.91	0.92	0.91	384	
1	0.94	0.87	0.90	54	
2	0.98	0.92	0.95	59	
3	0.81	0.87	0.84	39	
4	0.88	0.94	0.91	52	
5	0.88	0.86	0.87	58	
6	1.00	0.90	0.95	20	
7	0.92	0.96	0.94	25	
8	0.91	0.89	0.90	35	
9	0.90	1.00	0.95	19	
accuracy			0.91	745	
macro avg	0.91	0.91	0.91	745	**Figure 9.17**
weighted avg	0.91	0.91	0.91	745	**Classification report**

Listing 9.14 Calculating the tweet count and retweet ratio for each user

```
from sklearn.metrics import ConfusionMatrixDisplay

ConfusionMatrixDisplay.from_predictions(y_test, y_pred,
  normalize="true", cmap="Greys")
```

The code in listing 9.14 produces the visualization in figure 9.18. Remember, the English language is mapped to 0. By examining the confusion matrix in figure 9.18, you can observe that the model only misclassified between English and other languages. For example, the model never incorrectly classified Korean as Portuguese. This makes sense, as English is the most common language on the internet, so many people can speak at least a bit of English in addition to their native language.

Exercise 9.2

Try out various configurations of the node2vec algorithm to observe how it affects the cosine distance between embeddings of connected nodes and the accuracy of the classification model. You can remove the relationship weight parameter to observe how the unweighted variant of the node2vec algorithm behaves or fine-tune the `embeddingDimension`, `inOutFactor`, and `returnFactor` parameters. Check out the official documentation (http://mng.bz/lVXo) for the complete list of node2vec parameters.

Congratulations! You have successfully trained your first node classification model based on node2vec embeddings. Remember, since node2vec is a transductive model, you should retrain the model when new nodes are added to the graph. Therefore, models like node2vec are used in batch processing pipelines that run, for example, once a day.

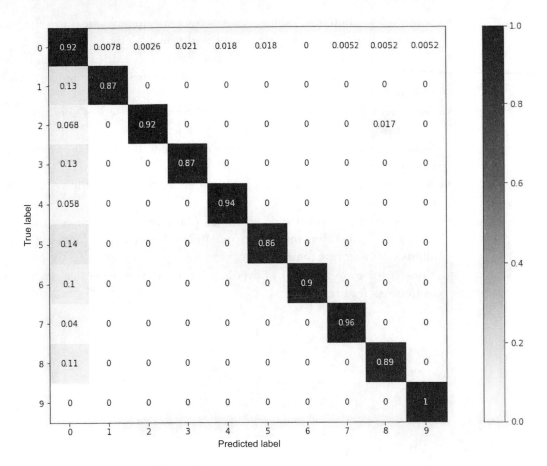

Figure 9.18 Confusion matrix

9.4 Solutions to exercises

The solution to exercise 9.1 is as follows.

Listing 9.15 Counting the `Stream` nodes with no incoming or outgoing relationships

```
MATCH (n:Stream)
WHERE NOT EXISTS { (n)--() }
RETURN count(*) AS result
```

Summary

- Node embedding models use a dimensionality reduction technique to produce node representations of arbitrary sizes.
- Node embedding models can encode nodes based on their structural roles in the network or can follow a more homophily-based design.

- Some of the node embedding models are transductive, meaning they cannot produce embeddings for nodes not seen during training.
- The node2vec algorithm is inspired by the word2vec skip-gram model.
- The node2vec algorithm uses random walks to produce sentences, which are then fed into the skip-gram model.
- Second-order random walks consider the previous step of the random walk when calculating the next traversal possibilities.
- Node2vec can be fine-tuned to produced embeddings based on node structural roles or homophily.
- The embedding dimension parameter defines the size of the vector that represents nodes.
- Pay special attention to isolated nodes when using node embedding models. Most node embedding models encode isolated nodes identically, so ensure that aligns with your task requirements.
- Node classification is a task of predicting a property or label of a node based on its network features.

Link prediction

10

This chapter covers

- Discussing the link prediction workflow
- Introducing link prediction dataset split
- Constructing link prediction features based on node pairs
- Training and evaluating a supervised link prediction classification model

Most real-world networks are dynamic and evolve through time. Take, for example, a friendship network of people. People's friends change over time. They might meet new people or cease to associate with others. You might assume new connections form randomly in a friendship network; however, it turns out that most real-world networks have a profound organizing principle. The studies around link prediction are focused on identifying and understanding various network-evolving mechanisms and applying them to predict future links.

Figure 10.1 shows a small network of people, where the relationships represent friendships. Solid lines represent existing connections. As mentioned, friendship networks evolve over time, and people form new connections. Intuitively, you might assume that Luke and Rajiv in figure 10.1 are more likely to form a future

247

connection, visualized with a dotted line, than Jose and Alice, due to being closer in the network. Unsurprisingly, the number of common friends between a pair of individuals is a good indicator of whether they are likely to meet in the future. Simply put, the closer two individuals are in the network, the higher the probability of forming future links. Predicting future links within a network is the main objective of the link prediction field. Accurately predicting future links can be used in recommender systems, or it can be used to better understand the network organizing principles. Imagine a bipartite network composed of users and products in which the connections represent the products they purchased. In this example, link prediction techniques could be instrumental in predicting future user–product relations, allowing you to implement personalized product recommendations.

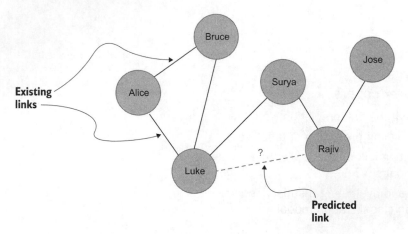

Figure 10.1   Link prediction

On the other hand, there are networks that do not necessarily evolve over time, but we have a limited understanding of their connections. One such example is a biological network of drugs and diseases. A drug often has a narrow variety of diseases it can treat. A clinical trial must be conducted to determine whether a drug can treat any new disease; however, clinical trials are very costly. The other problem with drug repurposing is that there is a vast number of combinations of drugs and diseases on which one could conduct clinical trials. Link prediction techniques can be used to identify missing links in the network. The process of predicting missing links in the network can be thought of as *link completion*.

The biomedical network visualized in figure 10.2 consists of drugs and diseases. The solid lines indicate for which diseases a drug can be used. For example, aspirin can be used to treat headaches, Kawasaki disease, and coronary artery disease. On the other hand, ramipril is known to treat coronary artery disease and hypertension. Since both aspirin and ramipril can be used to treat coronary artery disease, it might make sense to explore if ramipril can treat other diseases than aspirin can. Again, you are simply looking at the number of common neighbors between drugs to base your predictions. Note that this is a simplified version of a drug repurposing scenario. In the real world, much more information about human genes, pathways, and other biological processes is considered. Additionally, you would need to include biomedical domain experts in the process to help construct the graph, evaluate the results, and more.

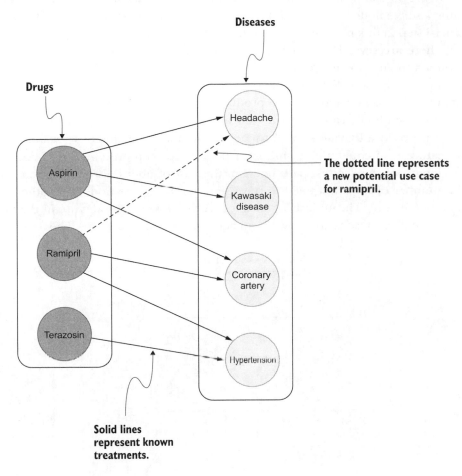

Figure 10.2   Link completion

10.1 Link prediction workflow

As mentioned, most networks follow various organizing principles, intentionally or unintentionally, which you can use in your analysis to predict the probability of a new link between a pair of nodes. For example, in a social network, you might assume people are more likely to become friends if they are of similar age. However, looking only at personal characteristics might be unsatisfactory, as this approach might lose a lot of information about a relationship between two persons. Two people might be of similar age, but they don't mingle in the same social groups, so the probability of them becoming friends is lower. On the other hand, if two people have many common friends, it is more likely they will meet and become friends. It also turns out that if a person has a lot of friends, they are more likely to form new connections than if they have fewer friends.

When predicting whether a new connection will be established, you are never examining a single node in isolation but, rather, a pair of nodes in the graph. Therefore, the crucial step in link prediction is to design features that encode a pair of nodes.

There are several approaches you could take to encode a pair of nodes. I have grouped them into three categories, presented in figure 10.3. First, you can combine any node properties. For instance, I have used the age difference in the social network example. You could also take the product of node degrees or the cosine similarity of node embeddings. However, you can also simply concatenate embeddings or any other property if that might perform better. Distance-based metrics are another group of features you could use in link prediction. A typical representative of this group is the length of the shortest path between the pair of nodes. Essentially, you calculate the number of hops you need to traverse to get from one node to another and use that as a feature. The underlying idea is that the closer the nodes are in the network, the more likely it is that a link will form between them in the future. The third group of

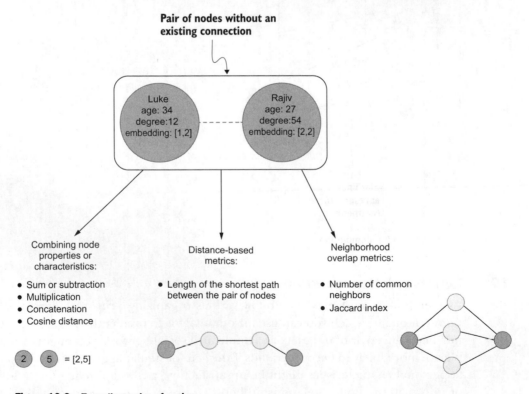

Figure 10.3   Encoding pairs of nodes

features focuses on evaluating the neighborhood overlap between two nodes. For example, the higher the number of common friends is, the greater the likelihood is that the pair will meet sometime in the future. You could also calculate the Jaccard similarity index, which would simply be a normalized version of the common friends count. There are also other metrics that encode the overlap of the local neighborhood, which you will learn later in the chapter.

The three categories and their examples presented in figure 10.3 do not offer an exhaustive list of possible features. There are other ways of combining metrics into link prediction features. However, the groups presented in figure 10.3 cover most of the methods to generate features you will encounter in your link prediction tasks.

One simple way to predict links is calculating the link prediction metrics between pairs of nodes and simply taking the arbitrary top number of them as links probable to happen in the future. On the other hand, you could also decide to train the classification model using those link prediction metrics. An added value of training a classification model is that it can learn to identify patterns that you might miss when taking an unsupervised approach. For instance, the model could identify that certain link prediction metrics carry more weight than others. Additionally, a particular combination of metrics may significantly forecast the outcome. These details might be overlooked if one only considers the top scores of a single similarity metric. In this chapter, you will learn how to calculate several link prediction metrics and train and evaluate a classification model based on those metrics.

Now, imagine you are still working at Twitch as a data scientist. You have been tasked with finding ways to improve channel recommendations. So far, you are already using the recommendation system based on shared audiences between different channels. If there is a significant audience overlap between two channels, you can use that information to provide recommendations to users. As a user, you will see those recommendations in the Users of This Channel Also Watch section. What could you do to try to improve these recommendations? One idea is to predict which channels will share audiences in the future. Then, you could provide these predictions as recommendations to users. This approach might improve the overall recommendations, as you would recommend channels with existing audience overlap as well as channels with a high probability of future audience overlap.

Figure 10.4 shows the network of Twitch channels or streams, where the relationships represent the audience overlap. The solid lines represent existing shared audience overlap and could be used to populate one section of recommendations. As a data scientist, you could use the information about the existing relationships to predict future audience overlap. The future audience overlap predictions can then be used to power your recommendation engine.

Interestingly, using future link predictions as recommendations could, in turn, be thought of as self-fulfilling projections. Similar approaches have been used to recommend movies (Lakshmi & Bhavani, 2021), products (Darke et al., 2017), and even links between medical concepts (Kastrin et al., 2014). Link prediction can also be

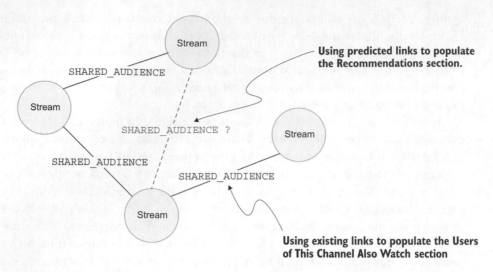

Figure 10.4   **Link prediction flow**

used with other techniques to construct a hybrid recommendation engine (Çano & Morisio, 2017). How would you go about training a classification model that could be used to predict future overlap of audiences between channels?

The high-level overview of the process of training a link prediction classification model is presented in figure 10.5. The first step is to split the relationships into three distinct sets. One set is used to generate network features, while the other two are used to train and evaluate the classification model. You might run into data leakage problems if you used the same relationships to both generate the network features and train the classification model. *Data leakage* occurs when your training data contains information about the output but similar data will not be available when the model is used for predictions. Leakage frequently leads to high performance during training and possibly evaluation of the model, but unfortunately, it doesn't perform well for new predictions. If you are using any graph features with the link prediction model, you must take extra care to prevent any feature leakage. *Feature leakage* refers to

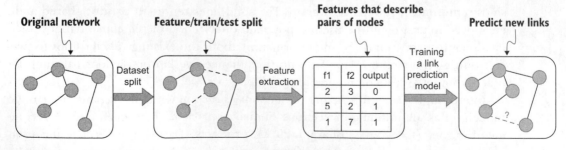

Figure 10.5   **Building a link prediction model to recommend Twitch channels**

when a feature contains the same or comparable information as the output. For example, imagine you are using the distance-based shortest path feature between two nodes. By using the same relationships to generate features and train the model, the model would simply learn to classify or predict a connection between all pairs of nodes with a network distance of 1. In other words, when the network distance between a pair of nodes is 1, there is a relationship between the pair of nodes. Therefore, the network distance feature and the classification output would contain the same information, introducing feature leakage. Essentially, you can think of feature leakage as cheating on your model evaluation by peeking at the results during training. To avoid feature and data leakage, you need to use one relationship set to calculate the network features and another relationship set to provide supervised classification examples for training and evaluating the model.

Once the dataset split is done, you need to calculate the link prediction metrics that will be used to train a model. As previously mentioned, you could calculate network distance, calculate the number of common neighbors, or simply aggregate node properties. You need to calculate the features for both the positive and negative examples of links in the network. Finally, use these link prediction features to train a classification model to predict whether a link is probable to happen in the future or not. Given that the dataset was split into training and test relationship sets, you can evaluate your model on the test set of the dataset. Once you determine that the classification model performs well enough, you can use it in production to generate recommendations for users of your platform.

To follow the exercises in this chapter, you need to have the Twitch network imported into the Neo4j database, as described in chapter 9. The Jupyter notebook with all the code examples in this chapter is available on the following GitHub web page: http://mng.bz/Y1JA.

10.2 Dataset split

You need to split the dataset accordingly to evaluate the trained classification model. If your model used no graph-based features, like distance-based or neighborhood-based metrics, then you could follow the traditional test/train data split. Assume you are trying to predict new links between people based on their age and education. Since both of those features are node properties that are not graph-based, you could simply take 80% of existing relationships as the training set and evaluate your model on the remaining 20% of relationships. Obviously, you need to add some negative examples, as the model otherwise cannot learn to differentiate between the two outputs and might produce inaccurate predictions. Producing negative examples is not a problem, as there are many pairs of nodes that are not connected. In practice, positive link examples scale linearly with the number of nodes in the graph, while negative examples scale quadratically. This could lead to a considerable class imbalance problem; however, it is a frequent step in the link prediction process to subsample the negative classification samples to around the same number as the positive ones. You will learn more about negative example subsampling in the next section.

As soon as you add any graph-based features that capture the similarity or closeness of nodes in the graph, you need to be very mindful of data leakage. Remember, when a feature contains the same or comparable information as the output variable but is unavailable when making predictions, you have introduced data leakage into the workflow. The most obvious example is the network distance between nodes in the graph. If the network features and training examples are calculated on the same set of relationships, then the model will simply learn that relationships exist between nodes that are only one hop away. However, none of the pairs of nodes without a link in the network will be classified as probable to form a connection, as none are one hop away. Even node embeddings based on the homophily principle, introduced in chapter 9, could be problematic if you didn't perform a proper dataset split. Overall, most of the graph-based features might introduce some data leakage issues. It is common to split relationships into three sets to avoid data leakage problems:

- Relationship set used to generate features
- Relationship set used to train the model
- Relationship set used to evaluate the model

Using separate sets of relationships to generate network features and then train and evaluate the classification, you can avoid feature leakage issues with graph-based features. Therefore, none of the calculated network features will have identical or very comparable information as the output variable. With the network distance example, supervised classification examples will have a minimum network distance of 2. Both negative and positive classification examples can have a network distance of 2. In turn, the network distance feature is not identical to the output variable, and you prevent any feature leakage.

There are many options for going about performing the dataset split. In this section, you will learn about the *time-based* and *random* dataset split techniques.

10.2.1 *Time-based split*

In theory, link prediction is a technique used to predict future connections based on past ones. You could produce a dataset split based on the time component if you know when the links were created.

The original network in figure 10.6 has relationships created between 2020 and 2021. In this simple graph example, you can use the relationships from 2020 to generate network features. There should be a significant number of relationships in the feature set, as you don't want the network to be too disconnected or have too many isolated nodes. Having too few relationships in the feature set might produce poor network features, which might, in turn, not be predictive of future links. Relationships created in 2021 in figure 10.6 are then used to construct the test and train sets. For example, you could use 80% of the newer relationships as the training set and the remaining 20%

to evaluate the model. Remember that the relationships used to generate network features should not be used in either the train or the test sets. Optionally, you could also introduce a validation set from the newer relationships created in 2021 if you plan to perform any hyperparameter optimization of the classification model.

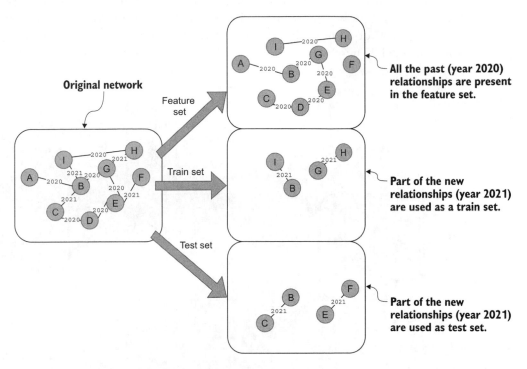

Figure 10.6   Time-based approach to relationship split for a link prediction task

Use the time-based split, if possible, as it accurately mimics the scenario of predicting future links. In the example in figure 10.6, you take existing knowledge about relationships (from 2020) and try to predict the future (in 2021). The additional benefit is that the model should learn to capture the underlying organizing mechanism of the network as the time-based split follows network evolution, which should, in turn, provide better predictions. Unfortunately, the Twitch dataset of shared audiences doesn't have the time component of relationships available, so you will have to resort to another method.

10.2.2   *Random split*

Random split is similar to time-based split, in that you need to produce train and test sets as well as the feature set of relationships. You can't differentiate between past and future relationships, since no time information is available. Instead, you randomly take a subset of relationships in the graph as the train and test sets you will use to train and evaluate the classification model. Random split is also useful for link completion tasks, where you predict missing links in the network and have no time component available.

You can see that figure 10.7 is almost identical to figure 10.6. The only difference is how to select which relationships belong to which set. With the time-based approach, you can choose the set the relationship belongs to based on the time property. However, since you don't have the time information available, you need to take the random approach. Therefore, you select to which set a relationship belongs at random.

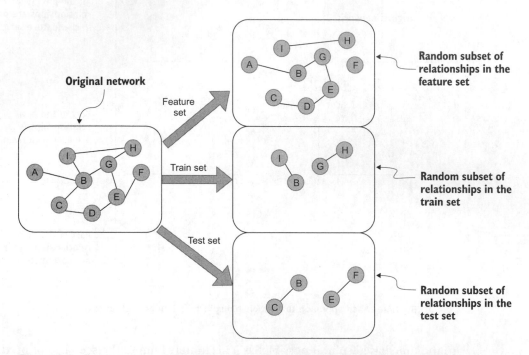

Figure 10.7   Random approach to relationship split for the link prediction task

NOTE   The key concept with the link prediction dataset split is that to avoid data leakage, the links used to calculate network features should differ from the supervised link samples used for training and evaluating a classification model. *Feature leakage* occurs when a feature contains the same or comparable information as the output variable. For example, if you were to avoid introducing a separate feature set to calculate network features like the network distance, the classification model would learn that pairs of nodes that are one hop or traversal away have 100% probability of forming or having a link. In turn, the model accuracy on the training and test sets would be 100%, as the network distance contains the same information as the output variable. However, the model would be terrible at predicting missing or future links. Optionally, you can introduce a validation set if you plan to perform any hyperparameter optimization.

Now, you will perform the random split for link prediction on the Twitch shared audience network. You need to have the Neo4j environment up and running with the Twitch dataset defined in chapter 9 loaded. Next, you need to open a Jupyter notebook to define the connection to the Neo4j database.

Listing 10.1   Defining the connection to Neo4j

```
from neo4j import GraphDatabase

url = "bolt://localhost:7687"
username = "neo4j"
password = "letmein"

# Connect to Neo4j
driver = GraphDatabase.driver(url, auth=(username, password))

def run_query(query, params={}):
  with driver.session() as session:
    result = session.run(query, params)
    return result.to_df()
```

The code in listing 10.1 defines the connections with the Neo4j database and the run_query function used to execute any Cypher statement. Make any necessary changes to the url, username, and password variables.

> **Exercise 10.1**
> Count the number of relationships in the Twitch shared audience network.

There are 131,427 relationships in the dataset. You will begin by constructing the feature set of relationships. Remember, the feature set needs to be the largest, as you want to retain as connected a network as possible without too many isolated nodes or disconnected components. In this instance, you can use 90% of all relationships in the feature set, leaving you with around 13,000 positive examples for the train and test sets. To construct the feature set, you will create new relationships with a FEATURE_REL type. Cypher offers a rand() that returns a random floating-point number in the range from 0 to 1 and follows an approximate uniform distribution. To select a random subset of relationships for the feature set, you will use the rand() function in the Cypher statement. The following Cypher statement takes approximately 90% of existing SHARED_AUDIENCE relationships and creates a new connection with the FEATURE_REL between those pairs of nodes.

Listing 10.2   Constructing a relationship feature set

```
run_query("""
MATCH (s1:Stream)-[:SHARED_AUDIENCE]->(s2:Stream)
WITH s1, s2
```

```
WHERE rand() <= 0.9
MERGE (s1)-[:FEATURE_REL]->(s2);
""")
```

The code in listing 10.2 selects and creates a random, nondeterministic set of relation-ships. Make sure to run it only once, as the relationship split would not be acceptable otherwise. If you have run the query multiple times for any reason, simply delete the FEATURE_REL relationships and rerun the Cypher statement in listing 10.2. Note that you might get a slightly different count of FEATURE_REL relationships when rerunning the query, due to using the rand() function.

> ### Exercise 10.2
>
> Now, you will select the relationships for the train and test set. You will start by produc-ing positive samples for the classification model. The positive samples are relation-ships between the pairs of nodes between which the SHARED_AUDIENCE relationships exist but not the FEATURE_REL ones.
>
> Match the pairs of nodes between which the SHARED_AUDIENCE exists but not the FEATURE_REL ones. Next, use the MERGE clause to create new relationships between those pairs of nodes with the TEST_TRAIN type. Finally, return the count of newly cre-ated relationships.

I got the result of 13,082 created relationships. You will probably get a different num-ber, but it should be in the same ballpark, around 13,000. You have prepared the posi-tive samples for the classification model. Now, it is time to select some negative examples where the relationship does not exist.

10.2.3 *Negative samples*

When training a binary classifier like the link prediction model, you should include both positive and negative examples in the training and test sets. Without negative examples, the model cannot learn to differentiate between the two outputs and might produce inaccurate predictions.

A common characteristic of real-world graphs is that they are sparse. Imagine any large social platform on the internet. You might have hundreds or thousands of friends on the platform; however, there are millions or, in some cases, billions of users on the platform. That means you have only a thousand out of a billion relationships possible. In the machine learning context, every user has up to a few thousand posi-tive examples and, possibly, around a billion negative examples. If you used all the negative examples, you would have to deal with a considerable class imbalance, as the positive examples of relationships scale linearly with the number of nodes, while the negative examples scale quadratically. Most machine learning models perform best when the number of samples in each class is about the same. However, if the data-set is heavily imbalanced, then you might get a high accuracy by just predicting the majority class every time. With link prediction, if you would predict that no link exists between any pair of nodes, you would probably get around 99% accuracy in most cases. Thus, there would be a high probability of misclassification of the minority class and, consequently, poor classification model performance. Therefore, it is common to subsample the negative examples and use about the same number of positive and negative samples in most link prediction workflows.

Exercise 10.3

In this exercise, you will select pairs of nodes to construct the negative examples for the classification model. You must select about the same number of negative samples as the positive ones produced in exercise 10.2. You can use the count of 13,082 positive examples, or the count you got in exercise 10.2. The negative examples should be produced in a way that ensures no relationship exists between the pair of nodes in feature, train, or test sets.

Start by matching a pair of nodes where the SHARED_AUDIENCE relationship does not exist between them. Next, ensure you have matched two different nodes and will avoid running into situations in which both the source and target node are the same. Filter pairs of nodes where the randomly generated value is higher than 0.9 (rand() > 0.9) to guarantee that the negative examples are somewhat random and representative of the graph as a whole. Once the pairs of nodes are correctly matched, use the LIMIT clause to limit the number of negative examples to around 13,000. Finally, create a relationship between the selected pairs of nodes with the NEGATIVE_TEST _TRAIN type.

10.3 *Network feature engineering*

Now, you will produce network features that capture the closeness or similarity of pairs of nodes in the network. The idea is that the closer or more similar a pair of nodes are given the network metrics, the more likely they are to form a future connection. The future connections will then be used to provide better recommendations to Twitch users.

You might have noticed that the train and test sets are lumped together under the TEST_TRAIN and NEGATIVE_TEST_TRAIN relationship types. As you need to calculate the link prediction features for both the train and test sets, there is no need to differentiate between the two just yet. Remember, all the graph-based features for the train and test sets will be calculated strictly on the feature set of relationships, to prevent any data leakage.

Again, you have the option to choose between learned or manually defined features. For example, you could use the node2vec algorithm to calculate node embeddings and then use the cosine similarity of embeddings between pairs of nodes as a feature of the classification model. However, since you would be using transductive node embeddings to calculate link prediction features, you would need to retrain the classification model every time a new node is added to the graph. While that might be satisfactory in some scenarios, you probably don't want to retrain a model every time a new streamer shows up on the platform. Luckily, a lot of research has been done about link prediction features from which you can borrow some ideas for feature engineering. It makes sense to start by selecting straightforward and uncomplicated features and evaluating their performance. If there is a need, you can always later use more complex techniques, like inductive node embeddings. You must finish exercises 10.2 and 10.3 before continuing with the code examples to generate features.

10.3.1 *Network distance*

The first feature you will calculate is the *network distance*. The network distance is calculated by finding the shortest path between a pair of nodes and then counting the number of relationships in the shortest path.

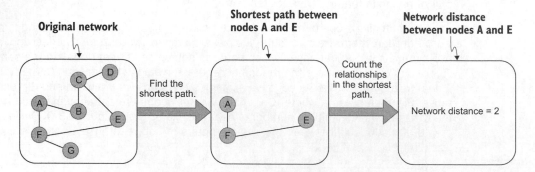

Figure 10.8   Calculating network distance between a pair of nodes A and E

Figure 10.8 shows the process of finding the network distance between nodes A and E. In the first step, you need to calculate the shortest path between the pair of nodes. When dealing with an unweighted network, the shortest path represents the path that traverses the fewest relationships to get from one node to another. In the example in figure 10.8, you must traverse two relationships to get from node A to node E. In other words, the network distance between nodes A and E is 2.

The idea behind the network distance is that the closer the two nodes are in the network, the more likely they are to form future connections. For example, imagine you are dealing with a link prediction in a social network. The network distance between a pair of persons in the train or test set should never be 1, as this would mean you haven't performed the relationship split correctly. However, if the network distance is 2, that would mean the pair of persons have at least one common friend. If the distance is greater than 2, the two persons don't have any common friends and are less likely to form future connections. In theory, the higher the network distance is, the less likely a future connection is. In your use case, the closer the two streams are in the network, the more likely it is there will be a significant audience overlap in the future.

Using Cypher query language, you can find the shortest unweighted path with the `shortestPath()` function. In an unweighted path, the traversal of each relationship has an identical cost, so the shortest path between two nodes will always be the count of the total relationships in a path between them. The `shortestPath()` function expects as input a Cypher pattern that defines the source and target nodes as well as the optional allowed relationship types in the path. For more advanced use cases, you can also define the minimum or the maximum number of traversals or relationships in the path. The following Cypher statement finds the shortest path between Surya and Jim.

Listing 10.3   Finding shortest unweighted paths with Cypher

```
MATCH (source:Person {name:"Surya"}),          Defines the source and target
      (target:Person {name:"Jim"})             nodes of the shortest path
MATCH p = shortestPath((source)-[:FRIEND|COWORKER*1..10]->(target))
RETURN p
                                               Identifies the shortest path between
                                               the source and target nodes under
                                               the p reference variable
```

The first part of listing 10.3 is a simple `MATCH` clause used to identify the source and target nodes. Next, you need to define the shortest path constraints using Cypher syntax. The defined graph pattern that defines the shortest path constrains in listing 10.3 is shown in the following listing.

Listing 10.4   Graph pattern used to define the shortest path constraints

```
(source)-[:FRIEND|COWORKER*]->(target)
```

The Cypher syntax in listing 10.4 defines the shortest path between the `source` and `target` nodes. One constraint of the shortest path is that it can only traverse `FRIEND` or `COWORKER` relationships. The function ignores all the other relationship types. Note that the relationship direction is also essential. In the example in listing 10.4, the shortest path algorithm can only traverse outgoing relationships throughout the path. Finally, you need to add the * symbol to allow the algorithm to traverse multiple relationships. If the * symbol were missing, one of the shortest path constraints would be that the algorithm can only traverse a single relationship.

Now, you will calculate the network distance for all pairs of nodes in the train and test sets of relationships (listing 10.5). The test and train sets of pairs of nodes are tagged with the `TEST_TRAIN` and `NEGATIVE_TEST_TRAIN` relationship types. Then, you must find the shortest path between all pairs of nodes in the two sets. In the last step, you will calculate the length of the shortest path, which is equivalent to the number of relationships, with the `length()` function.

Listing 10.5   Calculating the network distance between pairs of nodes in the train and test sets

Matches all the pairs of nodes
connected with the TEST_TRAIN or
NEGATIVE_TEST_TRAIN relationships

Identifies the shortest path between the pairs of
nodes. The shortest path is constrained to be only
allowed to traverse the FEATURE_REL relationships
to prevent data leakage.

```
run_query("""
MATCH (s1)-[r:TEST_TRAIN|NEGATIVE_TEST_TRAIN]->(s2)
MATCH p = shortestPath((s1)-[:FEATURE_REL*]-(s2))
WITH r, length(p) AS networkDistance
SET r.networkDistance = networkDistance
""")
```

Calculates the length of the
shortest paths using the
length() function

Stores the network distance result
as the relationship property

You may notice that there is no direction indicator in the shortest path graph pattern definition in listing 10.5. Therefore, the shortest path algorithm can traverse the relationship in the opposite direction as well, effectively treating the relationships as undirected.

10.3.2 *Preferential attachment*

Another popular metric used in link prediction is preferential attachment. *Preferential attachment* is an underlying organizing principle occurring in real-world networks, where nodes with a higher number of relationships are more likely to make new relationships. In the social network example, people with more friends are more likely to make new connections. They might be invited to more social events or be introduced more, due to having many friends. The preferential attachment model was first described by Barabási and Albert (1999).

Figure 10.9 shows two `Stream` nodes in the center with a relatively large node degree. The preferential attachment mechanism assumes streams that already share a significant audience with many other streams are more likely to form future connections. So following the preferential attachment principle, you could assume that the two central `Stream` nodes are likely to have a shared audience overlap, as indicated by the dotted line in figure 10.9.

To calculate the preferential attachment metric between the pair of nodes, you need to multiply their node degrees. Essentially, you take the node degree of the first node and multiply it by the node degree of the second node. When a pair of nodes has a high preferential attachment metric, the nodes are more likely to form a connection in the future.

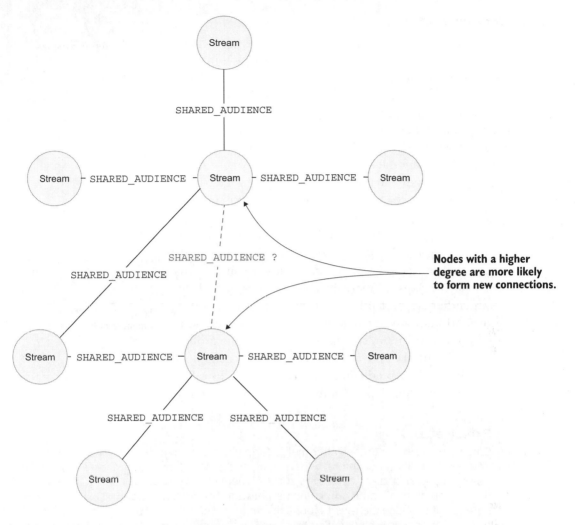

Figure 10.9 Nodes with higher degrees are more likely to form new connections.

Exercise 10.4

Calculate the preferential attachment metric for pairs of nodes in the train and test sets. Similar to network distance metric calculation, you start by matching the pairs of nodes connected with the TEST_TRAIN or NEGATIVE_TEST_TRAIN relationships. Next, you calculate the node degrees for both nodes. Make sure to count both incoming and outgoing relationships as the node degree and to only count the FEATURE_REL relationships. Finally, multiply the two node degrees and store the results under the preferentialAttachment property of relationships.

10.3.3 *Common neighbors*

The next metric you will calculate as a link prediction feature is the *common neighbors* metric. The intuition behind the common neighbors metric is simple. The more common neighbors two nodes have, the higher the chance is of a link forming in the future. In the context of social networks, the more mutual friends two people have, the greater the chance they will meet or be introduced in the future.

Remember, due to the relationship split, none of the pairs of nodes in the train or test set has a direct connection. However, many nodes might have several common friends, as shown in figure 10.10. Imagine that all the nodes in figure 10.10 represent Twitch streams. If stream A has an audience overlap with stream B and stream B overlaps with stream C, then there will likely be an audience overlap between stream A and C in the future. Additionally, the higher the number of common neighbors between two streams is, the higher the probability is of a future link. To use the common neighbor metric in the link prediction model, you need to calculate the number of common neighbors between all pairs of nodes in the train and test sets.

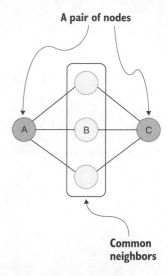

Figure 10.10   Common neighbors between a pair of nodes

> **Exercise 10.5**
>
> Calculate the common neighbor metric for pairs of nodes in the train and test sets. You start similarly to before by matching the pairs of nodes connected with the `TEST_TRAIN` or `NEGATIVE_TEST_TRAIN` relationships. Then, you need to count the distinct number of common neighbors between the matched pairs of nodes. Make sure to also include the results for pairs of nodes with no common neighbors by using the `OPTIONAL MATCH` clause. Finally, store the number of common neighbors between pairs of nodes under the `commonNeighbor` property of relationships.

10.3.4 *Adamic–Adar index*

The *Adamic–Adar index* is a link prediction metric first described by Adamic and Adar (2003). The idea behind the Adamic–Adar index is that the smaller the node degree common neighbors between a pair of nodes have, the more likely it is that they will form a connection in the future. Again, imagine you are dealing with a social network. A pair of people have one friend in common. If that common friend has 1,000 other friends, it is less likely they will introduce the particular pair of people than if they only had two friends in total.

In example A in figure 10.11, nodes A and B have two common neighbors or friends. The common friends are nodes C and D. Both nodes C and D have 1,000 friends in

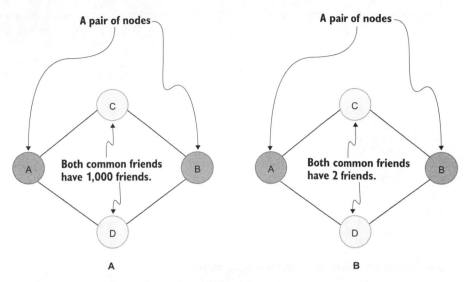

Figure 10.11   Intuition behind the Adamic–Adar index

total. Since common friends of nodes A and B have a broad group of friends themselves, it is less likely that either of the common friends will introduce nodes A and B.
On the other hand, in example B in figure 10.11, common friends of nodes A and B
have only two friends in total. Essentially, nodes C and D are only friends with nodes A
and B. Therefore, since the friend circle of common friends is much smaller, it is more
likely that, for example, nodes A and B are both invited to social events that nodes C or
D might host. Similar logic could be applied to the Twitch overlap network.

The Adamic–Adar index is calculated using the equation shown in figure 10.12.

$$A(x, y) = \sum_{u \in N(x) \cap N(y)} \frac{1}{log \mid N(u) \mid}$$

Where N(u) is the set of
nodes adjacent to u

Figure 10.12   Adamic–Adar index equation

Don't worry if you don't understand all the symbols in figure 10.12. The Adamic–Adar
index is defined as the sum of the inverse logarithmic node degree of common neighbors shared by a pair of nodes. The following are the main steps of the Adamic–Adar
index calculation:

1 Start by finding all the common neighbors of nodes x and y.
2 Calculate the node degree of all common neighbors.
3 Sum the inverse logarithm of node degrees of all common neighbors.

The following Cypher statement calculates the Adamic–Adar index between pairs of
nodes in the train and test sets.

> **Listing 10.6   Calculating the Adamic–Adar index between pairs of nodes in the train and test sets**

Identifies all the common neighbors of nodes s1 and s2

```
run_query("""
MATCH (s1:Stream)-[r:TEST_TRAIN|NEGATIVE_TEST_TRAIN]->(s2:Stream)
OPTIONAL MATCH (s1)-[:FEATURE_REL]-(neighbor)-[:FEATURE_REL]-(s2)
WITH r, collect(distinct neighbor) AS commonNeighbors      <—
UNWIND commonNeighbors AS cn
WITH r, count{ (cn)-[:FEATURE_REL]-() } AS neighborDegree  <—
WITH r, sum(1 / log(neighborDegree)) AS adamicAdar  <—
SET r.adamicAdar = adamicAdar;
""")
```

Stores the results as the relationship property

Calculates the sum of the inverse logarithmic degree

Calculates the node degree for each common neighbor, including both incoming and outgoing relationships

10.3.5 *Clustering coefficient of common neighbors*

The last link prediction you will calculate is the *clustering coefficient of common neighbors*. A clustering coefficient measures the connectedness of the neighbors of a particular node, with the values ranging from 0 to 1. A value of 0 indicates the neighboring nodes have no connections with each other. On the other hand, a value of 1 indicates the network of neighbors forms a complete graph, where all the neighbors are connected.

The clustering coefficient of common neighbors is a link prediction variant, where you only calculate how connected the common neighbors of a particular pair of nodes are. Researchers have shown (Wu et al., 2015) that the clustering coefficient of common neighbors can improve the accuracy of link prediction models.

To calculate the local clustering coefficient of common neighbors between a pair of nodes, you need to identify the number of common neighbors as well as the number of links between common neighbors. Once you have those numbers, you only need to divide the number of existing links between neighbors by the potential number of connections. The number of potential connections between neighbors equals the number of links if all neighbors are connected. The following Cypher statement calculates the clustering coefficient of common neighbors and stores the results as a relationship property.

> **Listing 10.7   Calculating the clustering coefficient of common neighbors between pairs of nodes in the train and test sets**

Identifies and counts the number of common neighbors between a pair of nodes

```
run_query("""
MATCH (s1:Stream)-[r:TEST_TRAIN|NEGATIVE_TEST_TRAIN]->(s2:Stream)
OPTIONAL MATCH (s1)-[:FEATURE_REL]-(neighbor)-[:FEATURE_REL]-(s2)
WITH r, collect(distinct neighbor) AS commonNeighbors,
     count(distinct neighbor) AS commonNeighborCount      <—
```

```
OPTIONAL MATCH (x)-[cr:FEATURE_REL]->(y)
WHERE x IN commonNeighbors AND y IN commonNeighbors
WITH r, commonNeighborCount, count(cr) AS commonNeighborRels
WITH r, CASE WHEN commonNeighborCount < 2 THEN 0 ELSE
    toFloat(commonNeighborRels) / (commonNeighborCount *
                    (commonNeighborCount - 1) / 2) END as clusteringCoefficient
SET r.clusteringCoefficient = clusteringCoefficient
""")
```

◁ — **Identifies all existing relationships between common neighbors**

Calculates the clustering coefficient by dividing the number of existing relationships by the number of potential relationships

◁ **Stores the results as a relationship property**

You might have noticed that you treat relationships in the feature set as undirected at query time throughout the example in this section. The Cypher statement in listing 10.7 is no different. At first, you ignore the relationship direction when identifying common neighbors. Since the relationships are treated as undirected, the number of potential connections is also 50% fewer than if you had a directed network. Therefore, the number of potential relationships in the Cypher statement is divided by 2 in the second-last line of listing 10.7.

10.4 Link prediction classification model

The only thing left to do is to train and evaluate a link prediction model. *Link prediction* is a binary classification problem where you predict whether a link is likely to form in the future. You will train a random forest classification model to solve the link prediction task based on the features you calculated for the train and test sets of relationships. The random forest classification model is used here because it is relatively robust to feature scaling and collinearity issues. However, you could have chosen other classification models, like the logistic regression or support vector machine.

Use the following Cypher statement to retrieve link prediction features and output from the database.

Listing 10.8   Retrieving link prediction features and class output

```
data = run_query("""
MATCH (s1)-[r:TEST_TRAIN|NEGATIVE_TEST_TRAIN]->(s2)
WITH r.networkDistance AS networkDistance,
    r.preferentialAttachment AS preferentialAttachment,
    r.commonNeighbor AS commonNeighbor,
    r.adamicAdar AS adamicAdar,
    r.clusteringCoefficient AS clusteringCoefficient,
    CASE WHEN r:TEST_TRAIN THEN 1 ELSE 0 END as output
RETURN networkDistance, preferentialAttachment, commonNeighbor,
    adamicAdar, clusteringCoefficient, output
""")
```

The Cypher statement in listing 10.8 retrieves the features stored on the TEST_TRAIN and NEGATIVE_TEST_TRAIN relationships. The last column in the results of listing 10.8

is the `output` column, which differentiates between positive and negative classification examples. Positive examples are tagged with the `TEST_TRAIN` relationship type and are represented with a value of 1, while the negative examples are marked with `NEGA-TIVE_TEST_TRAIN` and are represented as 0.

Examining the distribution of relevant features is advisable, as with any other machine learning task. The pandas dataframe has a `describe()` method that calculates the distributions of values in columns.

Listing 10.9   Defining the connection to Neo4j

```
data.describe()
```

Figure 10.13 shows the distribution of link prediction features. Interestingly, the network distance feature ranges from 2 to 4; however, it is mainly 2, as the mean network distance is barely 2.055. Moreover, it might not be the most predictable feature in this example, due to its low variance. The preferential attachment has a wide range, from 0 to nearly 3,000,000. Remember, the preferential attachment is calculated by multiplying the degrees of both nodes in the pair. The only way a preferential attachment can be 0 is if some nodes have zero connections. While all nodes have relationships in the original network, that might not be so in the feature set, where some connections are missing, due to the data split. Interestingly, the clustering coefficient is relatively high, on average.

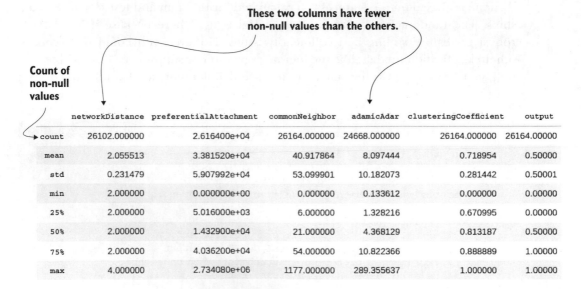

	networkDistance	preferentialAttachment	commonNeighbor	adamicAdar	clusteringCoefficient	output
count	26102.000000	2.616400e+04	26164.000000	24668.000000	26164.000000	26164.00000
mean	2.055513	3.381520e+04	40.917864	8.097444	0.718954	0.50000
std	0.231479	5.907992e+04	53.099901	10.182073	0.281442	0.50001
min	2.000000	0.000000e+00	0.000000	0.133612	0.000000	0.00000
25%	2.000000	5.016000e+03	6.000000	1.328216	0.670995	0.00000
50%	2.000000	1.432900e+04	21.000000	4.368129	0.813187	0.50000
75%	2.000000	4.036200e+04	54.000000	10.822366	0.888889	1.00000
max	4.000000	2.734080e+06	1177.000000	289.355637	1.000000	1.00000

Count of non-null values

These two columns have fewer non-null values than the others.

Figure 10.13   Distribution of link prediction features

10.4.1 Missing values

In total, there are 26,164 training and test samples. However, figure 10.13 also indicates that some values are missing in the `networkDistance` and `adamicAdar` columns. For example, there are only 26,102 non-null values under the `networkDistance` feature. The network distance is undefined because the two nodes are not in the same component. Therefore, no path exists between the two. As mentioned, isolated nodes in the network might be the leading cause of missing network distance values. You can fill in the missing values with a maximum distance value of 4. Remember, the higher the network distance is between a pair of nodes, the less likely a link will be formed between them, at least in theory. So if a pair of nodes is not in the same component, which is a null network distance in this example, you want to choose a value representing a significant network distance to fill in missing values. Therefore, you may decide to pick the maximum value of the network distance (4) in the dataset to fill in the missing values.

Another column with missing values is `adamicAdar`, which might happen when a pair of nodes have no common neighbors. You can fill in the missing values of the `adamicAdar` column with a mean Adamic–Adar value of about 8.

Listing 10.10 Filling in the missing values

```
data['networkDistance'].fillna(4, inplace=True)
data['adamicAdar'].fillna(8.097444, inplace=True)
```

10.4.2 Training the model

With all the preprocessing steps done, you can go ahead and train the link prediction model. The `data` dataframe contains both the train and test sets of relationships. Therefore, you will first use the `train_test_split` from the scikit-learn library to split the test and train sets. You will use 80% of the samples as training examples and the remaining 20% to evaluate the model. If you were planning to perform any hyperparameter optimization of the classification model, you could also produce a validation set. However, optimizing the classification model itself is beyond the scope of this book, so you will skip creating a validation set. After the dataset split, you will feed the training samples into the random forest model, which will learn to predict whether a link is probable in the future.

Listing 10.11 Splitting the train and test sets and training the link prediction model

```
from sklearn.model_selection import train_test_split
from sklearn.ensemble import RandomForestClassifier

X = data.drop("output", axis=1)
y = data["output"].to_list()

X_train, X_test, y_train, y_test = train_test_split(
  X, y, test_size=0.2, random_state=0)
```

```
rfc = RandomForestClassifier()
rfc.fit(X_train, y_train)
```

The code in listing 10.11 starts by defining the feature and target columns. The output column is used as the target, while all the other columns are used as model features. Next, you perform a test/train split with the train_test_split function. Finally, you instantiate a random forest model and learn it based on the training samples.

10.4.3 *Evaluating the model*

As with all machine learning tasks, you should evaluate the performance of your link prediction model using the test set. In the following listing, you will generate a classification report using a built-in scikit-learn function.

Listing 10.12   Generating the classification report

```
from sklearn.metrics import classification_report

y_pred = rfc.predict(X_test)
print(classification_report(y_test, y_pred))
```

The code in listing 10.12 produces the classification report shown in figure 10.14, which can be used to evaluate the model.

	precision	recall	f1-score	support
0	0.91	0.93	0.92	2578
1	0.93	0.91	0.92	2655
accuracy			0.92	5233
macro avg	0.92	0.92	0.92	5233
weighted avg	0.92	0.92	0.92	5233

Figure 10.14   Classification report of the link prediction model

Congratulations! You have trained a link prediction model with an accuracy of 92%. The accuracy is a good metric, as the ratio between negative and positive samples is even.

Finally, you can evaluate the feature importance of the trained link prediction model. The following code will produce an ordered dataframe with the features ordered by their importance, descending.

Listing 10.13   Evaluating feature importance

```
def feature_importance(columns, classifier):
    features = list(zip(columns, classifier.feature_importances_))
    sorted_features = sorted(features, key = lambda x: x[1]*-1)

    keys = [value[0] for value in sorted_features]
    values = [value[1] for value in sorted_features]
    return pd.DataFrame(data={'feature': keys, 'value': values})

feature_importance(X.columns, rfc)
```

Table figure 10.15 shows that the network distance is the least important feature, by a wide margin. That was somewhat expected, due to the low variance of the network distance feature. Interestingly, the most relevant feature is the Adamic–Adar index, followed by the common neighbor and preferential attachment features. Note that you might get slightly different results due to the random dataset split used at the beginning of this chapter.

	feature	value
0	adamicAdar	0.348872
1	commonNeighbor	0.266738
2	preferentialAttachment	0.256368
3	clusteringCoefficient	0.123113
4	networkDistance	0.004909

Figure 10.15   Feature importance

10.5   Solutions to exercises

The solution to exercise 10.1 is as follows.

Listing 10.14   Counting the number of relationships

```
run_query("""
MATCH (n)-[:SHARED_AUDIENCE]->()
RETURN count(*) AS result
""")
```

The solution to exercise 10.2 is as follows.

Listing 10.15   Constructing the positive example for the test and train sets

```
# Create test/train rel
# Take the remaining 10%
train_test_size = run_query("""
MATCH (s1)-[:SHARED_AUDIENCE]->(s2)
WHERE NOT EXISTS {(s1)-[:FEATURE_REL]->(s2)}
MERGE (s1)-[r:TEST_TRAIN]->(s2)
RETURN count(r) AS result;
""")
print(train_test_size)
```

The solution to exercise 10.3 is as follows.

Listing 10.16   Constructing the negative example for the test and train sets

```
# Create negative test/train pairs
run_query("""
MATCH (s1:Stream),(s2:Stream)
```

```
WHERE NOT EXISTS {(s1)-[:SHARED_AUDIENCE]-(s2)}
      AND s1 < s2
      AND rand() > 0.9
WITH s1,s2
LIMIT 13082
MERGE (s1)-[:NEGATIVE_TEST_TRAIN]->(s2);
""")
```

The solution to exercise 10.4 is as follows.

Listing 10.17   Calculating the preferential attachment feature for pairs of nodes in the train and test sets

```
run_query("""
MATCH (s1:Stream)-[r:TEST_TRAIN|NEGATIVE_TEST_TRAIN]->(s2)
WITH r, count{ (s1)-[:FEATURE_REL]-() } *
        count{ (s2)-[:FEATURE_REL]-() } AS preferentialAttachment
SET r.preferentialAttachment = preferentialAttachment
""")
```

The solution to exercise 10.5 is as follows.

Listing 10.18   Calculating the common neighbors feature for pairs of nodes in the train and test sets

```
run_query("""
MATCH (s1:Stream)-[r:TEST_TRAIN|NEGATIVE_TEST_TRAIN]->(s2)
OPTIONAL MATCH (s1)-[:FEATURE_REL]-(neighbor)-[:FEATURE_REL]-(s2)
WITH r, count(distinct neighbor) AS commonNeighbor
SET r.commonNeighbor = commonNeighbor
""")
```

Summary

- Link prediction is a task of predicting future or missing links in the network.
- Link prediction models are frequently used in recommender systems.
- Link prediction features are designed to encode similarity or distance between pairs of nodes.
- Link prediction features can be constructed by aggregating node properties, evaluating network distance, or examining local or global neighborhood overlap.
- If you use transductive node embeddings in link prediction workflows, you cannot generate node embeddings for new unseen nodes during training and, therefore, cannot predict future links for nodes that weren't present during the training.
- Feature leakage occurs when a feature contains the same or comparable information as the output variable. You could run into leakage problems if you used the same relationships to generate network features as well as train and evaluate a classification model. Therefore, it is necessary to split the dataset into feature, train, and test sets. Optionally, you can introduce a validation set if you plan to perform any hyperparameter optimization.

- The feature set is used to calculate network features, while the test and train sets provide classification samples to train and evaluate a model. Optionally, you can also introduce a validation set if you plan to implement any hyperparameter optimization techniques.
- Using all the negative examples during training would lead to a considerable class imbalance. Therefore, it is common to subsample the negative examples and use about the same number of positive and negative samples.
- The network distance encodes how close a pair of nodes are in the network. The theory states that the closer a pair of nodes is, the more likely it is they will form a future link.
- The preferential attachment principle nicely captures how most real-world networks evolve. The underlying idea is that the rich get richer. Therefore, nodes with a higher number of existing links are more likely to form new links in the future.
- Local neighborhood overlap features can be as simple as the number of common neighbors two nodes have or as advanced as the Adamic–Adar index, which assumes the smaller degree the common neighbors between a pair of nodes have, the more likely the pair is to form a connection in the future.

Knowledge
graph completion

- Introducing heterogeneous graphs
- Explaining knowledge graph embeddings
- Describing knowledge graph completion workflow
- Examining knowledge graph completion results

Chapter 10 was an introduction to link prediction and completion techniques. The difference between link prediction and completion is that the first is a workflow to predict future links, while the latter deals with predicting missing links. However, in practice, link prediction and completion workflows are very similar. What wasn't explicitly mentioned is that the link prediction features used in chapter 10 do not differentiate between various node or relationship types. For example, the number of common neighbors does not differentiate between different relationship or node types. Therefore, the link prediction features used in chapter 10 work best with monopartite or *homogeneous* graphs. A monopartite or homogenous graph consists of a single node and relationship type. The visualization in figure 11.1 depicts a homogeneous graph that consists of a single node type `Stream` and a single relationship type `SHARED_AUDIENCE`.

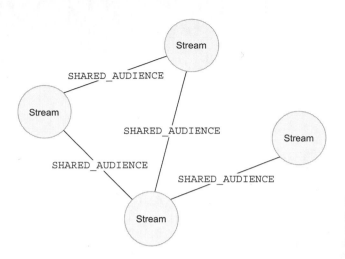

Figure 11.1 Homogeneous graph consisting of `Stream` **nodes and** `SHARED_AUDIENCE` **relationships**

Suppose you work at a large pharmaceutical company as a data scientist. You have been tasked with predicting additional use cases for existing drugs the company produces. The strategy of identifying new use cases for existing approved drugs is called *drug repurposing*. The oldest example of drug repurposing is for acetylsalicylic acid, better known as *aspirin*. It was initially used in 1899 as an analgesic to relieve pain. Later, it was repurposed to be used as an antiplatelet aggregation drug. An antiplatelet drug decreases the ability of blood clots to form (Vane, 1971). Aspirin was later repurposed again, as it has been shown that daily administration of aspirin can help prevent the development of cancers, particularly colorectal cancer (Rüschoff et al., 1998; Rothwell et al., 2011). Despite the potential of drug repurposing, it's crucial to remember it can be a prolonged process, taking many years to get the drug accepted due to costly and time-consuming clinical trials, and it's not as simple as a data scientist predicting a new connection and instantly moving the product to production.

It is very likely that, as a data scientist, you don't have a biomedical background and, therefore, cannot manually pick new potential use cases based on domain expertise. What are your options? You can model known connections between drugs and diseases as a bipartite graph.

Figure 11.2 shows a bipartite network of approved drugs and diseases. The relationships indicate existing applications of drugs for treating conditions. For example, aspirin can be used to treat headaches, Kawasaki disease, coronary artery disease, and hypertension.

You could create a drug repurposing workflow by first determining similar drugs. The similarity between drugs is frequently calculated based on their chemical structure and the overlap of diseases they treat (Luo et al., 2016). Once similar drugs have been identified, you can use that information to predict or recommend new applications for existing drugs.

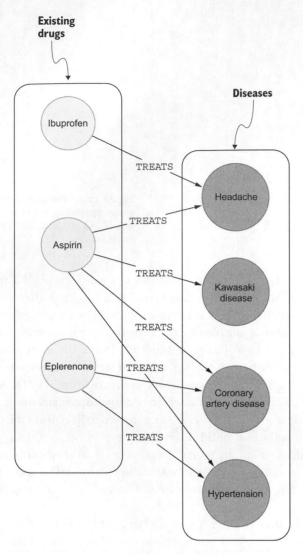

Figure 11.2   Bipartite network of existing drugs and known treatments

The drug repurposing workflow shown in figure 11.3 has two steps:

1   Identifying similar relationships
2   Recommending new drug applications based on drug similarity

The first step is to identify similar drugs. For this exercise, one idea could be that the more common diseases are that two drugs treat, the higher the drug similarity between the two will be. There are several approaches you could take to infer the similarity relationship. You could use the Jaccard similarity coefficient, described in chapter 7, to calculate the drug similarity. Another idea would be to use a node embedding model like node2vec, presented in chapter 9, to calculate node embeddings and compare

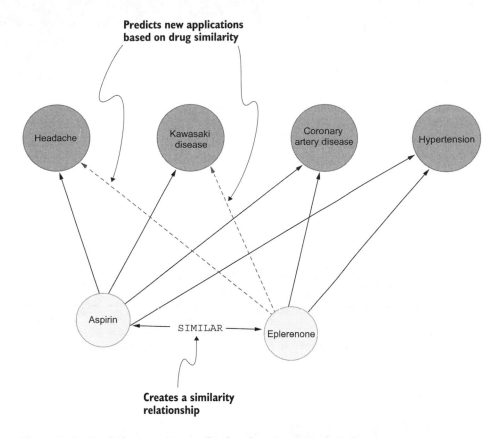

Figure 11.3 Predicting new drug applications based on drug similarity

drugs using the cosine similarity of node embeddings. Finally, you could also borrow some of the link prediction features described in chapter 10 to calculate drug similarity. Using any of the mentioned approaches, you would create a similarity relationship with some sort of score between pairs of drugs.

In the second step, you could recommend new drug applications based on the calculated similarity relationships. In the example in figure 11.3, aspirin and eplerenone are tagged as similar drugs. Therefore, you could predict potential applications for eplerenone by examining which conditions drugs like aspirin treat. In this example, you might predict that eplerenone potentially could be used to treat Kawasaki disease and headaches.

NOTE Remember, the link prediction workflow only suggests the priority of evaluating new applications, while the domain experts then decide and potentially conduct clinical trials to determine new drug applications.

The described drug repurposing workflow is valid; however, with this approach, you would overlook a lot of existing biomedical knowledge. There is a lot of data about genes, biological processes, anatomy, and other biomedical information you could incorporate into your graph and, consequently, into drug repurposing analysis.

Medical researchers have accrued a lot of knowledge over the years. There are many official medical databases you can borrow information from to construct a biomedical graph. For example, the graph schema in figure 11.4 contains several types of nodes, spanning from drugs to diseases to genes to side effects and many others. Additionally, there are several types of relationships present. Sometimes, multiple types of relationships are available between particular types of nodes. In figure 11.4, you can observe that a drug can either upregulate or downregulate a gene.

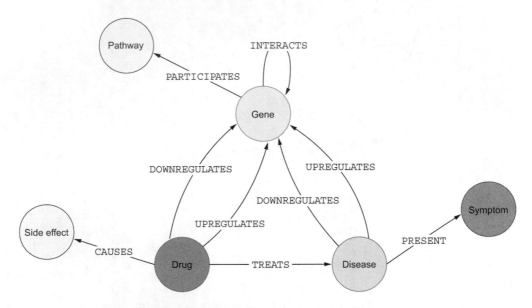

Figure 11.4   Example schema of a complex biomedical graph

A complex biomedical graph is an example of a *heterogeneous graph*, where multiple node and relationship types are present. In a drug repurposing workflow, you could use all the available information in a biomedical graph to predict new TREATS relationships. However, since the graph schema is more complicated, it requires a different approach to feature engineering than those we've discussed. If you were inclined to perform a manual feature engineering workflow like the one described in chapter 10, you would need to find a way to encode various node and relationship types. For example, the number of common neighbors used in chapter 10 does not differentiate between various node and relationship types. A disease can upregulate or downregulate a gene, and you want to somehow encode them differently. Therefore, manual feature engineering would likely be tedious and labor intensive, while requiring domain expertise. While node embedding algorithms like the node2vec algorithm remove the need for manual feature engineering, they are not designed to differentiate between various node and relationship types. Luckily, you are not the first person to run into this problem. The solution to avoid manual feature engineering while having a model that differentiates between various node and relationship types is to use *knowledge graph embedding* models. Unlike node embedding models, knowledge graph embedding models encode nodes as well as relationships in the embedding space. The added benefit of encoding relationships in the embedding space is that the embedding model can learn to differentiate between different relationship types.

11.1 Knowledge graph embedding model

As mentioned, the key difference between node embeddings and knowledge graph embedding models is that the latter embeds relationships as well as nodes. Before delving into theory, you need to familiarize yourself with knowledge graph embedding terminology.

11.1.1 Triple

Knowledge graph embedding models use *triples* to describe graphs. A triple consists of two nodes, known as a *head* (h) and *tail* (t), and a labeled-directed relationship (r).

Figure 11.5 shows a visualization of a sample graph on the left side and a triple representation of the same graph on the right. A triple consists of two nodes, a head (h) and tail (t), and a directed labeled relationship (r). The head node is the source or start node of the relationship, while the target or end node is marked as the tail node. In the example in figure 11.5, Ana is considered the head, while Paris is the tail node. The idea behind knowledge graph embeddings is to support heterogeneous graphs and differentiate between various types of relationships. Therefore, the relation label in a triple defines its type. The relation label in figure 11.5 is LIVES_IN.

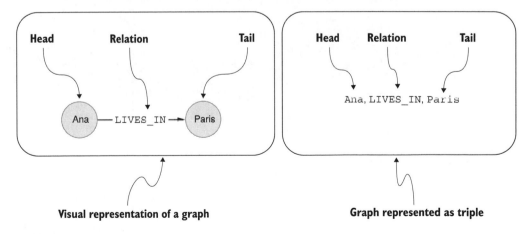

Figure 11.5   Triple representation

Exercise 11.1

Construct two triples to define your location. The first triple should contain information about the city you live in, while the second triple should connect your city to the country it belongs to. Choose the relation labels you find the most appropriate.

NOTE   The triple is defined to differentiate between various relationship types or labels. However, there is no explicit definition of node labels. Therefore, the knowledge graph embedding models do not explicitly differentiate between different node types.

11.1.2   *TransE*

TransE (Bordes et al., 2013) is one of the earliest and most intuitive knowledge graph embedding models. The objective of the TransE method is to calculate low-dimensional vector representations, also known as *embeddings*, for all the nodes and relationships in the graph. The TransE method is frequently used to demonstrate knowledge graph embeddings, as it is simple to illustrate and relatively cheap to calculate.

Figure 11.6 shows the concept of encoding nodes and relationships in the embedding space. The key idea behind the TransE method is to encode nodes and relationships in the embedding space so that the embedding of the head plus relation should be close to the tail. In figure 11.6, you can observe that the embedding of the head node plus the embedding of the relationship is precisely equal to the embedding of the tail node.

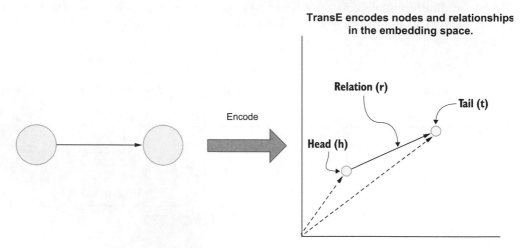

Figure 11.6   TransE encoding intuition

The TransE method tries to produce embeddings so that for every triple in the training set, it minimizes the distance between the sum of the head and the relationship to the tail embedding. This optimization score can be written as h + r ≈ t, as shown in figure 11.7. On the other hand, if a relationship between the head and tail node does not exist, then the sum of head and relation embedding should not be close to the tail (h + r != t). You can read more about the mathematical implementation in the original article (Bordes et al., 2013).

h + r ≈ t if relation is present
h + r ≠ t if relation is not present   **Figure 11.7   TransE optimization metric**

11.1.3 TransE limitations

While TransE implementation is simple and intuitive, it has some drawbacks. There are three categories of relationships you will use to evaluate the TransE method.

The first category of relationships is the *symmetric* relations. The triple data structure does not allow undirected relationships; however, a category of relationships could be treated as undirected. The undirected relationships are referred to as *symmetric* within the field of knowledge graph embedding models. Some example triple symmetric relationships are

```
Tomaž, SIBLING, Blaž
Blaž, SIBLING, Tomaž
```

If Tomaž is a sibling of Blaž, then Blaž is also a sibling of Tomaž. There is no way around this simple fact. The question is, can TransE encode symmetric relationships?

The TransE method produces a vector representation for each relationship type. Therefore, the SIBLING vector representation in figure 11.8 has the same direction in both instances. The problem is that a vector representation of the same relationship type cannot point in the opposite direction. One SIBLING vector points from the head to the tail node. However, the second SIBLING vector starts from the second node and has the same direction as the first SIBLING vector. Therefore, the second SIBLING vector does not and cannot point back to the first node. Consequently, TransE does not support symmetric relationships from a theoretical point of view.

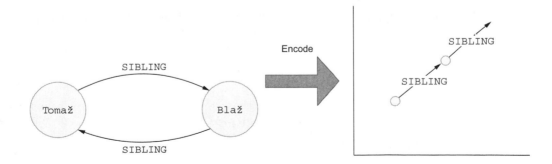

Figure 11.8   Encoding symmetric relationships with TransE

The second category of relationships you will evaluate is the *composition* relations. One example of the composition relation is the following:

```
John, MOTHER, Alicia
Alicia, SPOUSE, Michael
John, FATHER, Michael
```

A composition relationship can be constructed by combining two or more relationships. In the example in figure 11.9, the FATHER relationship can be composed by adding the MOTHER and SPOUSE relationships. You can observe that one can fit the relationship vectors to fit this graph pattern. Therefore, the TransE method supports composite relations.

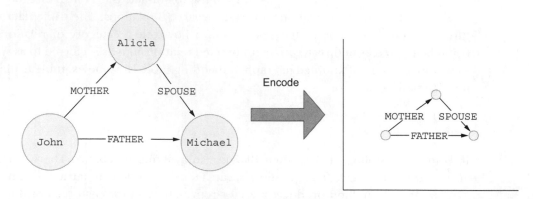

Figure 11.9   Encoding composition relationships with TransE

The last category is the *1-to-N* relationships. Essentially, this scenario happens when a node has the same relationship to multiple other nodes. Some examples of 1-to-N relations are

```
Surya, FRIEND, Rajiv
Surya, FRIEND, Jane
```

The only way TransE could encode that Surya is friends with both Jane and Rajiv is if the vector representation of Jane and Rajiv is equal. Having the identical vector representation for Jane and Rajiv does not make sense, as they are different entities in the graph and, therefore, should have different embeddings. The only other solution would be that the FRIEND relationship vector would have different directions, as shown in figure 11.10. However, the TransE method implements only a single vector representation for a given relationship type. Consequently, the TransE method does not support 1-to-N relationships.

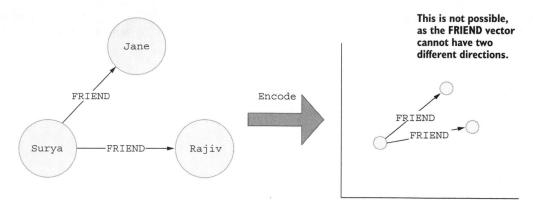

Figure 11.10   Encoding 1-to-N relationships with TransE

11.2   *Knowledge graph completion*

Now that you have gained a theoretical background in knowledge graph embeddings, you can continue with your task of predicting new applications for existing drugs. Imagine you work at a large pharmaceutical company that produces aspirin. Aspirin is a mass-produced drug, and therefore, a new application could rake in a lot of revenue. The idea is to use existing biomedical knowledge to predict new applications. You have determined that the best course of action would be to apply *knowledge graph completion* techniques to find new potential drug applications, also known as *drug repurposing*. Knowledge graph completion can be thought of as multiclass link prediction, where you predict new links and their types. You will train a knowledge graph embedding model to encode nodes and relationships in the biomedical graph and then use those embeddings to identify new potential applications for aspirin.

The drug repurposing workflow is shown in figure 11.11. The basis of the whole flow is a rich and complex biomedical knowledge graph that contains existing drugs; their treatments; and other biomedical entities, like genes and pathways. As you are working for a large company, other great people at the company have already mapped and constructed the required biomedical graph. Next, you need to feed the biomedical graph into a knowledge graph embedding model. Since you won't need to perform any graph transformations or manipulations, you can skip using a graph database altogether. While multiple Python libraries feature knowledge graph embedding models, I prefer *PyKEEN* (Ali et al., 2021) due to its simplicity and easy-to-use interface. Additionally, PyKEEN implements more than 40 different knowledge graph embedding models along with out-of-the-box support for hyperparameter optimization. Finally, you will use a built-in PyKEEN method to predict new applications for aspirin. You need to install the PyKEEN and pandas libraries, as shown in listing 11.11, to follow along with the code examples.

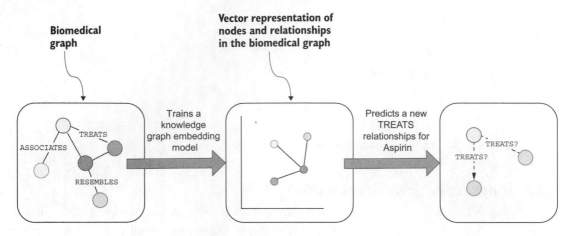

Figure 11.11   Drug repurposing workflow

Listing 11.1   Installing PyKEEN

```
pip install pykeen==1.9.0 pandas
```

All the code is available as a Jupyter notebook (http://mng.bz/zXNQ).

11.2.1   Hetionet

Your coworkers have prepared a subset of the Hetionet dataset (Himmelstein et al., 2017) to use. The original Hetionet dataset contains 47,031 nodes (11 types) and 2,250,197 relationships (24 types).

The graph schema of the Hetionet dataset is presented in figure 11.12. The graph contains various entities, like genes, pathways, compounds, and diseases. Additionally, there are 24 different types of relationships present in the graph. Explaining all the medical terminology behind medical entities and their relationships could take a whole book. The most important relationship for a drug repurposing workflow is the TREATS relationship that starts from the Compound node and ends at the Disease node. Essentially, the TREATS relationship encapsulates existing approved drug treatments. You will use knowledge graph completion techniques to predict new TREATS relationships originating from the aspirin or acetylsalicylic acid node.

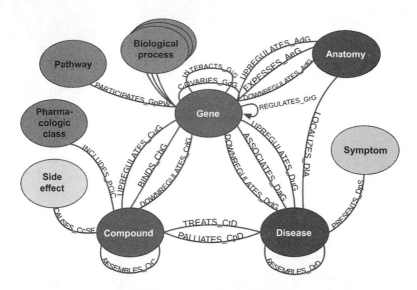

Figure 11.12 Hetionet schema (Source: Himmelstein et al. Licensed under CC BY 4.0)

You will use a subset of the Hetionet dataset in this example. The subset has the schema shown in figure 11.13.

Figure 11.13 presents a subset of the Hetionet dataset you will use in the drug repurposing workflow. The given subset contains 22,634 nodes (3 types) and 561,716 relationships (12 types). The graph contains existing approved drug treatments that can be found under the TREATS relationship, along with some additional information about how compounds and diseases interact with genes. The genes can also interact with other genes. The subset of the Hetionet dataset is available on GitHub (http://mng.bz/ddww) and has the structure shown in table 11.1.

Table 11.1 Structure of the Hetionet relationship CSV file

source_name	source_label	target_name	target_label	type
SERPINF2	Gene	KLK13	Gene	interacts
SERPINF2	Gene	SSR1	Gene	interacts
SERPINF2	Gene	TGM2	Gene	interacts
SERPINF2	Gene	UBC	Gene	interacts
SERPINF2	Gene	SERPINB12	Gene	interacts

You will use the pandas library to load the CSV file from GitHub, shown in listing 11.13, which first imports the pandas library. Next, it uses the built-in `read_csv` method to load the Hetionet dataset from GitHub.

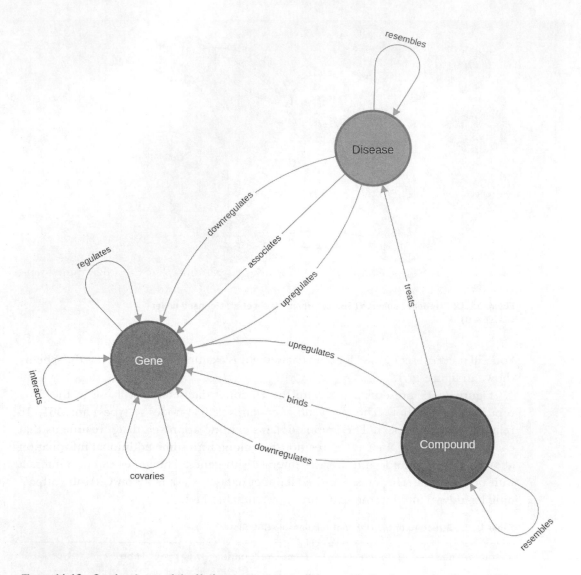

Figure 11.13   Graph schema of the Hetionet subset that will be used in the drug repurposing workflow

Listing 11.2   Loading the Hetionet subset as a pandas dataframe

```
import pandas as pd

data = pd.read_csv(
    "https://bit.ly/3X2qp1r"
)
```

11.2.2 Dataset split

As with all machine learning workflows, you need to perform a test-train dataset split. You can feed a graph structure to PyKEEN with a list of triples, as shown in the following listing. Remember, the triple data object consists of head, label, and tail elements.

Listing 11.3   Inputting triples to PyKEEN

```
from pykeen.triples import TriplesFactory

tf = TriplesFactory.from_labeled_triples(
    data[["source_name", "type", "target_name"]].values,
)
```

The `TriplesFactory` is a PyKEEN class designed to store triples used for training and evaluating the model. The code in listing 11.3 uses the `from_labeled_triples` method to input a list of triples from the pandas dataframe. The `data` dataframe contains additional information about node labels, which you need to filter out. Therefore, the code in listing 11.3 specifies using columns `source_name`, `type`, and `target_name` as triples. Now that the triples are loaded into PyKEEN, you can perform a dataset split with the following code.

Listing 11.4   Splitting the dataset into train, test, and validation sets

```
training, testing, validation = tf.split([0.8, 0.1, 0.1], random_state=0)
```

The dataset split is performed with the `split` method, as demonstrated in listing 11.4. While the primary goal is to predict new `treats` relationships, the dataset, including all data splits, contains all available relationships, such as `interacts`, `upregulates`, and more, to provide as much relevant information to the model as possible. The method takes in an array of three values as a parameter that defines the ratio of the training, testing, and validation sets. The first value defines the ratio of the training set, the second value represents the testing set ratio, and the final number specifies the size of the validation set. The third value can be omitted, as it can be calculated from the first two.

11.2.3 Train a PairRE model

While the TransE model is great for an introduction to knowledge graph embedding models, it has its limitations. For example, a single drug can be used to treat multiple diseases. However, as mentioned in the TransE introduction, the TransE method cannot encode 1-to-N relationships, making it a lousy model for biomedical knowledge graphs. Therefore, you will use a later and better model called *PairRE* (Chao et al., 2020). PairRE is capable of encoding symmetry, composition, and 1-to-N relationships, which makes it a great model to use for biomedical knowledge graphs. I encourage you to read the article at https://arxiv.org/abs/2011.03798 if you are interested in details of the mathematical implementation. The following code trains the PairRE model based on the subset of the Hetionet dataset you were provided.

Listing 11.5   Training a PairRE model

```
from pykeen.pipeline import pipeline

result = pipeline(
    training=training,
    testing=testing,
    validation=validation,
    model="PairRE",              ← Specifies the PairRE model
    stopper="early",             ← Defines the stopping strategy
    epochs=100,
    random_seed=0,               ← The random seed is set for reproducibility.
)
```

The PairRE model can be trained with a single function, as shown in listing 11.5. The training, testing, and validation sets are loaded via separate arguments. You can select the model with the `model` argument; there are more than 40 models you can pick from. Check the documentation (http://mng.bz/rj2y) for a complete list of available models. The `early` value for the stopper argument evaluates the model every 10 epochs by default. Using the stopper option with the `early` value, the training pipeline stops the training if the model accuracy does not improve with additional epochs. Finally, the `random_seed` parameter is used to ensure result reproducibility. The complete list of available pipeline parameters is available in the official documentation (http://mng.bz/0K86).

> **NOTE**   The training can be performed on either CPU or GPU devices. However, the training will be faster if you have a GPU device available. If you don't have a local GPU available, you can always try out free cloud environments, like the Google Colab.

11.2.4 Drug application predictions

With the PairRE model trained, you can predict new applications for acetylsalicylic acid, better known as aspirin. The PyKEEN library offers a `predict_target` function, which allows you to input the head and relation of a triple and output the predictions for the tail node. In your example, you input `acetylsalicylic acid` as the head and `treats` as the relation element, as shown in the following listing. The output of the most probable `tail` nodes is given in a pandas dataframe structure.

Listing 11.6   Predicting new use cases for acetylsalicylic acid

```
from pykeen.predict import predict_target

pred = predict_target(
    result.model,
    head="Acetylsalicylic acid",
```

```
      relation="treats",
      triples_factory=result.training,
).df
pred_filtered = pred.filter_triples(result.training)
print(pred_filtered.head())
```

Table 11.2 shows the resulting predicted use cases.

Table 11.2   The top five predictions for acetylsalicylic acid

tail_id	tail_label	score
19,912	Systemic lupus erythematosus	·9.228726
19,827	Breast cancer	·9.510363
19,913	Systemic scleroderma	·9.543921
19,887	Pancreatic cancer	·9.711681
19,919	Type 1 diabetes mellitus	·9.731101

Predictions with a `score` value closer to zero are more probable. Your model predicted that aspirin potentially could be used to treat systemic lupus erythematosus, systemic scleroderma, and some forms of cancer. These predictions can be used to recommend a clinical trial for a particular drug use case. The clinical trials must be carefully planned, as they take a long time and are incredibly costly (Schlander et al., 2021). Therefore, it is essential to produce as accurate recommendations as possible, as the cost of clinical trials can reach more than a billion dollars.

> **Exercise 11.2**
> Predict potential new applications for `Caffeine` with the `predict_target` function.

11.2.5 *Explaining predictions*

After the predictions have been made, you can search the medical literature for supporting or invalidating research. Again, the importance of including a domain expert in the process cannot be overstated, as they play a critical role in interpreting both the results and relevant medical literature. For example, if you search for a combination of aspirin and pancreatic cancer, you can find some articles that might validate your predictions (Sun et al., 2019). Given that the Hetionet article was published in 2017, it probably does not contain new medical information from 2019. Hetionet is an aging resource that was restricted to fewer than 200 diseases. In practice, pharmaceutical and other companies use various text-mining systems deployed at scale to extract knowledge from various medical research articles and trials to keep their biomedical graphs updated with all the latest available information (Bachman et al., 2022).

Having supporting evidence for your predictions shows that the method of using knowledge graph embedding models for knowledge graph completion can yield great results. Suppose you found no supporting literature for your predictions. In that case, you could present existing biomedical connections to domain experts and let them decide whether they hold any merit. Even though you didn't need a graph database for the drug repurposing workflow, it would still be great for explaining predictions. Luckily, your coworkers at the large pharmaceutical company have you covered, or in reality, the authors of the Hetionet have made it available through a read-only Neo4j Browser interface. The Hetionet browser interface is available at https://neo4j.het .io/browser/.

The following Cypher query will visualize the first 25 paths between acetylsalicylic acid and pancreatic cancer that are up to three hops away.

Listing 11.7   Predicting new potential use cases for acetylsalicylic acid

```
MATCH (c:Compound {name:"Acetylsalicylic acid"}),
      (d:Disease {name:"pancreatic cancer"})
MATCH p=(c)-[* ..3]-(d)
RETURN p LIMIT 25
```

The Cypher statement in listing 11.7 produces the visualization in figure 11.14. On the left side of the figure, you will see `acetylsalicylic acid`, while `prostate cancer` is on the right. Acetylsalicylic acid can be used to palliate osteoarthritis and gout. Interestingly, osteoarthritis associates with genes similar to those of prostate cancer. In any case, a domain expert can evaluate existing connections and make up their own mind. There are 1,716 distinct paths with a length of up to three hops between acetylsalicylic acid and pancreatic cancer. Therefore, it is hard to visualize them all in a single image, and a domain expert could prioritize connections based on node or relationship types.

Exercise 11.3

Visualize the first 25 paths with a length of up to three hops between acetylsalicylic acid and autistic disorder. Use the existing Neo4j version of the Hetionet graph, which is available through Neo4j Browser at https://neo4j.het.io/browser/.

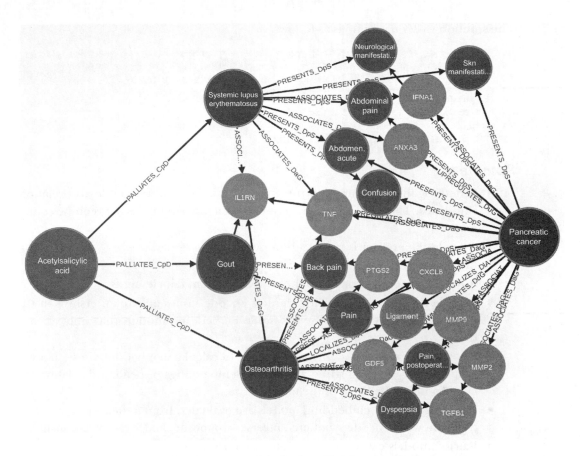

Figure 11.14   Existing connections between acetylsalicylic acid and pancreatic cancer

11.3   Solutions to exercises

One possible solution to exercise 11.1 is as follows.

```
Tomaz, LIVES_IN, Ljubljana
Ljubljana, PART_OF, Slovenia
```

The solution to exercise 11.2 is as follows.

Listing 11.8   Predicting new use cases for caffeine

```
pred_df = get_prediction_df(
    result.model,
    head_label="Caffeine",
    relation_label="treats",
    remove_known=True,
    triples_factory=result.training,
)
pred_df.head()
```

The solution to exercise 11.3 is as follows.

> **Listing 11.9 Visualizing the first 25 paths with a length of up to three hops between acetylsalicylic acid and autistic disorder**

```
MATCH (c:Compound {name:"Acetylsalicylic acid"}),
      (d:Disease {name:"autistic disorder"})
MATCH p=(c)-[* ..3]-(d)
RETURN p LIMIT 25
```

Summary

- A heterogeneous or multipartite graph consists of multiple node and relationship types. There could also be numerous relationship types between two entity types.
- A triple data object is used to represent directed graphs, where multiple relationship types are present.
- A triple data object consists of head, relation, and tail elements.
- Knowledge graph embedding models encode nodes and relationships in the embedding space, as opposed to node embedding models that only encode nodes.
- Knowledge graph embedding models try to calculate embedding in such a way that for every existing triple, the sum of embeddings of head and relation are close to the embedding of the tail node.
- Knowledge graph embedding models are evaluated from a theoretical perspective if they can encode symmetry, inverse, composite, and 1-to-N relationships.
- PairRE models can encode all four categories (symmetry, inverse, composite, and 1-to-N) of different relationships.
- Knowledge graph completion can be thought of as a multiclass link prediction problem, where you are predicting new links and their type.
- In a drug repurposing workflow, the predictions must be evaluated by domain experts and then go through clinical trials to be approved. Knowledge graph completion is only used to prioritize the most likely candidates.

Constructing a graph using natural language processing techniques

The amount of text-based information available on the internet is astounding. It is hard to imagine the number of social media posts, blogs, and news articles published daily. However, despite the wealth of information available, much of it remains unstructured and difficult to extract valuable insights from. This is where natural language processing (NLP) comes into play. NLP is a rapidly growing field that has seen a significant increase in attention in recent years, especially since transformer models (Vaswani, 2017) and, more recently, the GPT-3 (Brown et al., 2020) and GPT-4 models (OpenAI, 2023) were introduced. One particularly important area of NLP is the field of information extraction, which focuses on the task of extracting structured information from unstructured text.

In the example provided in figure 12.1, the text describes the founding of a company and contains information such as the company name, the founders' names, and the founding date. The information extraction process would involve identifying and extracting this information from the text. This output of the information extraction pipeline would be a set of triples. Each triple represents a piece of information and consists of a head, relation, and tail object. The triple object definition is identical to the previous chapter, where you implemented a knowledge graph completion pipeline. In the example in figure 12.1, the extracted information might be represented in the following triples:

- `Steve Jobs, FOUNDED, Apple`
- `Steve Wozniak, FOUNDED, Apple`
- `Apple, FOUNDED_ON, April 1. 1976`

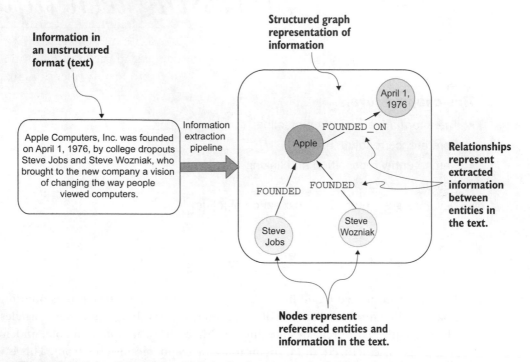

Figure 12.1   Extracting structured information from text and using it to construct a graph

Creating a graph based on given triples is a straightforward process. Each triple can be used to construct a graph, where the head of the triple is the starting node, the relation represents the relationship type, and the tail is the ending node. There are some exceptions for which you might want to store the triple as a node property in a labeled property graph model. For example, you could store the founding date of Apple as a node property. By connecting these nodes and relationships together, you can create a graph that represents the extracted information. This graph can be used for various purposes, such as data analysis, knowledge representation, and information retrieval.

Suppose you are working as a data scientist at a venture capital firm. A venture capital firm needs to stay informed of the latest developments in the field. Given the vast amount of news produced daily in multiple languages, it is virtually impossible to manually read every article; therefore, you have been assigned to develop a system that automatically reads the news and extracts information about new companies being founded, mergers, and acquisitions. In this scenario, you present the idea of developing an information extraction pipeline to accomplish this goal. This pipeline would extract relevant data from text and store it as a graph.

This approach would allow you to easily identify patterns of new companies being founded, merged, or acquired. Additionally, you would have the context of those events readily available. For example, you could retrieve who founded the companies, when they were founded, whether the founder is notable, and so on. With enough data processed, this approach would also allow exploration of the history or progression of various entities within the graph. Therefore, you could create a notification system when new relationships of a particular type appear in the graph. Additionally, the graph would also allow you to explore the context and history of entities involved in various corporate events. This will enable the venture capital firm to stay informed of the latest developments in the field and make informed investment decisions. You propose the design of the information extraction pipeline shown in figure 12.2.

The proposed information extraction pipeline in figure 12.2 is a multistep process to extract structured information from unstructured text. The pipeline consists of several NLP techniques, such as *coreference resolution, named entity recognition* (NER), and *relation extraction* (RE):

- Coreference resolution models identify all the references to the same entity. In practice, the coreference resolution is most often represented as the task of replacing pronouns with referenced entities, although it could be a more complicated process than that. For example, in the text *He lives in Bahamas,* the pronoun *He* would be replaced with the referenced entity *Jon.*

- Next, the pipeline identifies entities and concepts in the text using NER models. In figure 12.2, the model identified `Jon`, `W3C`, and `Bahamas` as entities. The NER model can also be trained to detect types of entities like `Person`, `Organization`, and `Location`.

- The last NLP technique in the pipeline is relation extraction. It is used to extract various connections between recognized entities. In this example, the pipeline would extract the following two triples:
  - `Jon, WORKS_AT, W3C`
  - `Jon, RESIDES, Bahamas`

- Using a graph database to store the relationships between entities extracted by the NLP process allows the information to be easily stored, queried, and visualized. Additionally, using a graph database allows for more complex queries, such as finding patterns and connections between entities, which can be difficult to

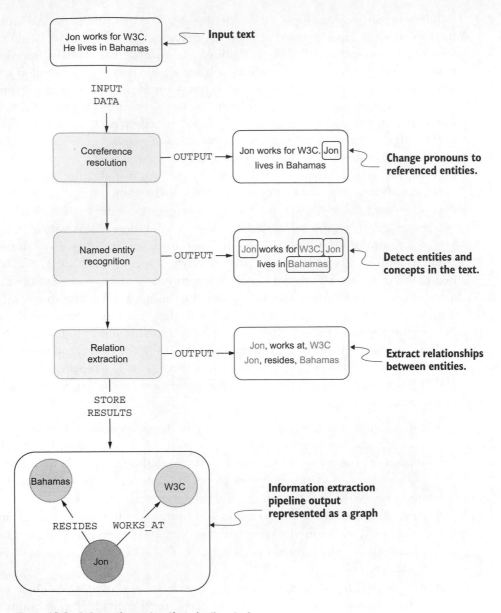

Figure 12.2   Information extraction pipeline design

perform using traditional database structures. As you have some experience with graph machine learning, you could also use the graph in node classification or link prediction workflows.

12.1   Coreference resolution

The first step in the pipeline is a coreference resolution model. *Coreference resolution* is the task of identifying all expressions in a text referring to the same entity.

In the first sentence of the example in figure 12.3, *Google* and *they* refer to the same entity. The second sentence starts with a reference to a *company*. Interestingly, the *company* reference is a bit ambiguous, as it could refer to either *Google* or *YouTube* when no other information is present. This is only one example of a more challenging problem coreference resolution models must solve. However, if you knew that Eric Schmidt is the CEO of Google, it would be reasonably easy to resolve the reference of the *company* to Google. Sometimes, you are dealing with plural pronouns or references, as in the case of *both companies*. Therefore, the ideal output of a coreference resolution model would be a reference to both *Google* and *YouTube*.

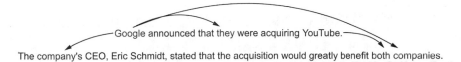

Figure 12.3   Coreference resolution

Coreference resolution can be approached in two main ways:

- Rule-based
- Neural networks

Rule-based coreference resolution (Haghighi & Klein, 2009; Raghunathan et al., 2010) involves using a set of predefined rules and heuristics to identify and link coreferent expressions in a text. These rules can be based on syntactic, semantic, and contextual information, such as the gender or number agreement between expressions, the distance between expressions in the text, or the presence of certain keywords. However, rule-based systems have several limitations when applied to real-world applications, as it is virtually impossible to define the rules for each possible variation. On the other hand, neural coreference resolution (Clark & Manning, 2016; Lee et al., 2017) involves training a neural network to identify and link coreferent expressions in a text. The neural network learns to identify coreferent expressions by recognizing patterns and relationships in the data rather than relying on predefined rules.

Coreference resolution is a crucial component of most NLP pipelines. It is used as a preprocessing step of various NLP workflows, ranging from information extraction to text summarization and question-answering tasks (Singh, 2018).

12.2   Named entity recognition

Named entity recognition (NER) is a task that involves identifying and classifying named entities in a text into predefined categories. The named entities and categories depend heavily on the domain you are working with. For example, at a venture capital firm, you might want to identify people, organizations, and locations in the text. However, if you were at a biomedical company, the focus would be more on genes, proteins, diseases, drugs, and so on. In most cases, the NER models are fine-tuned for a specific domain. In the proposed information extraction pipeline, you want to identify people, organizations, locations, and dates.

In the example in figure 12.4, the NER model identified the entities `Google` and `YouTube` as an organization and `Eric Schmidt` as a person. The extracted named entities are visualized with displaCy (https://spacy.io/universe/project/display).

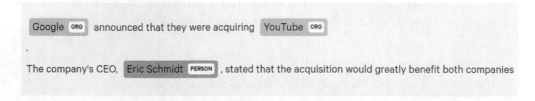

Figure 12.4   Named entity recognition

12.2.1 *Entity linking*

Frequently, disambiguating which entities are mentioned in the text can be challenging. For example, there is only one organization named *Google*, but there are probably multiple people named *Eric Schmidt*. Techniques like entity linking have been introduced to solve the problem of disambiguating named entities. *Entity linking* is the task of connecting named entities to their corresponding ID in a knowledge base. The target knowledge base depends on the use case domain. For example, entity linking is popular in biomedical domains, where it is used to connect identified genes, drugs, and other entities in the text to various biomedical knowledge bases. On the other hand, for the general purpose of disambiguating people and organizations, knowledge bases like *Wikipedia* or *DBpedia* are most frequently used.

Figure 12.5 shows an example of linking entities to Wikipedia. As you can see, Wikipedia URLs are used as unique identifiers of entities. Interestingly, even on Wikipedia, there are multiple entries for Eric Schmidt (https://en.wikipedia.org/wiki/Eric_Schmidt_(disambiguation)). Picking the correct entity when there are multiple entries with the same name is a challenging task. Abbreviations and aliases of entities are some of the other challenges you face when performing entity linking.

Most of the recently proposed entity linking models are based on a deep learning approach. Some models are so-called *end-to-end entity linking models*, which perform both named entity recognition and linking in a single step (Brank et al., 2017). Other models perform only entity linking and need to have the identified named entities provided along with the text (Barba et al., 2022).

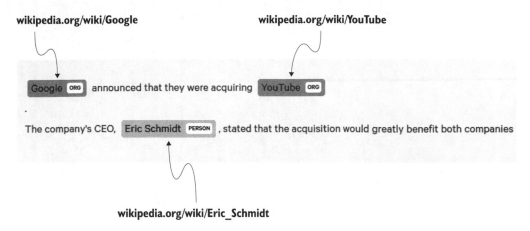

Figure 12.5 Named entity linking

12.3 *Relation extraction*

As the name suggests, *relation extraction models* extract relationships between entities in the text. The proposed information extraction pipeline for the venture capital firm should focus on extracting relationships between companies and people. The most frequent output of relation extraction models is a list of triples. You have already used triples in the previous chapter. As the name suggests, triples contain three elements that specify the start node, end node, and relationship type.

There are several approaches to extracting relationships from text. You could take a rule-based approach and extract relationships by using a set of predefined heuristics. One example of a rule-based approach to extracting relation is to define rules based on part of speech and tagging and dependency parsing.

Figure 12.6 visualizes the output of the part of speech and dependency parsing. For example, you can observe that each word is tagged according to its function in English. The tags signify whether the word is a noun, adjective, verb, and so on. On the other hand, the dependency parser calculates the dependencies between words. For example, *acquiring* is a verb. The verb refers to the object *YouTube*, while the subject points to *they*. In this case, *they* refers to *Google*. Therefore, a rule that would simply take the subject and objects of a verb and construct triples based on that could be defined. However, in practice, rules can get much more complicated. I found that rule-based approaches are used in domains like biomedicine (Rindflesch & Fiszman, 2003; Rindflesch et al., 2011).

Another approach you could take is to train a deep learning model based on training data to identify and extract relationships. There is a lot of research based on neural network approaches to extracting relationships, as it offers a remarkable ability to extract relationships and achieve excellent performance. There are models trained to detect relationships within a single sentence (Zhou et al., 2016; Han et al., 2019) as

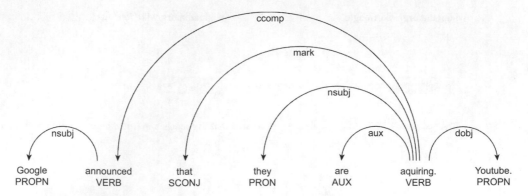

Figure 12.6   Part of speech tagging and dependency tagging

well as document-level relationship extraction (Yao et al., 2019). In the end, you would want a model that would extract the following relationships from the example in figure 12.5.

Listing 12.1   Extracted triples from the example in figure 12.5

```
Google, ACQUIRED, YouTube
Eric Schmidt, CEO, Google
```

12.4   *Implementation of information extraction pipeline*

Now that you have some theoretical knowledge about information extraction workflow, you will develop a pipeline that will identify organizations and people and the relevant relationships between them. You will use existing NLP models for the initial pipeline implementation, so you don't need to worry about training any custom NLP models. The pipeline will be evaluated using the following text.

Listing 12.2   Text used to evaluate the information extraction pipeline

```
Apple Inc was founded on April 1, 1976, by Steve Jobs, Steve Wozniak, and
Ronald Wayne as a partnership. They started the company in California. The
company's first product was the Apple I, a computer designed and hand-built
entirely by Wozniak. To finance the company's creation, Jobs sold his
Volkswagen Bus, and Wozniak sold his HP-65 calculator. Wozniak debuted the
first prototype Apple I at the Homebrew Computer Club in July 1976. The Apple
I was sold as a motherboard with CPU, RAM, and basic textual-video chips—a
base kit concept which would not yet be marketed as a complete personal
computer. It went on sale soon after debut for US$666.66 (equivalent to
$3,175 in 2021). Wozniak later said he was unaware of the coincidental mark
of the beast in the number 666, and that he came up with the price because he
liked "repeating digits". Later in 2013 Apple acquired AlgoTrim. Then in 2015
the company also bought Semetric, which is in music analytics category.
```

The text in listing 12.2 was copied from Wikipedia (https://en.wikipedia.org/wiki/Apple_Inc.) and contains information about Apple Inc., its founders, and their first product. I added two sentences at the end that mention various acquisitions so that you can evaluate the model on how it processes information about company acquisitions. This text will be used to evaluate the coreference resolution model as well as the relationship extraction process. The implementation of the proposed information extraction pipeline is available as a Jupyter notebook on GitHub (http://mng.bz/KeJ0).

12.4.1 SpaCy

You will be using SpaCy to develop the information extraction pipeline. SpaCy is a free, open source Python library for NLP workflows. The advantage of SpaCy is that it offers a beginner-friendly interface to perform various NLP tasks and can also be used in production environments.

The following Python code installs the required Python libraries.

Listing 12.3 Installing the required Python libraries

```
pip install spacy==3.4.4 coreferee==1.3.1 transformers==4.25.1
```

The code in listing 12.3 installs SpaCy along with the `coreferee` and `transformers` libraries. The `coreferee` library (https://github.com/explosion/coreferee) is a SpaCy plugin that provides a coreference resolution model. The code in listing 12.3 installs the `transformers` library that will be used for relation extraction. Next, you need to install the pretrained models `en_core_web_lg` and the `coreferee` with the following Python code.

Listing 12.4 Downloading NLP models

```
python -m spacy download en_core_web_lg
python -m coreferee install en
```

12.4.2 Corefence resolution

As mentioned, you will use the `coreferee` plugin to perform coreference resolution. You can load the coreference model in SpaCy with the following code.

Listing 12.5 Loading the coreference model

```
import spacy, coreferee

coref_nlp = spacy.load('en_core_web_lg')
coref_nlp.add_pipe('coreferee')
```

The `coreferee` model does not provide a method that resolves the coreference text out of the box. Therefore, you need to define a function using the coreference resolution method to identify references and then replace references with referred entities in the text.

Listing 12.6   Using the coreference model to resolve text references

```
def coref_text(text):
    coref_doc = coref_nlp(text)
    resolved_text = ""

    for token in coref_doc:
        repres = coref_doc._.coref_chains.resolve(token)
        if repres:
            resolved_text += " " + " and ".join(
                [
                    t.text
                    if t.ent_type_ == ""
                    else [e.text for e in coref_doc.ents if t in e][0]
                    for t in repres
                ]
            )
        else:
            resolved_text += " " + token.text

    return resolved_text

ctext = coref_text(text)
print(ctext)
```

The `coref_text` function in listing 12.6 resolves entity coreferences and replaces them in the text accordingly. Without going into too much detail, the code checks if the resolved token `repres` is part of a named entity, and if it is, it replaces the reference with the named entity's text instead of only the token's text.

The code in listing 12.6 produces the following output.

Listing 12.7   Coreference resolved text

```
Apple Inc was founded on April 1 , 1976 , by Steve Jobs , Steve Wozniak , and
Ronald Wayne as a partnership .Steve Jobs and Steve Wozniak and Ronald Wayne
started the Apple Inc in California . The Apple Inc 's first product was the
Apple I , a computer designed and hand - built entirely by Steve Wozniak . To
finance the Apple Inc 's creation , Jobs sold Ronald Wayne Volkswagen Bus ,
and Steve Wozniak sold Ronald Wayne HP-65 calculator . Steve Wozniak debuted
the first prototype Apple I at the Homebrew Computer Club in July 1976 . The
Apple I was sold as a motherboard with CPU , RAM , and basic textual - video
chips — a base kit concept which would not yet be marketed as a complete
personal computer . Apple went on sale soon after debut for US$ 666.66 (
equivalent to $ 3,175 in 2021 ) . Wozniak later said Wozniak was unaware of
the coincidental mark of the beast in the number 666 , and that Wozniak came
up with the price because Wozniak liked " repeating digits " . Later in 2013
Apple Inc acquired AlgoTrim . Then in 2015 the AlgoTrim also bought Semetric ,
which is in music  analytics category .
```

At first sight of the output in listing 12.7, it seems the coreference model did a solid job. For example, you may notice that *They* in the second line was replaced with *Steve Jobs and Steve Wozniak and Ronald Wayne*, while the *company* was replaced with *Apple Inc.* However, the model is not perfect. On the fourth line, the model replaced both instances of *his* with *Ronald Wayne.* The results are wrong as Jobs sold his Volkswagen Bus, not Ronald Wayne's. Additionally, you will likely notice that the resolved text does not bother with proper possessive nouns and articles, as generating grammatically correct text based on the coreference model output is a significant problem on its own. Also, the text on the last line of listing 12.7 is a bit ambiguous about which company bought Semetric. The model could choose between Apple Inc. and AlgoTrim. While you might know that Apple Inc. acquired Semetric, the coreference model went with AlgoTrim.

12.4.3 End-to-end relation extraction

You will use the REBEL model (Huguet Cabot & Navigli, 2021) for the relation extraction step in the pipeline. The REBEL model is an end-to-end relation extraction model, which means it detects both entities and relationships in a single model. The model has state-of-the-art performance on various datasets, as indicated on its GitHub repository (https://github.com/Babelscape/rebel).

> **NOTE** Large language models, such as GPT-4 from OpenAI (2023), have been a game-changing advancement in the world of NLP. Their ability to understand human-like text has presented remarkable opportunities in the field of information extraction. With a model trained on diverse internet text, they can sift through massive amounts of data, understand the context, and pull out relevant details, making the information extraction pipelines more accessible. Their ability to generalize allows them to be applied to a variety of domains, from academic research to business analytics, extracting valuable insights from unstructured data (Li et al., 2023; Wei et al., 2023).

The model can be used directly with the `transformers` library or as a SpaCy component. You will use the SpaCy variant. Unlike the `coreferee` model that can be installed using pip, you must copy the SpaCy component definition from the repository (http://mng.bz/VR8G). The SpaCy component definition is too long to include in the book; however, you can copy the code without changing anything. The SpaCy component definition is also included in the accompanying Jupyter notebook.

Next, you load the REBEL model in SpaCy with the following code.

Listing 12.8   Loading the REBEL model

```
nlp = spacy.load("en_core_web_lg")

nlp.add_pipe(
    "rebel",
    after="senter",
```

```
    config={
        "device": -1,  # Number of the GPU, -1 if want to use CPU
        "model_name": "Babelscape/rebel-large",
    },
)
```

Once the model is loaded, the code to extract the relationships is trivial.

Listing 12.9 Extracting relationships from text

```
doc = nlp(ctext)
for value, rel_dict in doc._.rel.items():
    print(rel_dict)
```

The Python code in listing 12.9 processes the `ctext`, and the REBEL component results can be retrieved with the `doc._.rel.items()` method. The code in listing 12.9 produces the following output.

Listing 12.10 Results of the relation extraction step

```
{'relation': 'founded by', 'head_span': Apple Inc, 'tail_span': Steve Jobs}
{'relation': 'founded by', 'head_span': Apple Inc,
➡ 'tail_span': Steve Wozniak}
{'relation': 'founded by', 'head_span': Apple Inc,
➡ 'tail_span': Ronald Wayne}
{'relation': 'employer', 'head_span': Steve Jobs, 'tail_span': Apple Inc}
{'relation': 'employer', 'head_span': Steve Wozniak, 'tail_span': Apple Inc}
{'relation': 'employer', 'head_span': Ronald Wayne, 'tail_span': Apple Inc}
{'relation': 'manufacturer', 'head_span': Apple Inc, 'tail_span': Apple Inc}
{'relation': 'member of', 'head_span': Steve Wozniak,
➡ 'tail_span': Homebrew Computer Club}
{'relation': 'founded by', 'head_span': Homebrew Computer Club,
➡ 'tail_span': Steve Wozniak}
{'relation': 'has part', 'head_span': motherboard, 'tail_span': CPU}
{'relation': 'has part', 'head_span': motherboard, 'tail_span': RAM}
{'relation': 'part of', 'head_span': CPU, 'tail_span': motherboard}
{'relation': 'part of', 'head_span': RAM, 'tail_span': motherboard}
{'relation': 'said to be the same as', 'head_span': mark of the beast,
➡ 'tail_span': 666.66}
{'relation': 'said to be the same as', 'head_span': 666.66
➡, 'tail_span': mark of the beast}
{'relation': 'parent organization', 'head_span': AlgoTrim,
➡ 'tail_span': Apple Inc}
{'relation': 'subsidiary', 'head_span': AlgoTrim, 'tail_span': Semetric}
{'relation': 'parent organization', 'head_span': Semetric,
➡ 'tail_span': AlgoTrim}
```

The extracted relationships in listing 12.10 look satisfactory. The REBEL model identified that Apple was founded by Steve Jobs, Steve Wozniak, and Ronald Wayne. In turn, it parsed that they are also employed by Apple. Unfortunately, the model can *hallucinate* some results. A hallucination is a result that cannot be found in the text.

For example, the model identified that Steve Wozniak founded the Homebrew Computer Club. While the fact is true, it cannot be verified through the text; therefore the model hallucinated that fact. The acquisitions are identified with the `parent organization` and `subsidiary` relationships. The model extracted both relationships from the text. The last relationship is incorrect; that is not a problem of the REBEL model but, rather, of the coreference resolution step.

> ### Exercise 12.1
>
> Construct a graph in Neo4j using the relationships extracted from listing 12.10. Since you don't have information about node types, you can use a generic `Entity` label for all nodes.

Figure 12.7 presents a visual representation of the output of the information extraction pipelines. Entities are represented as nodes, while the relations are represented with relationships.

> ### Exercise 12.2
>
> Search for news articles about business foundations or acquisitions, and then run them through the implemented information extraction pipeline. You can experiment with including or excluding the coreference resolution step and evaluate how it affects the output.

12.4.4 Entity linking

The final step in our information extraction process is linking entities to their corresponding WikiData IDs. As a part of the Wikipedia ecosystem, WikiData serves as a repository for structured data across all Wikipedia projects. To gain a better understanding of the available data, you can visit the page dedicated to Steve Jobs (https://www.wikidata.org/wiki/Q19837) on WikiData. The WikiData ID, which can be found at the end of the URL, for Steve Jobs is Q19837. For the initial version, there won't be any advanced entity disambiguation. You will simply use the WikiData API to search for entities and choose the first result from the list. Later, you can implement more advanced entity linking, including entity disambiguation using the sentence context (Barba et al., 2022).

The code in listing 12.11 searches WikiData for given entities and returns the URL and the description of the first entity of the list.

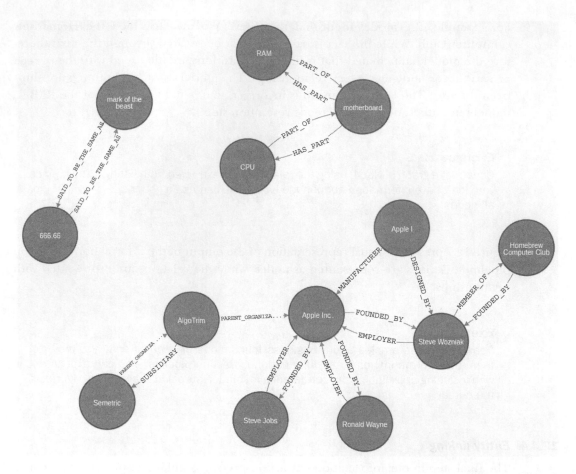

Figure 12.7   Information extraction pipeline results

Listing 12.11   Defining a function that searches for entities on WikiData

```
import requests

def retrieve_wiki_id(item):
    try:
        url = "https://www.wikidata.org/w/api.php?action=wbsearchentities"
        params = f"&search={item}&language=en&format=json"
        data = requests.get(url + params).json()
        return {
            "id": data["search"][0]["url"],
            "description": data["search"][0]["display"]["description"]["value"],
        }
    except Exception as e:
        return None
```

You can now use the function defined in listing 12.11 to match the entities from the information extraction pipeline to WikiData IDs.

Listing 12.12 A basic entity linking workflow

```
entities = set()
for value, rel_dict in doc._.rel.items():
    entities.update([rel_dict["head_span"], rel_dict["tail_span"]])

for entity in entities:
    wiki_data = retrieve_wiki_id(entity)
    print(entity, wiki_data)
```

The code in listing 12.12 outputs the following results.

Listing 12.13 Results of entity linking

```
CPU {'id': '//www.wikidata.org/wiki/Q5300', 'description': 'electronic
➥ circuitry within a computer that carries out the instructions of a
➥ computer program by performing the basic arithmetic, logical, control
➥ and input/output (I/O) operations specified by the instructions and
➥ coordinates the other components'}
motherboard {'id': '//www.wikidata.org/wiki/Q4321', 'description': 'main
➥ printed circuit board (PCB) for a computing device'}
Steve Jobs {'id': '//www.wikidata.org/wiki/Q19837', 'description':
➥ 'American entrepreneur; co-founder of Apple Inc. (1955-2011)'}
Steve Wozniak {'id': '//www.wikidata.org/wiki/Q483382', 'description':
➥ 'American computer pioneer, inventor, computer engineer and
➥ programmer; co-founder of Apple Inc.'}
AlgoTrim None
Ronald Wayne {'id': '//www.wikidata.org/wiki/Q332591', 'description':
➥ 'co-founder of Apple Inc.'}
Apple I {'id': '//www.wikidata.org/wiki/Q18981', 'description': 'computer
➥ built by the Apple Computer Company'}
Semetric None
mark of the beast {'id': '//www.wikidata.org/wiki/Q6770514', 'description':
➥ 'album by Manilla Road'}
666.66 {'id': '//www.wikidata.org/wiki/Q2778183', 'description': 'album
➥ by Noir Désir'}
RAM {'id': '//www.wikidata.org/wiki/Q5295', 'description': 'form of
➥ computer data storage'}
Apple Inc {'id': '//www.wikidata.org/wiki/Q312', 'description': 'American
➥ multinational technology company'}
Homebrew Computer Club {'id': '//www.wikidata.org/wiki/Q1195191',
➥ 'description': "computer hobbyist users' group in California"}
```

Overall, the entity linking results in listing 12.13 appear satisfactory. Luckily, there are no ambiguous entity references where, for example, there were two different persons with the same name mentioned, and you would need to determine which one is intended. For example, imagine Eric Schmidt was mentioned in the text. You would need to identify whether this was Eric Schmidt the American businessman or Eric Schmidt the American footballer who played for the 2001 North Dakota Fighting

Sioux team. Additionally, it should be noted that not all entities can be linked to Wiki-Data. For example, AlgoTrim and Semetric have no entry in the WikiData knowledge base. Interestingly, both the mark of the beast and 666.66 are linked to entities representing albums. Having mark of the beast and 666.66 linking results is a consequence of completely ignoring text context. The process of information extraction can be extremely valuable yet equally challenging, requiring precise techniques to achieve reliable results.

12.4.5 *External data enrichment*

While the implemented WikiData linking method offers little help with entity disambiguation, it opens up the options for external data enrichment. WikiData offers a plethora of information. For example, WikiData offers various data about Apple Inc., ranging from its board members to subsidiaries and more (https://www.wikidata.org/wiki/Q312). Since the REBEL model does not provide entity types, you could use WikiData to fetch linked entity types. However, retrieving information from WikiData is beyond the scope of this book, as it requires some basic knowledge of SPARQL. Nonetheless, I wanted to give you some hints about how you could enrich your venture capital firm graph with various external data sources.

Congratulations! You have successfully implemented an information extraction pipeline to extract information about organizations and people from unstructured text.

12.5 *Solutions to exercises*

The solution to exercise 12.1 is as follows.

> **Listing 12.14   Cypher statement to import the extracted relationships into Neo4j database**

```
WITH [
  {relation:'founded by',head_span:'Apple Inc',tail_span:'Steve Jobs'},
  {relation:'founded by',head_span:'Apple Inc',tail_span:'Steve Wozniak'},
  {relation:'founded by',head_span:'Apple Inc',tail_span:'Ronald Wayne'},
  {relation:'employer',head_span:'Steve Jobs',tail_span:'Apple Inc'},
  {relation:'employer',head_span:'Steve Wozniak',tail_span:'Apple Inc'},
  {relation:'employer',head_span:'Ronald Wayne',tail_span: 'Apple Inc'},
  {relation:'manufacturer',head_span:'Apple Inc',tail_span:'Apple Inc'},
  {relation:'member of',head_span:'Steve Wozniak',
    tail_span: 'Homebrew Computer Club'},
  {relation: 'founded by', head_span: 'Homebrew Computer Club',
    tail_span: 'Steve Wozniak'},
  {relation: 'has part', head_span: 'motherboard', tail_span: 'CPU'},
  {relation: 'has part', head_span: 'motherboard', tail_span: 'RAM'},
  {relation: 'part of', head_span: 'CPU', tail_span: 'motherboard'},
  {relation: 'part of', head_span: 'RAM', tail_span: 'motherboard'},
  {relation: 'said to be the same as',head_span: 'mark of the beast',
    tail_span: '666.66'},
  {relation: 'said to be the same as',head_span: '666.66',
    tail_span: 'mark of the beast'},
  {relation:'parent organization',head_span:'AlgoTrim',
    tail_span:'Apple Inc'},
```

```
    {relation:'subsidiary',head_span:'AlgoTrim',tail_span:'Semetric'},
    {relation: 'parent organization', head_span: 'Semetric',
      tail_span: 'AlgoTrim'}] AS data
UNWIND data AS row
MERGE(head: Entity {id: row.head_span})
MERGE(tail: Entity {id: row.tail_span})
WITH head, tail, row.relation AS relationType
CALL apoc.merge.relationship(head, relationType, {}, {}, tail) YIELD rel
RETURN distinct 'done'
```

Plain Cypher syntax does not support importing relationships with dynamic types. You can use the `apoc.merge.relationship` procedure, as shown in listing 12.14, to avoid having to import each relationship type separately. You can learn more about the procedure in the documentation (http://mng.bz/xjrX).

Summary

- Information extraction is a natural language task that extracts structured information from unstructured text.
- Coreference resolution is used to identify all the references to the same entity within the text.
- Named entity recognition identifies various entities within the text along with their type.
- Entity linking is a process of linking entities to a target knowledge base (WikiData, MeSH, etc.).
- The entity linking process opens up options for additional external data enrichment, as you can identify entities with a unique ID.
- Entity linking models use the context of the sentence or a paragraph to disambiguate entities.
- Relation extraction models extract relationships between entities.
- There are two types of relation extraction models: rule-based and deep-learning approaches.
- The named entity recognition and relation extraction models are heavily dependent on the use case domain.
- Relation extraction models produce a list of triples that can be used to construct a graph.
- The triples can be used to construct a graph representation of the information.
- An end-to-end relation extraction model like REBEL performs both named entity recognition and relation extraction in a single step.
- Mapping entities to target knowledge bases like WikiData allows you to use the information in from these knowledge bases to enrich your graph.

appendix
The Neo4j environment

In this book, you will learn graph theory and algorithms through practical examples using Neo4j. I chose Neo4j because I have more than five years of experience with it, building and analyzing graphs.

Neo4j is a native graph database, built from the ground up to store, query, and manipulate graph data. It is implemented in Java and accessible from software written in other languages using Cypher query language, through a transactional HTTP endpoint or the binary Bolt Protocol. In Neo4j, data is stored as nodes and relationships, which are both first-class citizens in the database. Nodes represent entities, such as people or businesses, and relationships represent the connections between these entities. Nodes and relationships can have properties, which are key–value pairs that provide additional information about the nodes and relationships.

Neo4j is designed to be highly scalable. It uses a flexible indexing system to efficiently query and manipulate data and supports atomicity, consistency, isolation, and durability (ACID) transactions to ensure data consistency. It also has a built-in query language, called Cypher, which is designed to be expressive and easy to use for querying and manipulating graph data.

Another benefit of using Neo4j is that it has two practical plugins you will be using:

- *The Awesome Procedures on Cypher (APOC) plugin*—A library of procedures, functions, and plugins for Neo4j that provide a wide range of capabilities, including data import/export, data transformation and manipulation, date-time interval processing, geospatial processing, text processing, and others.

- *The Graph Data Science (GDS) plugin*—A set of graph algorithms and procedures for Neo4j that allow users to perform advanced analytics on their graph data. GDS provides efficient, parallel implementations of common graph algorithms, such as shortest path, PageRank, and community detection. In addition, the plugin includes node embedding algorithms and machine learning workflows that support node classification and link prediction workflows.

A.1 Cypher query language

Cypher is a declarative query language for graph databases used to retrieve and manipulate data stored in a graph database. Cypher queries are written in a simple, human-readable syntax. Here is an example of a simple Cypher query that uses ASCII-art-style diagramming to illustrate the relationships being queried.

Listing A.1 A sample Cypher statement

```
MATCH (a:Person)-[:FOLLOWS]->(b:Person)
WHERE a.name = "Alice"
RETURN b.name
```

The openCypher initiative is a collaboration between Neo4j and several other organizations to promote the use of Cypher query language as a standard for working with graph data. The goal of the openCypher initiative is to create a common language that can be used to query any graph database, regardless of the underlying technology. To achieve this goal, the openCypher initiative is making the Cypher language specification and related resources available under an open source license and is encouraging the development of Cypher implementations by a variety of organizations. So far, the Cypher query language has been adopted by Amazon, Agens Graph, Katana Graph, Memgraph, RedisGraph, and SAP HANA (openCypher Implementers Group; https://opencypher.org/projects/).

There is also an official ISO project to propose a unified Graph Query Language (GQL) to interact with graph databases (GQL Standards Committee). The GQL aims to build on the foundation of SQL and integrate proven ideas from existing graph query languages, including Cypher. That makes learning Cypher a great start to interact with graph databases, as it is already integrated with many of them and will also be part of the official ISO Graph Query Language. Take a look at the graph pattern matching proposal for GQL (Deutsch et al., 2022) for more information.

A.2 Neo4j installation

There are a few different options to set up your Neo4j environment:

- Neo4j Desktop
- Neo4j Docker
- Neo4j Aura

I would advise you to use Neo4j Desktop if you are new to Neo4j.

A.2.1 Neo4j Desktop installation

Neo4j Desktop is a local Neo4j graph database management application. It allows you to create database instances and install official plugins with only a few clicks. If you decide to use Neo4j Desktop, follow these steps to successfully start a Neo4j database instance with installed APOC and GDS plugins:

1 Download the Neo4j Desktop application from the official website (https://neo4j.com/download; figure A.1).

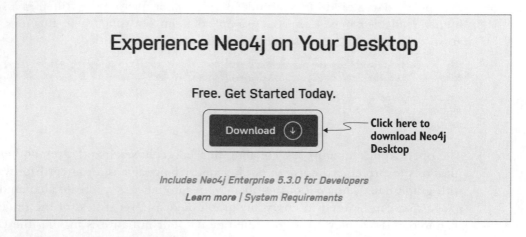

Figure A.1   Download Neo4j Desktop.

2 Install the Neo4j Desktop application on your computer, and then open it.
3 Complete the registration step. You can enter the software key you were assigned when you downloaded the application or skip this step by clicking Register Later (figure A.2).

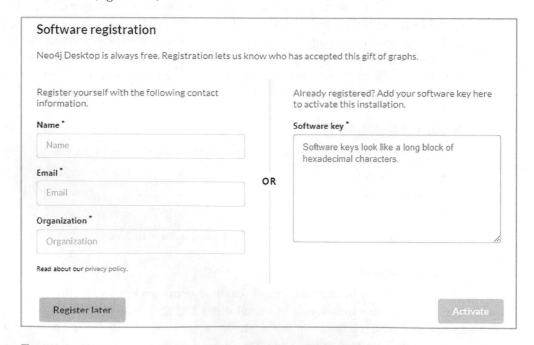

Figure A.2   Enter your personal information, or skip the registration step.

4 The Movie Database Management System (DBMS) is automatically started on the first execution of Neo4j Desktop. Stop the Movie DBMS if it is running (figure A.3).

Figure A.3   Stop the default Movie DBMS database.

5 Add a new local DBMS (figure A.4).

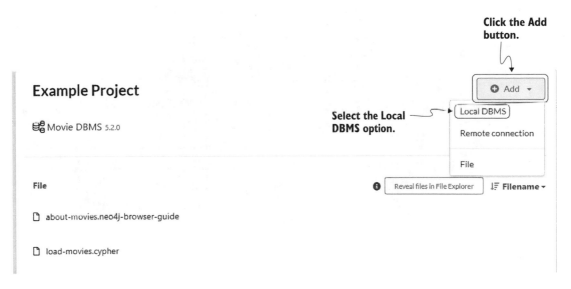

Figure A.4   Add a Local DBMS.

6 Type in any values for the DBMS name and password. Make sure to select version 5.12.0 or greater (figure A.5).

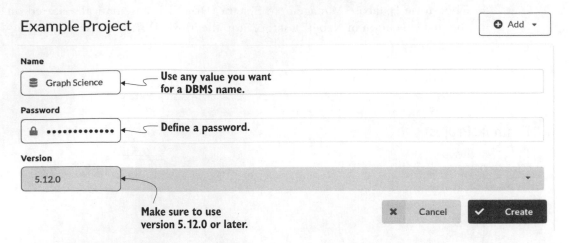

Figure A.5   Define a DBMS password and version.

7   Install the APOC and GDS plugins by selecting the DBMS, which opens a right-hand pane with Details, Plugins, and Upgrade tabs. Select the Plugins tab, and then install the APOC and GDS plugins (figure A.6).

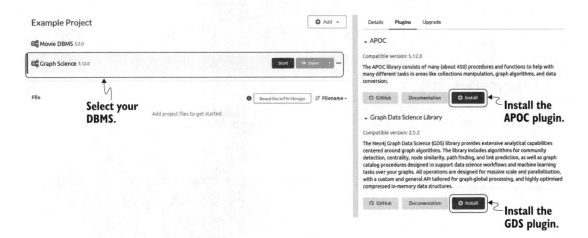

Figure A.6   Install the APOC and GDS plugins.

8   Start the database (figure A.7).
9   Open Neo4j Browser (figure A.8).

Figure A.7   Start the database.

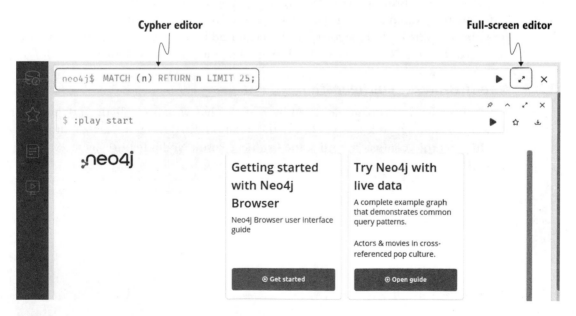

Figure A.8   Open Neo4j Browser.

10 Execute Cypher queries by typing them in the Cypher editor. For longer
    Cypher statements, you can use the full-screen editor option (figure A.9).

Figure A.9   The Cypher query editor in Neo4j Browser

A.2.2   *Neo4j Docker installation*

If you select the Neo4j Docker installation, you need to run the command in the following listing in your command prompt.

Listing A.2   Starting Neo4j Docker

```
docker run \
  -p 7474:7474 -p 7687:7687 \
  -d \
  -v $HOME/neo4j/data:/data \
  -e NEO4J_AUTH=neo4j/pleaseletmein \
  -e 'NEO4J_PLUGINS=["apoc", "graph-data-science"]' \
    neo4j:5.12.0
```

This command starts a dockerized Neo4j in the background. The APOC and GDS plugins are automatically added by defining the NEO4J_PLUGINS environment variable. It is a good practice to mount the data volume to persist the database files. The database username and password are specified with the NEO4J_AUTH variable.

Visit http://localhost:7474 in your web browser after you have executed the command in listing A.2. Type in the password, specified with the NEO4J_AUTH variable. The password in the example is pleaseletmein.

A.2.3   *Neo4j Aura*

Neo4j Aura is a hosted cloud instance of the Neo4j database. Unfortunately, the free version does not provide the GDS library. If you want to use cloud-hosted Neo4j Aura to follow the examples in this book, you will need to use the AuraDS version, which provides support for GDS algorithms. You can find more information on Neo4j's official website: https://neo4j.com/cloud/platform/aura-graph-database/.

A.3   *Neo4j Browser configuration*

Neo4j Browser has a beginner-friendly feature that visualizes all the relationships between resulting nodes, even when the relationships are not part of the query results. To avoid confusion, untick the Connect Result Nodes feature, as shown in figure A.10.

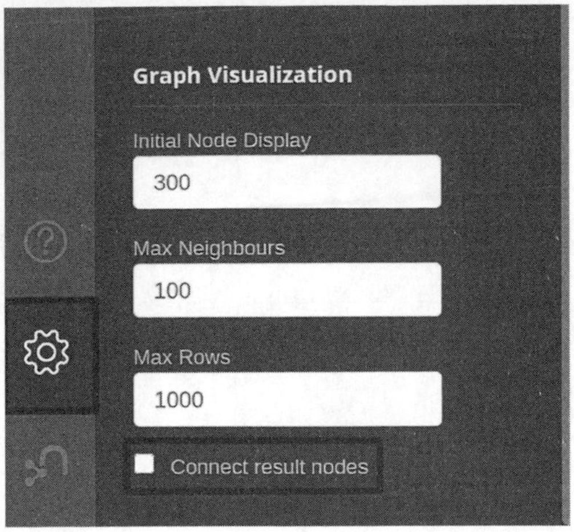

Figure A.10   Untick Connect Result Nodes in Neo4j Browser.

references

Adamic, L. A., & Adar, E. (2003). Friends and neighbors on the web. *Social Networks, 25*, 211–230.
Al-Zaman, S. (2021). A bibliometric and co-occurrence analysis of COVID-19-related literature published between December 2019 to June 2020. *Science Editing. 8*, 57–63. https://doi.org/10.6087/kcse.230

Albert, R., Jeong, H. & Barabási, A. L. (1999). Diameter of the World-Wide Web. *Nature, 401*, 130–131. https://doi.org/10.1038/43601

Ali, M., Berrendorf, M., Hoyt, C., Vermue, L., Sharifzadeh, S., Tresp, V., & Lehmann, J. (2021). PyKEEN 1.0: A Python library for training and evaluating knowledge graph embeddings. *Journal of Machine Learning Research, 22*(82), 1–6.

Andersen, N. et al. (2020). The emerging COVID-19 research: Dynamic and regularly updated science maps and analyses. *BMC Medical Informatics and Decision Making, 20*(1), 309. 30. https://doi.org/10.1186/s12911-020-01321-9

Bachman, J., Gyori, B., & Sorger, P. (2022). *Automated assembly of molecular mechanisms at scale from text mining and curated databases*. bioRxiv. Barabási, A. L., & Albert, R. (1999). Emergence of scaling in random networks. *Science, 286*(5439), 509–512.

Barba, E., Procopio, L., & Navigli, R. (2022). ExtEnD: Extractive entity disambiguation. *Proceedings of the 60th Annual Meeting of the Association for Computational Linguistics, Ireland, 1* (Long Papers), 2478–2488. Association for Computational Linguistics.

Beguerisse-Díaz, Mariano et al. (2014). Interest communities and flow roles in directed networks: The Twitter network of the UK riots. *Journal of the Royal Society Interface, 11*(101), 20140940. https://doi.org/10.1098/rsif.2014.0940

Beveridge, A. & Chemers, M. M. (2018). *The game of Game of Thrones: Networked concordances and fractal dramaturgy*. Taylor and Francis.

Blondel, V. D., Guillaume, J.-L., Lambiotte, R., & Lefebvre, E. (2008). Fast unfolding of communities in large networks. *Journal of Statistical Mechanics: Theory and Experiment*, (10), P10008.

Bordes, A., Usunier, N., Garcia-Duran, A., Weston, J., & Yakhnenko, O. (2013). Translating embeddings for modeling multi-relational data. *Advances in Neural Information Processing Systems, 26*.

Brank, J. , Leban, G., & Grobelnik, M. (2017). Annotating documents with relevant Wikipedia concepts. *Proceedings of the Slovenian Conference on Data Mining and Data Warehouses (SiKDD), Ljubljana, Slovenia*.

Brin, S., & Page, L. (1998). The anatomy of a large-scale hypertextual web search engine. *Computer Networks and ISDN Systems, 30*(1–7), 107–117.

Brown, T. B. , Mann, B., Ryder, N., Subbiah, M., Kaplan, J., Dhariwal, P., Neelakantan, A., Pranav Shyam, Girish Sastry, Amanda Askell, Sandhini Agarwal, Ariel Herbert-Voss, Gretchen Krueger, Tom Henighan, Rewon Child, Aditya Ramesh, Daniel M. Ziegler, Jeffrey Wu, Clemens Winter, … Dario Amodei. (2020). *Language models are few-shot learners*. arXiv.

Çano, E., & Morisio, M. (2017). Hybrid recommender systems: A systematic literature review. *Intelligent Data Analysis, 21*(6), 1487–1524.

Chao, L., He, J., Wang, T., & Chu, W. (2020). *PairRE: Knowledge graph embeddings via paired relation vectors.*

Chen, H., Sultan, S., Tian, Y., Chen, M., & Skiena, S. (2019). *Fast and accurate network embeddings via very sparse random projection.*

Cherepnalkoski, D., & Mozetic, I. (2015). A retweet network analysis of the European parliament. *11th International Conference on Signal-Image Technology & Internet-Based Systems (SITIS)*, 350–357, https://doi.org/10.1109/SITIS.2015.8

CKO News Staff. (2017). *NASA expert visualizes lessons learned*. APPEL. https://appel.nasa.gov/2017/08/29/nasa-expert-visualizes-lessons-learned/

Clark, K., & Manning, C. (2016). *Deep reinforcement learning for mention-ranking coreference models.* Cooper, K. M. (2020). The ingredient co-occurrence network of packaged foods distributed in the United States. *Journal of Food Composition and Analysis, 86*, 103391.

Darke, E., Zhuang, Z., & Wang, Z. (2017). *Applying link prediction to recommendation systems for Amazon products.*

Dhingra, S. et al. (2016). Finding SCCs in a Social Network Graph. *International Journal of Computer Applications, 136*, 1–5.

Ding, Y., Yan, E., Frazho, A., & Caverlee J . (2010). *PageRank for ranking authors in co-citation networks.*

Durazzi, F., Müller, M., Salathé, M. et al. (2021). Clusters of science and health related Twitter users become more isolated during the COVID-19 pandemic. *Scientific Reports, 11*, 19655. https://doi.org/10.1038/s41598-021-99301-0

Dutta, A., Riba, P., Lladós, J. et al. (2020). Hierarchical stochastic graphlet embedding for graph-based pattern recognition. *Neural Computing and Applications, 32*, 11579–11596. https://doi.org/10.1007/s00521-019-04642-7

Efstathiades, H. et al. (2016). Online social network evolution: Revisiting the Twitter graph. *2016 IEEE International Conference on Big Data (Big Data)*, 626–635.

Erdös, P., & Rényi, A. (1959). On random graphs. *Publicationes Mathematicae, 6*, 290–297.

Evkoski, B. & Mozetič, I., Ljubešić, N., & Kralj Novak, P. (2020). A Slovenian retweet network 2018–2020. *SiKDD.*

Evkoski, B. & Mozetič, I., Ljubešić, N., & Kralj Novak, P. (2021). Community evolution in retweet networks. *PLOS ONE, 16.* e0256175. https://doi.org/10.1371/journal.pone.0256175

Fukuda, S., & Tomiura, Y. (2018). Clustering of research papers based on sentence roles. *ICADL Poster Proceedings. Hamilton, New Zealand.* The University of Waikato.

Gleason, B. (2013). #Occupy Wall Street: Exploring informal learning about a social movement on Twitter. *American Behavioral Scientist, 57*(7), 966–982. https://doi.org/10.1177/0002764213479372

Grover, A., & Leskovec, J. (2016). *node2vec: Scalable feature learning for networks.*

Gábor I., Vince G. (2011). When the Web meets the cell: Using personalized PageRank for analyzing protein interaction networks. *Bioinformatics, 27*(3), 405–407. https://doi.org/10.1093/bioinformatics/btq680

Haghighi, A., & Klein, D. (2009). Simple coreference resolution with rich syntactic and semantic features. *Proceedings of the 2009 Conference on Empirical Methods in Natural Language Processing*, 1152–1161. Association for Computational Linguistics.

Hamilton, W. L. , Ying, R., & Leskovec, J. (2017). *Inductive representation learning on large graphs.* CoRR. abs/1706.02216.

Hamilton, W. L., Ying, R., & Leskovec, J. (2018). *Representation learning on graphs: Methods and applications.*

Han, X., Gao, T., Yao, Y., Ye, D., Liu, Z., & Sun, M. (2019). OpenNRE: An open and extensible toolkit for neural relation extraction. *Proceedings of EMNLP-IJCNLP: System Demonstrations*, pp. 169–174.

Han, Y.-S., Kim, L., & Cha, J.-W. (2009). Evaluation of user reputation on YouTube. *International Conference on Online Communities and Social Computing*, 346–353. https://doi.org/10.1007/978-3-642-02774-1_38

Hawthorne, J., Houston, J. B., & Mckinney, M. (2013). Live-tweeting a presidential primary debate exploring new political conversations. *Social Science Computer Review, 31*, 552–562. 10.1177/0894439313490643

Henderson, K., Gallagher, B., Eliassi-Rad, T., Tong, H., Basu, S., Akoglu, L., Koutra, D., Faloutsos, C., & Li, L. (2012). RolX: Structural role extraction & mining in large graphs. *Proceedings of the 18th ACM SIGKDD International Conference on Knowledge Discovery and Data Mining*, 1231–1239. Association for Computing Machinery.

Himmelstein, D., Lizee, A., Hessler, C., Brueggeman, L., Chen, S., Hadley, D., Green, A., Khankhanian, P., & Baranzini, S. (2017). Systematic integration of biomedical knowledge prioritizes drugs for repurposing. *eLife, 6*, e26726.

Huguet Cabot, P. L., & Navigli, R. (2021). REBEL: Relation extraction by end-to-end language generation. *Findings of the Association for Computational Linguistics: EMNLP 2021*, 2370–2381. Association for Computational Linguistics.

Kashwan, K. R., & Velu, C. (2013). Customer segmentation using clustering and data mining techniques. *International Journal of Computer Theory and Engineering, 5*, 856–861. https://doi.org/10.7763/IJCTE.2013.V5.811

Kastrin, A., Rindflesch, T., & Hristovski, D. (2014). Link prediction in a MeSH Co-occurrence Network: Preliminary results. *Studies in health technology and informatics, 205*, 579–583.

Kim, T.-H., Kim, J., Heslop-Harrison, P., & Cho, K.-H. (2011). Evolutionary design principles and functional characteristics based on kingdom-specific network motifs. *Bioinformatics, 27*(2), 245–251. https://doi.org/10.1093/bioinformatics/btq633

Kirkley, A., Barbosa, H., Barthelemy, M., & Ghoshal, G. (2018). From the betweenness centrality in street networks to structural invariants in random planar graphs. *Nature Communications, 9*, 2501. https://doi.org/10.1038/s41467-018-04978-z

Kular, D. K. , Menezes, R., & Ribeiro, E. (2011). Using network analysis to understand the relation between cuisine and culture. _IEEE Network Science Workshop, 38–45. https://doi.org/10.1109/NSW.2011.6004656

Lakshmi, T., & Bhavani, S. (2021). *Link prediction approach to recommender systems.* le Gorrec, L., Knight, P. A., & Caen, A. (2022). Learning network embeddings using small graphlets. *Social Network Analysis and Mining, 12*, 20. https://doi.org/10.1007/s13278-021-00846-9

Lee, K., He, L., Lewis, M., & Zettlemoyer, L. (2017). *End-to-end neural coreference resolution.*

Levy, Y. (2014). Dependency-based word embeddings. *Proceedings of the 52nd Annual Meeting of the Association for Computational Linguistics, 2* (Short Papers), 302–308. Association for Computational Linguistics.

Li, B., Fang, G., Yang, Y., Wang, Q., Ye, W., Zhao, W., & Zhang, S. (2023). *Evaluating ChatGPT's information extraction capabilities: An assessment of performance, explainability, calibration, and faithfulness.*

Luo, H., Wang, J., Li, M., Luo, J., Peng, X., Wu, F. X., & Pan, Y. (2016). Drug repositioning based on comprehensive similarity measures and Bi-Random walk algorithm. *Bioinformatics, 32*(17), 2664–2671.

Marr, B. (2017). *Big data: Why NASA can now visualize its lessons learned.* Forbes. https://www.forbes.com/sites/bernardmarr/2017/02/22/big-data-why-nasa-can-now-visualize-its-lessons-learned/?sh=7f39b78b2003

Mikolov, T., Chen, K., Corrado, G., Dean, J. (2013). *Efficient estimation of word representations in vector space.* arXiv:1301.3781

Minot J. R., Arnold M. V., Alshaabi T., Danforth C. M., & Dodds P. S. (2021). Ratioing the President: An exploration of public engagement with Obama and Trump on Twitter. *PLOS ONE, 16*(4), e0248880. https://doi.org/10.1371/journal.pone.024888

Myers, S., Sharma, A., Gupta, P., & Lin, J. (2014). Information network or social network? The structure of the Twitter follow graph. *Proceedings of the 23rd International Conference on World Wide Web*, 493–498. Association for Computing Machinery.

Newman, M. E. (2001). The structure of scientific collaboration networks. *Proceedings of the National Academy of Sciences, USA, 98*(2), 404–409. https://doi.org/10.1073/pnas.021544898. PMID: 11149952; PMCID: PMC14598.

Nicola, V. (2018). *Study on the Twitter hashtag-hashtag co-occurrence network and knowledge discovery application* (v1.0.0). Zenodo. https://doi.org/10.5281/zenodo.1289254

OpenAI. (2023). *GPT-4 technical report.*

Pervin, F. (2015). Hashtag popularity on Twitter: Analyzing co-occurrence of multiple hashtags. In G. Meiselwitz, *Social Computing and Social Media* (pp. 169–182). Springer International Publishing.

Piedra, N., Chicaiza, J., Lopez-Vargas, J., & Tovar, E. (2017). *Discovery of potential collaboration networks from open knowledge sources.*

Pinkert, S., Schultz, J., & Reichardt J. (2010). Protein interaction networks—More than mere modules. *PLoS Computational Biology, 6*(1), e1000659.

Priyanta, S., & Prayana Trisna, I. N. (2019). Social network analysis of Twitter to Identify issuer of topic using PageRank. *International Journal of Advanced Computer Science and Applications, 10*. https://doi.org/10.14569/IJACSA.2019.0100113.

Pržulj, N., Corneil, D. G., Jurisica, I. (2004). Modeling interactome: Scale-free or geometric? *Bioinformatics, 20*(18), 3508–3515. https://doi.org/10.1093/bioinformatics/bth436

Raghunathan, K., Lee, H., Rangarajan, S., Chambers, N., Surdeanu, M., Jurafsky, D., & Manning, C. (2010). A multi-pass sieve for coreference resolution. *Proceedings of the 2010 Conference on Empirical Methods in Natural Language Processing*, 492–501. Association for Computational Linguistics.

Rindflesch, T. C., Kilicoglu, H., Fiszman, M., Rosemblat, G., & Shin, D. (2011). Semantic MEDLINE: An advanced information management application for biomedicine. *Information Services and Use, 31*(1), 15–21.

Rindflesch, T. C, & Fiszman, M. (2003). The interaction of domain knowledge and linguistic structure in natural language processing: Interpreting hypernymic propositions in biomedical text. *Journal of Biomedical Informatics, 36*(6), 462–477. https://doi.org/10.1016/j.jbi.2003.11.003

Rossi, R. A., Zhou, R., & Ahmed, N. K. (2017). *Deep feature learning for graphs.*

Rothwell, Peter M. et al. (2011). Effect of daily aspirin on long-term risk of death due to cancer: Analysis of individual patient data from randomised trials. *Lancet, 377*(9759), 31–41. https://doi.org/10.1016/S0140-6736(10)62110-1

Rüschoff, J. et al. (1998). Aspirin suppresses the mutator phenotype associated with hereditary nonpolyposis colorectal cancer by genetic selection. *Proceedings of the National Academy of Sciences of the United States of America, 95*(19), 11301–11306. https://doi.org/10.1073/pnas.95.19.11301

Sanhueza, C. (2017, January). *The Marvel universe social network, version 1.* Kaggle. https://www.kaggle.com/datasets/csanhueza/the-marvel-universe-social-network

Schlander, M., Hernandez-Villafuerte, K., Cheng, C. Y. et al. (2021). How much does it cost to research and develop a new drug? A systematic review and assessment. *PharmacoEconomics, 39*, 1243–1269. https://doi.org/10.1007/s40273-021-01065-y

Shirazi, S., Albadvi, A., Akhondzadeh, E., Farzadfar, F., & Teimourpour B. (2020). A new application of community detection for identifying the real specialty of physicians. *International Journal of Medical Informatics, 140*, 104161.

Singh, S. (2018). *Natural language processing for information extraction.*

Sun, J., Li, Y., Liu, L., Jiang, Z., & Liu, G. (2019). *Aspirin use and pancreatic cancer risk: A systematic review of observational studies. Medicine, 98*(51), e18033. https://doi.org/10.1097/MD.0000000000018033. PMID: 31860953; PMCID: PMC6940047.

Tinati, R., Carr, L., Hall, W., & Bentwood, J. (2012). *Identifying communicator roles in Twitter.* 10.1145/2187980.2188256.

Türker, İlker, & Sulak, E. (2018). A multilayer network analysis of hashtags in twitter via co-occurrence and semantic links. *International Journal of Modern Physics B, 32*(04), 1850029.

Ugander, J., Karrer, B., Backstrom, L., & Marlow, C. (2011). *The anatomy of the Facebook social graph.* arXiv.

Vane, J. (1971). Inhibition of prostaglandin synthesis as a mechanism of action for aspirin-like drugs. *Nature New Biology*, 231, 232–235. https://doi.org/10.1038/newbio231232a0

Vaswani, A., Shazeer, N., Parmar, N., Uszkoreit, J., Jones, L., Gomez, A. N., Kaiser, L., & Polosukhin, I. (2017). *Attention is all you need.* CoRR. abs/1706.03762.

Voulodimos, A., Doulamis, A. Patrikakis, C., Sardis, E., & Karamolegkos, P. (2011). *Employing clustering algorithms to create user groups for personalized context aware services provision.* https://doi.org/10.1145/2072627.2072637

Wang, R., Liu, W. and Gao, S. (2016). Hashtags and information virality in networked social movement: Examining hashtag co-occurrence patterns. *Online Information Review, 40*(7), 850–866. https://doi.org/10.1108/OIR-12-2015-0378

Wasserman, S., & Faust, K. (1994). *Social network analysis: Methods and applications.* Cambridge University Press. https://doi.org/10.1017/CBO9780511815478

Wei, X., Cui, X., Cheng, N., Wang, X., Zhang, X., Huang, S., Xie, P., Xu, J., Chen, Y., Zhang, M., Jiang, Y., & Han, W. (2023). *Zero-shot information extraction via chatting with ChatGPT.*

Wu, Z., Lin, Y., Wang, J., & Gregory, S. (2015). *Efficient link prediction with node clustering coefficient.* CoRR. abs/1510.07819.

Yao, Y., Ye, D., Li, P., Han, X., Lin, Y., Liu, Z., Liu, Z., Huang, L., Zhou, J., & Sun, M. (2019). DocRED: A large-scale document-level relation extraction dataset. *Proceedings of the 57th Annual Meeting of the Association for Computational Linguistics,* 764–777. Association for Computational Linguistics.

Zhou, P., Shi, W., Tian, J., Qi, Z., Li, B., Hao, H., & Xu, B. (2016). Attention-based bidirectional long short-term memory networks for relation classification. *Proceedings of the 54th Annual Meeting of the Association for Computational Linguistics, 2* (Short Papers), 207–212. Association for Computational Linguistics.

index